Violence Against Women in South Asian Communities

Issues for Policy and Practice

Edited by Ravi K. Thiara and Aisha K. Gill

Foreword by Professor Liz Kelly

Jessica Kingsley Publishers
London and Philadelphia

First published in 2010
by Jessica Kingsley Publishers
116 Pentonville Road
London N1 9JB, UK
and
400 Market Street, Suite 400
Philadelphia, PA 19106, USA

www.jkp.com

Library of Congress Cataloging in Publication Data
Violence against women in South Asian communities : issues for policy and practice / edited by Ravi K. Thiara and Aisha K. Gill ; foreword by Liz Kelly.
    p. cm.
Includes bibliographical references and index.
ISBN 978-1-84310-670-8 (pb : alk. paper) 1. Women--Violence against--South Asia. 2. Women--Violence against--South Asia--Prevention. 3. Women--Government policy--South Asia. I. Thiara, Ravi K. II. Gill, Aisha K.
HV6250.4.W65V567635 2009
362.82'920954--dc22
                        2009014502

British Library Cataloguing in Publication Data
A CIP catalogue record for this book is available from the British Library

ISBN 978 1 84310 670 8

Printed and bound in Great Britain by
Athenaeum Press, Gateshead, Tyne and Wear

To Amarjeet, always in my heart,
for all the laughter and friendship

(R.K Thiara)

In memory of my mother, Surinder Kaur,
a victim of gender-based violence.

(A.K. Gill)

Acknowledgements

Listening to women and children since the late 1980s has been invaluable; to them I owe a huge debt of gratitude. A big thank you to those 'giants' of the violence against women movement whom I have learnt so much from. And all those courageous women who continue to transgress boundaries and remain an inspiration.

Deep gratitude to my nearest and dearest, you know who you are, and especially to my parents, Shiv Singh and Satwant Kaur, and to Maanuv, Jyot, and Bhavan, our future.

Ravi K. Thiara

I begin by acknowledging the contributions of the women in this book, and the committed efforts of South Asian women's groups who work on the frontline. The poignancy of these cases inspires me to continue to invest my professional energy in this often challenging and always humbling work.

Special thanks are offered to Sonia Bhola, Mary Venning, Roger Fokerd, Tabassum Sayani, Saira Shafi, Bilal Sayed, Tabitha Freeman, Rowena Macaulay, Suki Dhanda, Paminder Parbha, Saika Alam, Shazia Nizam, Meera Betab, Vidya Maharaj and Daljit Kang, for their belief in this project, which was inspirational, and to Vik Chaudhuri, whose patience and understanding was so valuable – especially during the final days of submission of this manuscript. Also, thanks to Edward Graham, Jeremy Lowe, Peter Bloom and Pathik Pathak, who were all willing to read some of my earlier drafts and respond promptly with insightful comments.

Most of all, I would like to thank my uncle, Santokh Singh, whose commitment to this whole process cannot be calculated. Thank you for constantly reminding me of my history, and for teaching me that nothing is beyond my reach. It is in memory of your sister, my mother, that I do this kind of work.

Aisha K. Gill

Contents

Foreword

As someone who has worked in the field of violence against women (VAW) for over thirty years, alongside a number of the contributors to this book, it is a profound honour to be asked to write this foreword. This is an historic collection that documents, recognises and renews the contributions to the UK movement against VAW by South Asian feminists; contributions made as researchers, as activists, as practitioners. Indeed, for three decades South Asian feminists in Britain have combined these categories in creative and inspirational ways, living the multiple identities which contemporary social theory is now engaging with. They have been activist scholars, activist practitioners and practitioner-researchers; seeking out and creating 'spaces in between' (Morris 2008). Neither margin nor centre, these are spaces in which challenge and change are the order of the day; where the separating boundaries and binaries between disciplines and forms of practice are resisted. Working in between as an academic involves having one foot outside the public we are part of, enabling critical reflection on how divisiveness and fragmentation in civil society is structured and repro-duced. The reflexivity demands here are considerable – reflection about self in movement (and I could write an entirely different introduction about my self in movement within an ever evolving understanding of racism).

Intersectionality has been at the core of the work of Asian feminists for decades; now recognised conceptually in academia through being named. As this becomes a dominant approach in critical social theory – more deservedly than many of its predecessors – there is a tendency inside and outside the academy (including in women's studies), to neglect to remember that Kimberley Crenshaw (as she was then) coined the term within a reflection about black American women's experiences of VAW and challenges to majority feminist organisations. This is but one of the many, frequently unmarked, contributions on VAW to critical scholarship and movements for social justice. Indeed, it is in the practices of VAW activists that some of the promise of feminist coalition has been most evident at national and international levels; not least the global coalition which worked to get women's rights mainstreamed into international human rights thinking (Kelly 2004). Too much of this vital and innovative theory in action work is yet to be documented, since all too often *doing* has precluded recording and reflecting. Yet another reason to welcome this collection.

Ravi K. Thiara and Aisha K. Gill pay tribute to the work of many women which has led to this collection, while acknowledging that the motor for their research and activism has tended to be intimate partner and family violence. There is an unwritten history here too, that is in danger of being lost. A number of South Asian women were active in developing feminist approaches to child sexual abuse in the late 1980s, daring to raise the issue of abuse within South Asian communities, and I would like particularly to remember the late Aqeela Alam.

I have personal–political connections to much of the content, not least being that many of the authors embrace the gender equality and human rights framing of VAW which the Child and Woman Abuse Studies Unit (CWASU) (the research unit I direct) and the End Violence Against Women (EVAW) campaign (the feminist coalition I chair) have promoted. All who work within the framework of VAW know that we cannot hope to reduce, let alone end, violence in the lives of girls and women without achieving social justice and equality, and that this has to be a global transformation. This requires that we think about connections: between developed and developing worlds; between feminists wherever they are located; between forms of VAW and the conducive contexts in which they occur. Many of the chapters in this book demand that we make connections, whilst simultaneously noting the differences diversity makes and retaining a vision of not just responding better to, but *preventing* VAW.

I cannot write this foreword without paying tribute to the inspirational activism that South Asian feminists have brought to British feminism. Never afraid to take to the streets, they have done so in a light-footed and imaginative way. They are the finest, most impertinent composers of songs and chants, challenging stereotypes of South Asian women with every fibre of their being. Their dedication to joyful protest – never leaving behind a sense of fun and irony – is undoubtedly one reason why black and minority ethnic (BME) groups working on VAW still increase 'space for action' for the women with whom they work, who frequently join public events and dissent. The voice of protest and resistance is as radical, if not more so, as the voice of testimony: in reality a both/and rather than an either/or. Enabling women who have had their agency brutally denied to be political actors, and enjoy the process, should surely be *the* empowerment performance indicator.

When, in teaching and presentations, I talk about feminism and feminists being argumentative to young women who imagine a unified past, I am often reminded of the many meetings in which women from BME organisations insisted that we debate and anticipate what the unintended consequences of certain positions might be, and whether proposals may have additional implications for marginalised groups of women. These meetings again represent the best of feminism – spaces that embrace open exploration and recognise judgement calls, rather than singular 'lines'. This book is a confirmation of that sensibility in its acknowledgment of ongoing debates, conversations, contradictions and paradoxes. Change has happened, 2009 is not 1979, but the outcomes have been mixed and uneven. To theorise what has changed and for whom, in order to make more nuanced arguments about the present and future, we need more of these reflective spaces.

The work of South Asian feminists has always demanded that those of us from majority communities think about the similarities and differences for women from minority communities. Engaging in this challenge often reveals new insights that apply across the piece, problematising current orthodoxies. Take Multi-Agency Risk Assessment Conferences (MARAC), the government-supported core response to domestic violence in the last couple of years. Modelled on child protection conferences, although unlike them excluding the adults whose lives they will impact on – victims do not attend MARACs, only agencies, they operate now in over 200 local areas, linking statutory and voluntary sectors, albeit dominated in terms of number of attendees by the former. Any case designated 'high risk' can be referred to MARAC, where the task for all professionals present is to share everything they know about the respective families in order to undertake actions that enhance safety. It is the high-risk designation, and the fact that women's consent should be sought before referral, which justifies overriding women's privacy rights (Douglas *et al.* 2004). But are the potential unintended consequences the same for all women? What are the implications of such total disclosure for women from communities where absolute confidentiality has been key to enabling them to speak, let alone to crafting effective safety strategies? What about women for whom gossip and carelessness can literally place their life and potential future at risk? Do we really know that MARAC members understand these differential potentials for minority women, and take the precautions necessary? Perhaps this raises wider issues about rights to privacy and participation that apply across all cases.

This collection also challenges simplistic notions of culture, whether drawn on to explain or 'otherise' certain forms of VAW or to position BME women and the organisations that support them outside the mainstream. At the same time, issues of culture form a backdrop to the experiences of minority women and to how they are responded to. A recent report by the UN Special Rapporteur on Violence Against Women, Yakin Ertürk (2007), cogently outlines the dangers of culturalising VAW, and echoes the concerns of many contributors that we should avoid representing cultures as fixed and unchanging, or suggesting that it is only minority communities who inhabit cultures. South Asian feminists have been among the most lucid and convincing in arguing the necessity for a more complex understanding of the connections between cultures and VAW. One contemporary example which is highlighted in a number of chapters is that of faith and faith communities, almost all of which have long-standing traditions that fail to afford women equality within the faith group and all too often blame women and girls for sexual violence. Recently some faith groups have responded to feminist challenges by creating guidelines and new forms of response, but this is by no means universal and, as in secular contexts, implementation remains patchy. Allowing faith-based groups with no track record of supporting abused women to become service providers funded by the public purse is fraught with contradictions, many of which are outlined in this book. Can communities of control, which have presided over weak protection for victims of violence and virtual impunity for perpetrators, transform overnight into communities of safety and care?

While there has always been a small group of South Asian feminist researchers and theorists making important contributions to our understanding of VAW, this book means that we can begin to talk of the emergence of a field of study and a network of researchers. There are challenges for the future, not least recognising the need to build the knowledge base on, and assess responses to, sexual violence in the lives of South Asian women and to understand how disability and sexuality intersect with racism. We also have to dare to ask whether VAW, and each of its forms, is more common for some groups of women, or in specific contexts, and if so, why? If we really believe that violence occurs in the context of men's social power and position and women's resistance to this, then we need to examine more carefully contexts where gender relations are in flux, since these present sites where we might see elevated levels of violence, at least in the short term. A number of these are contexts which BME women inhabit. We also need to understand more deeply than we currently do the longer-term meanings and consequences of VAW for diverse groups of women; the burdens they carry as a result, and what could enable them to shed the load.

As we ponder the next steps in research, practice and activism, this volume provides many stepping stones in the right direction.

Professor Liz Kelly
Child and Woman Abuse Studies Unit
London Metropolitan University

References

Douglas, N., Lilley, S., Kooper, L. & Diamond, A. (2004) 'Safety and Justice: Sharing personal information in the context of Domestic Violence – an overview.' *Home Office Development and Practice Report 30.* London: Home Office.

Ertük, Y. (2007) Intersections between culture and violence against women. *Annual Report to the UN Human Rights Council* (A/HRC/4/34).

Kelly, L. (2005) 'Inside Outsiders: Mainstreaming Violence Against Women into Human Rights Discourse and Practice.' *International Feminist Journal of Politics 7,* 4, 471–495.

Morris, A. (2008) *Optimising the 'Spaces In-between': The Maternal Alienation Project and the Politics of Gender in Macro and Micro Contexts.* PhD thesis, University of Adelaide.

Introduction

Ravi K. Thiara and Aisha K. Gill

Violence against women (VAW) has received unprecedented attention at international and national levels since the mid-1990s. Understood to be rooted in the historical inequalities between men and women, and recognised as an obstacle to equality, development and peace, VAW is seen as one of the major factors undermining the human rights of women and children worldwide. It is defined by the United Nations as:

> Any act of gender-based violence that results in, or is likely to result in, physical, sexual or psychological harm or suffering to women, including threats of such acts, coercion or arbitrary deprivation of liberty, whether occurring in public or private life. (The United Nations, Declaration on the Elimination of Violence Against Women Article 1, 1993)

In the UK, due to sustained pressure from feminists, VAW has been the focus of increased political and policy attention. While 'domestic violence' remains the dominant lens for officially defining and responding to this issue, feminists have pushed for the adoption of 'violence against women' (Horvath and Kelly 2007) to better frame the nature and continuum of gendered violence in an integrated approach which avoids 'silo thinking'. In particular, VAW feminists have increasingly begun to use international laws and covenants to hold the government accountable over its obligation to protect women from violence and ensure their full human rights (Sen, Humphreys and Kelly 2003). This strategy, somewhat different from the struggle against VAW since the 1970s, along with the increased attention to the issue, has resulted in a great deal of debate, opportunities and continuing challenges. Although the journey to get VAW onto mainstream political agendas has been fraught with difficulties, the secrecy which previously surrounded the issue has increasingly been questioned, and public and professional understanding of VAW been enhanced.

The two terms 'domestic violence' and 'VAW' are increasingly used interchangeably. We use the term 'violence against women' in this book to acknowledge that not only do women experience more severe and frequent abuse but also this is linked to other systems of inequality based on gender, 'race', and class. However, while conceptually favouring 'violence against women', the terms 'gendered violence' and 'gender-based violence' are also used interchangeably by the contributors to this volume. Thus, we adopt a gendered perspective of violence against women, generally viewed as a pattern of coercive control perpetrated by an adult (usually male) towards an intimate partner (usually female). While recognising that definitions are complex, contested and cannot be universally applied unmodified or without qualification to all women, as revealed by the experience of South Asian women, we nevertheless want to hold on to the gendered nature of violence against women. In particular, domestic violence is a gendered crime, most often perpetrated by men on women (Walby and Allen 2004).[1] However, we recognise that for some, including South Asian women, abuse is also perpetrated by family members, and is designed to assert and maintain power over women for the purposes of regulating their behaviour and actions to comply with prescribed patriarchal norms. At times, it also takes on culturally specific forms, especially forced marriage and 'honour'-related violence, which we view as part of a continuum of VAW. For all these reasons, the book is primarily concerned with women experiencing abuse from intimate partners and wider family members.

There have been a number of legislative and legal developments in the UK that have also added momentum to the cross-government strategic response to this issue.[2] The Domestic Violence Crime and Victims Act 2004 includes a range of protection and support measures for victims, the introduction of action plans on domestic and sexual violence, and the establishment of specialist domestic violence courts. Similarly, the Sexual Offences Act 2003 widened the definition of some offences, created new offences, extended the age of children from 16 to 18 for some offences, and introduced offences against trafficking people into, within, and out of the UK for the purposes of sexual exploitation. The Female Genital

Mutilation Act 2003 makes it an offence for UK nationals or permanent residents to carry out, aid, abet or procure female genital manipulation (FGM) abroad. Following the decision not to ban forced marriage, the Forced Marriage Civil Protection Act 2007 received royal assent in July 2007 (implemented on 25 November 2008) after it included a series of additions embedded within the Family Law Act Part 4A.[3]

The Gender Equality Duty 2007, introduced by the Equality Act 2006, which requires all public authorities to draw up and publish gender equality schemes, as well as to conduct gender impact assessments of all new policies and laws, including on employment and service delivery, provides an official channel for VAW to be addressed. The Race Relations (Amendment Act) 2000 and the Human Rights Act 1998 also place an obligation on public bodies to protect individuals without discrimination. To date, there is no national government strategy on VAW, urged by the Convention on the Elimination of All Forms of Discrimination Against Women, (CEDAW),[4] and the End Violence Against Women (EVAW) campaign, a consortium of activists and organisations. In response to these efforts, the government has launched a consultation process around a national strategy (CEDAW 2008; EVAW 2009).[5]

The issue of violence against South Asian women has been raised by feminists and activists from these communities and their supporters for some time, and especially as part of this broader scrutiny of the issue.[6] While the government and its agencies have made some provisions, policy attention has largely been focused on particular forms of abuse, namely forced marriage and honour-based violence.[7] Developments in VAW theory and research have also been somewhat inadequate, tending to add on issues of ethnicity and culture rather than scrutinise existing explanatory frameworks. In order to synthesise theory and practice in relation to VAW and ethnicity, this book places South Asian women at the centre and explores the impact of male power and violence, in tandem with other oppressions, on individual and collective selves. Through this exclusive focus on South Asian women and VAW, it adds to existing literature by addressing issues for research, policy and practice. The various contributions highlight the continuities and changes since the late 1970s. They further link past and present discourses (around 'race'/ethnicity, nation and VAW) showing how they combine to shape the lives of South Asian women and their experiences of violence and abuse. In challenging binaries, the book emphasises the importance of making connections, by linking theory and politics, research and practice, the personal and the structural, victimisation and agency, and cultures of patriarchy with the myriad forms of VAW. In addressing the existing fragmentary knowledge about South Asian women and VAW, the purpose of this book is also to bring together a body of writing by activists and researchers engaged in contemporary debates about gender, 'race'/racism, ethnicity, culture, and violence.

A key goal of the book is to present an understanding of violence against South Asian women which recognises the ways in which their abuse is complicated by and mediated through the intersection of systems of domination based on 'race', ethnicity, class, culture and nationality. Intersectionality – drawing on the critique by black feminists in the US and UK in the 1970s and 1980s about the primacy given to gender over other oppressions by white feminists – has become an internationally influential and increasingly utilised concept by feminist scholars and activists to signify and investigate the complex and intertwining nature of oppression and inequality (Brah and Phoenix 2004; Ferree 2008). This approach is introduced and further developed in Chapter 1, which sets out a critical framework based on the concept of intersectionality for understanding the issue of violence against South Asian women. In their discussion, Thiara and Gill underline the importance of placing emphasis on the structures of power and domination, rather than just cultural differences, to fully comprehend South Asian women's personal and collective experiences, both theoretically and in practice. Thus, the authors concur with Sokoloff and Dupont (2005, p.3), when they state the need to 'emphasise the structural underpinnings of abuse while not denying the existence of real differences among individual battered women from diverse backgrounds'.

Clearly 'culture' and faith are important in the lives of South Asian women. However, the contributions in this book all allude to the importance of considering culture as a dynamic and contested force rather than as a static and unchanging monolith. It is thus both a source of oppression and support for women. Indeed, the central role of South Asian women, as part of diasporic communities, in reproducing and reinventing cultural values and norms, as 'cultural entrepreneurs', has been noted by some writers (Bhachu 1993, p.225). At the same time, the expectation that South Asian women will guard and enact a version of 'culture' that perpetuates the interests of the patriarchal community, even if antithetical to their own requirements, has been recognised. This book urges the need to guard against the adoption of simplistic explanations of culture in VAW, as well as the necessity of seeing cultural experiences as mediated through structural systems of inequality ('race'/racism, class, nationality for instance). It also highlights that a focus on cultural differences alone rather than also racism can be 'an innocence that amounts to the transgressive refusal to know' (Williams 1998, cited in Andall 2003) and result in a form of power evasion (Frankenberg 1993).

South Asian feminists began to challenge VAW in their communities in the late 1970s, as part of the wider feminist movement of the 1970s, which placed the issue at its heart (see Thiara 2003). Presently, there are approximately 2.5 million South Asians living in the UK, constituting the largest minority ethnic group, from a total black and minority ethnic (BME) population of 4.6 million (7.9 per cent), with BME women making up about 4 per cent (2.3 million) of the UK's overall population.[8] The perceived cultural homogeneity of South Asian groups has been critiqued by those seeking to foreground the implicit heterogeneity and differential power relations within and between South Asian communities. This writing challenges the staticity accorded to cultures and communities which are instead seen to be in a constant process of contestation and reconfiguration (Anitha and Gill 2009; Gangoli 2007; Gupta 2003; Puwar and Raghuram 2003; Wilson 2006; Thiara 2003). South Asian women activists tread difficult terrain, in contesting the operation of patriarchal power within their communities and in exposing race and gender inequalities in the national community (Patel 1997; Thiara 2003). These issues are addressed by a number of contributors to this book.

As has been evident from these activist struggles, marginality creates opportunities for resistance and change as well as oppression, though these are by no means simplistic processes. In Chapter 2, Wilson charts the development of South Asian women's collective struggles against gendered violence within a context of changing state policies on 'race', ethnicity and gender, on the one hand, and the gradual demolition and privatisation of the welfare state, on the other. She concludes that despite increased attention being given to domestic violence, the development of new funding regimes for welfare services 'is endangering the lives of South Asian women and children fleeing domestic violence by closing down the routes to, and places of safety...it is doing away with the very mechanisms which make women stronger' (see Chapter 2 by Wilson). In particular, the location at the intersection of multiple dominatory systems creates numerous contradictions for South Asian women. As argued by Wilson, an aspect of the greater surveillance and focus on South Asian groups post-9/11 jeopardises the ability of South Asian women to challenge violence and abuse in their communities.

Chapter 4 by Patel and Siddiqui further explores the continuing struggles by South Asian women against gender-based violence, in particular the negative impact of state multicultural policies on the rights of minority women, which they argue are currently under threat from the 'faith' and cohesion agenda of the government. They expose the contradictions in state policy simultaneously designed to tackle VAW and tighten immigration (by increasing the age of those allowed to marry spouses overseas from 18 to 21 as a way of preventing forced marriage). They also question the government's emphasis on a 'faith'-based approach to minority communities, which further serves to reinforce gender inequality. In articulating a feminist critique of 'faith'-based policies, which seek to reconstruct minority groups as 'faith communities' and thus undermine black feminist struggles, they underline the importance for feminists of resisting the 'shrinking of secular spaces' and to challenge those who use both 'religion and racism to limit our freedoms' (see Chapter 4 by Patel and Siddiqui). While acknowledging the ability of black feminists to influence state policy relating to 'their' issues – forced marriage and honour-related violence – the disconnect this can create from wider debates on VAW and state responsibility, resulting in what they call 'parallel universes', is importantly underlined.

While the positive response made by South Asian women to address VAW through autonomous organisation is increasingly undermined, the state and its agencies have sought to protect certain women from their families and communities. This shifting terrain of racialised discourses *about* minority ethnic communities as well as the internal dynamics *within* communities, have increasingly begun to erode 'secular spaces' (Patel and Siddiqui, Chapter 4). The dichotomy of tradition and modernity, in particular, has been highlighted in current debates around forced marriage and honour-based violence. Forced marriage and its treatment by the government is elaborated on in Chapter 5 by Gill and Mitra-Kahn. They contend that the strategy is problematic due to its disassociation from the VAW agenda, its alignment with issues of immigration and the 'othering' of minority groups, and its acceptance of community cohesion over multiculturalism. This, they argue, reinforces a political agenda based on a woman's 'right to exit' from their communities rather than securing gender equality. Drawing on Phillips' theory of 'multiculturalism without culture', they advocate interventions that reconcile gender equality with minority group identity through a reworked human rights perspective for tackling forced marriage.

With the increased government focus on domestic violence, there has been heightened debate about the most effective responses to men's violence. Most notably, the current emphasis on the criminal justice system (CJS) has been criticised by some writers and activists, especially in relation to minority ethnic women. Indeed, it is possible that as well as offering protection, state policies can further endanger women by placing them at risk in their communities and thus create further disadvantage. Wilson notes, for instance, that the prioritisation of funding for criminal justice developments over support services run for and by South Asian women can serve to further silence some women about domestic violence. Although mainstream CJS responses may not sit comfortably with many South Asian women, the recent development of Muslim Arbitration Tribunals (MATs) and shariah law, as a way of resolving family disputes, including domestic violence, is a further complex and contested issue on which there is little consensus (as illustrated by the discussion in Chapter 7 by Bano).[9] As highlighted in the conclusion, these developments need to be studied in order to assess the ways in which they may reinforce women's victimisation and erode their safety and rights. Patel and Siddiqui argue that this is a clear attempt to contain the rights of women already under great pressures to agree to mediation and governance based on their religion.

The extent to which, if at all, the law should accommodate religious and cultural diversity in multicultural Britain has been the subject of heated debate. Bano's chapter focuses on this issue by exploring the debate about the right of religious communities to practise religious law in the context of family law. Critiquing the debate on universalism versus cultural relativism for ignoring the complexities of power, belonging, internal dissent, autonomy and individual choice, and by contesting the exclusion of Muslim women's voices from debates that attempt to define their rights and interests, she seeks to give voice to the heterogeneous group of Muslim women who choose to resolve matrimonial disputes through Shariah Councils. In exploring the interconnection between Shariah Councils, power and gender inequality, Bano highlights the agency of Muslim women in drawing on rather than simply submitting to patriarchal systems of law, thereby showing the highly contradictory and contested nature of these women's relationship to religious identity and traditional law. However, regarding wider questions concerning the use of parallel legal systems, especially those focused on mediation, she rightly brings the focus back to the inherent contradictions and ambiguities of these systems. Specifically, she notes how parallel legal systems both increase women's vulnerability and disadvantage while also providing them greater choice. This is an issue that illustrates the divergence among South Asian feminists and the inherent contradictions involved in foregrounding women's subjectivity.

The role of masculinity in the perpetuation of intimate violence has rarely been considered despite increased study of the concept of masculinity. Chapter 3 by Balzani aims to fill this gap by situating South Asian masculinity within the broader context of gendered social relations and globalisation. She highlights the discontinuities in the construction and expression of masculinity, connected to the dynamic reconfiguration of cultures internationally and as relational products, and its intersection with identities shaped by local and global social, cultural, and economic processes, as a product of Western modernity. Women's collusion with and performance of hegemonic masculinity, in upholding patriarchal relations through the perpetration of VAW, is considered and offered as an explanation for their role in reinforcing women's subordination. In doing so, she challenges the notion that South Asian men are somehow inherently more violent than white men, something used by the government to curb immigration. Instead, she underscores the tension confronting South Asian men in simultaneously exerting greater control over women while remaining disempowered and marginalised themselves. She explores how these men respond to this contradiction through expressions of hegemonic and protest masculinities. Seeing these processes as a continuation of colonial subjugation, Balzani interprets contemporary struggles over masculinity in the UK among different groups of men as evidence that 'structures of patriarchy are transferable across state borders and involve…men competing with men to the disadvantage of all women' (Chapter 3), whereby women are seen as the vessels for the safeguarding of not only family honour but also that of the community and faith. She raises some poignant points for practice interventions to challenge negative masculinities.

The prevailing assumption that domestic violence occurs only when people are living together, and ceases once separation occurs, has been widely contested (Humphreys and Thiara 2003; Radford and Hester 2006). In Chapter 6, Thiara's examination of child contact and post-separation violence shows that this clearly is not the case for a significant number of women dealing with child contact and custody issues. Here the continuing control by men and the continuum of violence for women is reinforced by legal and court processes emphasising the rights of fathers to have contact with their children at the expense of the safety of women and children. The response to South Asian women and children by professionals, based on a lack of insight about the issues faced by them at the hands of partners, families and communities, further multiply women's victimisation, while structural inequalities create additional constraints and difficulties.

Discourse on immigration and 'immigrants' – legal or illegal – has historically been racialised, located as it is within a context of public hostility further fanned by politicians and large sections of the media. Immigration law presents a key point of contradiction for the state, simultaneously concerned with restricting immigration while protecting individual human rights. It also reinforces the victimisation of minority ethnic women caught between draconian immigration measures and gendered violence. Chapter 8 by Sharma and Gill focuses on the precarious position and vulnerability of women affected by the government 'no recourse to public funds' policy. They draw on casework examples to strengthen their broader contention that despite recent measures introduced to address this problem, the conflicting government priorities, of protecting women from VAW while limiting immigration, continue to deny some abused South Asian women independence and security.

If we are to move towards a strategy aimed at eradicating VAW, then the structural inequalities which perpetuate this must be addressed. Moreover, wider solutions, focused on greater access to safe crisis accommodation and support services to safe long-term housing, to specialist counselling and therapy, to greater education, training and employment opportunities, and to fairer immigration and welfare systems are necessary. South Asian activists have sought to address VAW through existing policy and legal mechanisms, while also arguing for the need for adequate specialist support services. The point that South Asian women often require different and specific responses is highlighted by many of the contributors to this book. Research has consistently shown that a significant number of South Asian women prefer specialist support services which are sensitive to their issues, as well as address the cultural and structural constraints or barriers they face (Rai and Thiara 1997; Thiara and Hussain 2005). Research reveals that as many as 87 per cent of women preferred culturally specific domestic violence services and stated very clearly why they valued this support (Thiara and Roy 2009). Indeed, the need for effective interventions to consider the cultural specificities as well as the structural contexts of South Asian women is underlined in this book, and has been the central focus of the South Asian women's movement to end VAW. It is only through engagement at these multiple levels that greater safety and justice can be secured for South Asian women and children.

South Asian academics and activists have been central to challenging the essentialised construction of the passive South Asian woman, so widely aired in popular and political discourse (Brah 1996; Feminist Review 1984; Gangoli 2007; Gill 2005; Puwar and Raghuram 2003; Thiara 2003; Wilson 2006). The representation of women as merely 'victims' has been especially pernicious in relations to South Asian women affected by violence and abuse, where their agency has often been overlooked in the construction of a 'collective victimhood' (see Chapter 1 by Thiara and Gill). More recently, the construction of 'Muslim women' as part of the 'British Muslim' phenomena obscures the contested nature of these constructed identities and subsumes differences of language, denomination, geography and history (Samad 1998). Where South Asian women's agency has been asserted, it has often been used by patriarchal elements in these communities to dub women as 'homebreakers', a label positively appropriated by some activists (Gupta 2003). Although wider research has focused on the ways in which women resist abusive and controlling partners, this has not been explored for South Asian women. This lack points to the need for future work that foregrounds their subjectivity, in particular the ways in which they contest and draw on cultural resources, and, despite structural constraints, carve out independent lives.

This book represents the start of a critical conversation which we hope others will continue and develop in the future. Inevitably, a number of gaps remain and need to be addressed in future research and practice. To date, there is sparse research evidence about South Asian women's experiences of sexual abuse and violence. Although it is known that there are often overlaps between domestic violence and sexual violence, this has not been explored in any detailed way. It is important, then, not only to consider the range of women's experiences of these issues but also to explore the service responses to them. While children's experiences of domestic violence have been given visibility since the mid-1990s, research on South Asian children is limited, and practice is even less developed. Given that in many UK conurbations, the South Asian population is younger, it is likely that their experiences of abuse intersect with and multiply a sense of other oppressions. As part of diasporic communities, the unique location of children and young people within these processes also creates numerous tensions and opportunities, often heightened by the experiences of growing up in abusive contexts, living in single parent families, or being in contact with abusive fathers or family members. It is important for research and practice to consider these issues in greater detail. The recent emphasis on CJS responses presents particular challenges and dilemmas for South Asian and other minority ethnic women. Although the evidence base for assessing the impact of such approaches is starting to build, this remains a gap for South Asian women, which clearly needs to be addressed.

Moreover, since the separation of research and practice cannot so readily be made for South Asian feminists, we hope that this book highlights, in Mirza's words, the need for 'conscious alliances, critical dialogue and intellectual rigour...to reveal the operation of power in which we are implicated' (Mirza 1997, p.18).

Notes

1. A superficial analysis of the British Crime Survey self-completion section on interpersonal violence shows 13 per cent of women and 9 per cent of men were subjected to at least one incident of domestic violence in the past year. However, when the frequency of attacks, the range and forms of violence and the severity of injury are considered, then women are overwhelmingly the most victimised: of those subjected to four or more incidents, 89 per cent were women and 81 per cent of all incidents were attacks on women (Humphreys, Houghton and Ellis 2008).

2. The cost of domestic violence to key services (criminal justice system, health, social services, housing, civil legal) is estimated to be £3.1 billion, and its cost to the UK economy to be £2.7 billion; this has also led to the government imperative to address the issue. Similarly, the estimated cost of sexual offences in England and Wales in 2003–04 was estimated at £8.5 billion, with each rape costing £76,000 (Walby 2004).

3. A prevailing argument against a specific stand-alone criminal offence was that a criminal offence specifically targeting forced marriage would not be an effective deterrent to this practice nor would it provide adequate protection for its victims.

4. The same report also raised concerns about minority ethnic women suffering multiple discrimination in many aspects of life, and in particular pointed to high rates of depression and mental illness, and especially higher suicide and self-harm rates

among Asian women. It called for the state to adopt targeted and culturally appropriate strategies and programmes to address mental health issues faced by minority ethnic women (CEDAW 2008, p.12). It further called on the state to conduct 'regular and comprehensive studies on intersectional discrimination against minority ethnic women' (CEDAW 2008, pp.12–13). The issue of women with insecure immigration status not having access to public funds where affected by violence was also raised and the state urged to review the 'no recourse to public funds' policy to ensure protection and provision to victims of violence (CEDAW 2008, p.13).

5.   End Violence Against Women. Available at www.endviolenceagainstwomen.org.uk, accessed on 28 April 2009.

6.   The 'South Asian' term encompasses women from Indian, Pakistani, Bangladeshi and 'Other Asian' groups.

7.   Indeed, the Beijing Declaration Platform for Action in 1995 stated that women from minority groups are among those especially vulnerable to violence as part of their multiple discrimination (Beijing Declaration and Platform for Action 1995).

8.   The terminology used to identify groups with migration histories has changed over the years and is itself a reflection of the construction of the 'other' with roots in 'othered' places. The terminology adopted often expands or constricts membership of the category, as the adoption of the term BAMER – Black Asian Minority Ethnic and Refugee – illustrates. When we refer to all minority ethnic groups in the UK, we use the term 'black and minority ethnic', though minority ethnic and black (to signify a collective political voice) and BAMER are also used by contributors throughout the book.

9.   The role of religious organisations and leaders within South Asian communities in challenging violence against women has hardly been explored, although attempts by individual women's groups have been made to engage with religious groups in their localities.

References

Andall, J. (ed.) (2003) *Gender and Ethnicity in Contemporary Europe.* Oxford: Berg.

Anitha, S. and Gill, A. (2009) 'Coercion, consent and the forced marriage debate in the UK.' *Feminist Legal Studies 17,* 2.

Bhachu, P. (1993) 'New European Women and New Cultural Forms: Culture, Class and Consumption among British Asian Women.' In H. Rudolph and M. Morokvasic (eds) *Bridging States and Markets: International Migration in the Early 1990s.* Berlin: Edition Sigma.

Brah, A. (1996) *Cartographies of Diaspora: Contesting Identities.* London: Routledge.

Brah, A. and Phoenix, A. (2004) 'Ain't I a woman? Revisiting intersectionality.' *Journal of International Women's Studies 5,* 3, 74–87.

CEDAW (2008) Concluding Observations of the UK of Great Britain and Northern Ireland, Forty-first Session, 30 June to 18 July 2008. Available at www.un.org/womenwatch/daw/cedaw/41sess, accessed on 25 June 2009.

End Violence Against Women (EVAW) (2009) EVAW Campaign. Available at www.endviolenceagainstwomen.org.uk, accessed on 28 April 2009.

Feminist Review (1984) 'Many Voices One Chant: Black Feminist Perspectives.' *Feminist Review 17* (special issue).

Ferree, M. M. (2008) 'Inequality, Intersectionality and the Politics of Discourse: Framing Feminist Alliances.' In E. Lombardo, P. Meier and M. Verloo (eds) *The Discursive Politics of Gender Equality: Stretching, Bending and Policy-Making.* London: Routledge.

Frankenberg, R. (1993) *White Women, Race Matters: The Social Construction of Whiteness.* Minneapolis, MN: University of Minnesota Press.

Gangoli, G. (2007) *Indian Feminisms: Campaigns against Violence and Multiple Patriarchies.* Aldershot: Ashgate.

Gill, A. (2005) 'Governing violence: Gender, community, and state interventions.' *Journal of Community Safety 4*, 2, 37–45.

Gupta, R. (ed.) (2003) *From Homebreakers to Jailbreakers: Southall Black Sisters.* London: Zed Books.

Horvath, M. and Kelly, L. (2007) *From the Outset: Why Violence Should be a Core Cross-strand Priority Theme for the Commission for Equality and Human Rights.* London: End Violence Against Women Campaign.

Humphreys, C. and Thiara, R.K. (2003) 'Neither justice nor protection: Women's experiences of post-separation violence.' *Journal of Social Welfare and Family Law 25*, 3, 195–214.

Humphreys, C., Houghton, C. and Ellis, J. (2008) *Literature Review: Better Outcomes for Children and Young People Experiencing Domestic Abuse – Directions for Good Practice.* Edinburgh: The Scottish Government.

Mirza, H. (ed.) (1997) *Black British Feminism.* London: Routledge.

Patel, P. (1997) 'Third Wave Feminism and Black Women's Activism.' In H. Mirza (ed.) *Black British Feminism.* London: Routledge.

Puwar, N. and Raghuram, P. (eds) (2003) *South Asian Women in the Diaspora.* Oxford: Berg.

Radford, L. and Hester, M. (2006) *Mothering Through Domestic Violence.* London: Jessica Kingsley Publishers.

Rai, D. and Thiara, R.K. (1997) *Redefining Spaces: The Needs of Black Women and Children and Black Workers in Women's Aid.* Bristol: Women's Aid Federation England.

Samad, Y. (1998) 'Imagining a British Muslim Identification.' In S. Vertovec and A. Rogers (eds) *Muslim European Youth.* Aldershot: Ashgate.

Sen, P., Humphreys, C. and Kelly, L. (2003) *Violence Against Women in the UK: CEDAW Thematic Shadow Report.* London.

Sokoloff, N.J. and Dupont, I. (2005) 'Domestic violence at the intersections of race, class and gender.' *Violence Against Women 11*, 1, 38–64.

Thiara, R.K. (2003) 'South Asian Women and Collective Action in Britain.' In J. Andall (ed.) *Gender and Ethnicity in Contemporary Europe.* London: Berg.

Thiara, R.K. and Hussain, S. (2005) *Supporting Some People: Supporting People and Services for Asian Women and Children Affected by Domestic Violence.* London: Imkaan.

Thiara, R.K. and Roy, S. (2009) *BAMER Women and Children and Domestic Violence: Recent Findings.* London: Imkaan.

United Nations, *Beijing Declaration and Platform for Action,* Fourth World Conference on Women, 15 September 1995. Available at www.unesco.org/education/information/nfsunesco/pdf/BEIJIN_E.PDF.

United Nations General Assembly, *Declaration on the Elimination of Violence Against Women,* resolution 48/104, 20 December 1993. Available at www.un.org/documents/ga/res/48/a48r104, accessed on 25 June 2009.

Walby, S. (2004) *The Cost of Domestic Violence.* London: Department of Trade and Industry Women and Equality Unit.

Walby, S. and Allen, J. (2004) *Domestic Violence, Sexual Assault and Stalking: Findings from the British Crime Survey.* Home Office Research Study 276. London: Home Office.

Williams, P. (1998) *Seeing a Color-Blind Future: The Paradox of Race.* New York: Noonday Press.

Wilson, A. (2006) *Dreams, Questions, Struggles: South Asian Women in Britain.* London: Pluto Press.

Chapter 1

Understanding Violence against South Asian Women

What It Means for Practice

Ravi K. Thiara and Aisha K. Gill

Introduction

Issues of 'race' and ethnicity have rarely been discussed at a conceptual level in the literature on violence against women (VAW); similarly contemporary scholarship on 'race' and ethnicity has not engaged with issues of gendered violence. Consequently, there has been a lack of substantive discussion about the experiences of violence against black and minority ethnic (BME) women. Black feminists have challenged this in two significant ways. First, the development of 'black feminist thought', since the late 1970s and early 1980s, has impacted on how 'difference' is analysed and understood, creating a conceptual space for many feminists to think about these issues in diverse and original ways. In challenging the homogenising and universalising tendencies of feminism, this body of scholarship has helped to refine theoretical approaches to gendered power relations by revealing new ways of understanding the complexity of BME women's experiences and lives. Thus, through initiating critical conversations, notions of 'multiple oppression' and 'intersectionality' have influenced mainstream feminism in its examination of the complex interplay between systems of domination and control, and especially to show how these systems mark the lives of a range of subordinate groups. In its evolution, this theorising has questioned earlier additive approaches, which emphasised hierarchies of oppression and which were widely critiqued for their inherently essentialist and absolutist claims.

Second, an emerging body of writing by South Asian women has begun to highlight South Asian women's experiences of violence and abuse, an area thus far marginalised in the growing field of VAW and domestic violence (DV) scholarship. Even where given visibility, these attempts have remained uninformed by the theoretical developments mentioned above, and different experiences simply been 'added on', rather than used to critically engage with existing explanatory frameworks. This has been echoed in the areas of policy and practice which focus almost exclusively on assumed cultural attributes and associated oppressive practices within these communities. Efforts to 'mainstream' minority ethnic issues, part of a broader integrationist policy agenda, have led to a greater scrutiny of particular 'cultural' practices centring on the family and marriage systems of South Asian communities, reminiscent of the debates of the 1970s and 1980s about arranged marriages.

Current scholarship, as part of the second challenge to marginality, has raised concerns about the construction and representation of problems affecting the lives of South Asian women and their communities, along with the policy and practice responses to them (Batsleer et al. 2002; Gill 2004; Gupta 2003; Thiara 2005a). This literature, mainly (though not exclusively) generated by BME women, reflects a range of different motivations and positions – to highlight differences and specificity in women's experiences, often for policy and funding purposes; to raise issues affecting the organisations that exist to support specific needs; and to some extent raise critical conceptual issues as part of a critique of dominant feminist discourse. Unfortunately, much of this literature does little more than highlight the experiences of South Asian women while gesturing towards a nuanced understanding of the structural underpinnings of these experiences (race and class etc.). Although dialogue generated by this literature has been necessary for informing practice, we argue in this chapter that research, policy and practice on VAW and DV has continued to exist in parallel, so that BME women have primarily been left to 'do their bit' in their fight against VAW, both in challenging racism, especially the disconnect between ethnicity and gender in government policy, and patriarchal practices within their communities.

We suggest that although recent feminist scholarship has assisted us in understanding complex social relations, dominant research, policy and practice responses to South Asian women experiencing gendered violence remain deeply uninformed by this and continue to treat 'difference' merely as 'cultural differences'. Given the complexity of this issue and the various approaches to it, it is hardly surprising that the aims of this chapter are not straightforward, beset as it is by numerous dilemmas which raise many more questions than can be answered. How is it possible to call for the recognition of specificity and difference while at the same time retaining a sense of commonality in experiences of VAW? Even if a theoretical consensus was possible, how might this translate into effective practice? How can we reject an essentialist and absolutist construction of the South Asian woman yet still assert a commonality that is translatable into effective support for women and children?

By foregrounding the inherent complexity and contradiction, and by drawing on developments in research and practice, this chapter aims to explore some of these issues. The chapter is divided into three broad sections. In the first, we examine the theoretical developments that have allowed writers to conceptualise the links between 'race', ethnicity, gender as 'difference' and consider to what extent these have influenced explanations of gendered violence. In the second section we explore the development of the concept of 'intersectionality' and especially how it helps us explain gendered violence in South Asian communities, and what this might mean for the development of practice. Thus, it considers to what extent and in what ways an intersectional approach to gendered violence can be used to deliver improved services for survivors of violence and abuse from different racial, ethnic and socio-economic backgrounds? The suggestion that the response to VAW should be rooted in an understanding both of human rights and intersectionality has been made in recent years (Horvath and Kelly 2007), as part of the argument that VAW should be addressed across all equality strands. And in relation to South Asian women, we argue that this presents the most effective way of understanding and acting on issues of VAW.

In the third section, we examine the implications of the debate on 'difference' and the concept of intersectionality to South Asian women and VAW. We outline the dominant approaches to this issue, and look at the ways in which discussions of 'culture' and differences have shaped debates on ethnicity and gendered violence. In this context, we examine the ways in which religion, 'culture' and 'community' have come to be constructed and represented by the state, and consider how these absolutist constructions shape the responses of practitioners to South Asian women affected by violence and abuse. And so we pose the question: to what extent do religion and culture hinder or assist in furthering our understanding of the issues of VAW and South Asian women? We conclude the chapter by exploring the implications of our discussion for practice, and consider what, based on an intersectional understanding of VAW, the most effective responses are for addressing the issues confronting South Asian women.

'Difference' and feminist analyses: some critical issues

Feminist scholarship has been engaged with questions of 'difference' since the late 1970s, albeit in different ways.[1] Indeed, a consideration of differences has a long history in Western feminism, as both the first and second waves of feminist writing focused on women's experiences to challenge male knowledge and privilege (Barrett 1987). Since the late 1970s, women's studies has emphasised the differences among women, challenging the assumed homogeneity and universalism inherent in claims of sisterhood. Instead they stressed the complexity of oppressions which women experience in gendered ways – 'race'/ethnicity, class, nation, disability, age and sexuality. Consequently, black women's experiences were emphasised to correct their prior invisibility. To date, questions of 'difference', experience, and history remain central to feminist analysis in varied geo-sociopolitical contexts (Mohanty 1991). It was Lorde (1984) who raised the issue of 'difference', pointing out how human differences were organised into simplistic binary oppositions (e.g. dominant/subordinate, man/woman, black/white), and highlighted the institutionalised rejection of 'difference' (Lorde 1984). In language unaffected by postmodernist deconstructionism, she exposed the dangers inherent in not recognising differences both among black people themselves and between black and white. That same year in the UK, a special issue of *Feminist Review* was devoted to a black feminist critique of white feminism, highlighting some pertinent issues about the lived realities of black women in Britain (Feminist Review 1984).

Since this time, debate around 'difference' and diversity has been prolific; at times 'difference' (and its sister 'diversity') has become a catch-all phrase to signify any minor point of differences, with little attention being paid to an analysis of the implications of this concept in concrete settings (something we explore later in the chapter, in relation to VAW). Mainstream writing that explores the intersections between 'race', ethnicity and gender, and considers the consequences of racism for women, is still fairly scarce, as these issues tend to get marginalised in mainstream debates. This is despite some early work which sought to place 'race' and gender at the centre of discussion (see Afshar and Maynard 1994). Much of this critique aimed to challenge the view that 'race' is only a minority experience, in which the category of 'white' remains unanalysed and privileged, leading to the tendency to conflate 'race' with racism (seeing experiences of minority groups only in terms of oppression). Instead, it was pointed out that, as a social construction, the meaning of 'race' varies according to time, place and circumstances,[2] so that the construction of racialised categories ('black' or 'minority ethnic') is also determined by historical, political, policy and cultural contexts which dictate different choices in individual and collective definitions, often leading to contradictions and dilemmas (Afshar and Maynard 1994; Brah 1992).

The analytical concept of 'difference' – emphasising the different and intersecting systems of power and subordination (discursive and material) experienced at the individual and collective level – has led many writers to advocate for a move away from a unidimensional portrayal of the relationship between 'race' and gender. Instead, they stress the complex and contradictory ways in which these categories lead to a variety of forms and experiences of oppression (Afshar and Maynard 1994; Brah 1992; hooks 1984, 1989, 1991) and insist that these issues need to be understood in terms of 'difference' being not a static but dynamic process. The problem here, however, is that while feminists claim to have dealt with the issue of 'difference', there is little theoretical work which takes account of the intersections of 'race', ethnicity and racism within gender studies more generally and especially within the area of VAW. Generally, the concept of 'difference' has come to be seen as an antidote to the unitary term 'woman/en', but while highlighting differences among women, few explore what 'difference' as a concept actually means within empirical research, theoretical analysis or political action. To some extent, this is a reflection of the separate traditions of activism found within Britain on the issue of VAW, where 'handling BME women' has largely been left to BME activists and researchers operating on the margins. Nevertheless, it demonstrates the 'blind spot' in feminist analysis, which leaves VAW in minority ethnic communities as a largely unexamined problem, falling as it does at the intersection between two theoretical 'jurisdictions'.

We argue that to simply focus on different experiences ('difference' as experiential diversity) does not help to illuminate the processes that produce or result in specific forms of subordination. Though some have argued that experience opens the space for investigating similarities and contradictions in women's lives and to develop theories to understand these collectively, we see experience as useful 'data' rather than the 'truth' which requires no explanation (Brah 1992; Collins 1990; Maynard 1994). Indeed, debate over the relationship of structure, culture and experience has long been central to discussions of 'difference'. Brah (1992), for instance, has emphasised the role of experience while calling for a distinction to be made between the everyday of lived experience (individual biography) and experience as a social relation (collective histories and social structural location of groups) (Brah 1996). Highlighting the problems in discussing 'difference' purely in terms of experience, she argues that the two levels are interdependent, 'relationally irreducible', so that collective experience is not representative of individual experiences any more than individual experiences are a direct expression of the collective (Brah 1996, p.117). Furthermore, her emphasis on the idea that differentiation and diversity are at the heart of 'difference' is useful in challenging homogeneity, stressing as it does differences *within* groups as well as *between* them, thus enabling us to focus on the relational dynamics of social relations and power.

As warned by some writers, if 'difference' is taken only as experience and accepted uncritically, then it has 'us' and 'them' connotations. This marks BME women as different and fails to treat 'whiteness' as a privileged racialised identity in need of interrogation. This can result in discrete experiences being written about without challenging the frameworks within which they are couched. As Maynard (1994) argues, recognising that 'race' results in different forms of 'difference' is not the same as paying attention to racism within feminist work. According to Spelman (1988, p.162), this amounts to a 'setting of tolerance, which requires looking but not necessarily seeing, adding voices but not changing what has already been said', where the power remains with white women (hooks 1984).

Moreover, the idea of 'difference' as experience can denote endless possibilities for diversity, as implicit within the liberal-pluralist view of the social world as a collection of differing groups and individuals and encapsulated in the practice of British multiculturalism. This lumps all forms of diversity together as examples of 'difference', viewing them all as similar, and as requiring similar responses, thus making it hard to analyse the inequality between disparate groups and the relationships of power between them. According to Mohanty (1988), questions of historical interconnection are thereby transformed into questions of discrete and separate histories. The current discourse about 'Muslim women' and the splintering of their identities from other subject identities is a consequence of this pluralist approach, which divides women from one another rather than considers what they have in common and so encourages cultural relativism. It is therefore critical to understand the *relational* aspects of black and white women's experiences and not see them as just different experiences, because at times they are conflictual and at times cooperational (Mackinnon 1987). It is by way of this fluid and nuanced approach that we will learn most from our analysis of VAW experiences.

Others have also pointed to the limited analytical value of 'difference' in analyses of 'race' and gender, if 'difference' highlights only diversity, without accounting for power and inequality (Maynard 1994). Due to this limitation, the need to shift focus from 'difference' simply as experience to 'difference' as social relations, which translate differences into oppression, has been emphasised (Brah 1992; Maynard 1994). A number of writers have highlighted the issues that feminist analyses of 'race' and gender should consider, and these provide a useful framework for an investigation of VAW issues. Such a framework considers the material and cultural dimensions of life and the social relations that emerge from and interact with these. It also recognises that access to resources, and the restrictions resulting from the lack of them are integral to analysing situations of black and white women. Implicit to this framework is an acknowledgement that the category 'white' needs to be problematised in any consideration of 'race' and gender (Ware 1992), since a focus on the exercise and mechanisms of white privilege and power can enhance understanding of racism and racial oppression. It also emphasises the need to end the splitting of 'race' and gender identities and positions and instead looks at ways in which each is implied in and experienced through the other, are constitutive, as the ensuing discussion on intersectionality will show.

It is evident, then, that the crossover between feminist and 'race'/ethnic studies has generated important debate and development concerning the ways in which we theorise 'difference'. As it has come to be commonly used, 'difference' can allow theorisations of social divisions if used as an analytical concept, or it can be used to highlight differences in experience. In relation to the VAW literature, it is evident that 'difference' has been used in a limited way, to simply highlight experiential diversity, rather than to develop analytical tools for explaining the ways in which intersecting social divisions impact in given contexts.

Intersectionality

When feminist theory attempts to describe women's experiences through analysing patriarchy, sexuality, or separate spheres ideology, it often overlooks the role of race. Feminists thus ignore how their own race functions to mitigate some aspects of sexism and, moreover, how it often privileges them over and contributes to the domination of other women. Consequently, feminist theory remains white, and its potential to broaden and deepen its analysis by addressing non-privileged women remains unrealised. (Crenshaw 1989, p.154)

Debates about intersections have a long history in the UK, specifically within gender studies, race and ethnic studies, and cultural and diaspora studies. They have challenged the invisibility of black people and the absence of theoretical and analytical frameworks that can take account of the impact of intersecting social divisions on different groups within particular contexts. The common thread linking these accounts, and of importance for our argument, is the idea that in order to understand gendered violence we must take account of 'difference' (in terms of structure and culture), and that we must have the tools to explain this in ways that do not reproduce stereotypical representations of South Asian women's subjectivity or their everyday experiences of their cultures and communities.

The publication of bell hooks's (1981) seminal work *Ain't I a Woman* (as well as Angela Davis's *Women, Race and Class* in the same year) inspired black feminists and scholars in the UK and the US to put forward an analytical critique of the categories 'woman' and 'black' by highlighting the intersections of gender, 'race' and class (Brah and Phoenix 2004; Yuval-Davis 2006). Despite the academy's elision of the crucial contribution made by black feminists in the UK to this debate, the publication of *The Empire Strikes Back* in 1982, a book which included two important chapters on this issue, spearheaded a spate of critical conversations on the topic, leading to numerous publications in the 1980s and 1990s which made crucial contributions to the current formulation of intersectionality or, as many refer to it, intersectional analysis (Centre for Contemporary Cultural Studies (CCCS) 1982).

It can therefore be argued that the debate over what constitutes the core elements of intersectional analysis came before the term itself was first coined by Crenshaw in 1989. While 'intersections' had largely been used descriptively, the term 'intersectionality', incorporating some of the early debate about 'difference', implied a metaphorical and conceptual tool that could be utilised to explain different experiences based on intersecting social divisions and multiple systems of oppression.[3] However, despite providing a broad framework, debate around intersectionality has continued, not least because it is often used differently, creating some inconsistency and ambiguity (Phoenix and Pattynama 2006). More recently, this debate has focused on whether the 'intersectionality of social divisions should be seen as an additive or as a constitutive process' (Yuval-Davis 2006, p.195), or whether the focus should be on systemic intersectionality (limiting representation of complexity) or constructionist intersectionality (giving greater scope for complexity and contradiction) (Prins 2006). Of course, some of these issues were also debated by feminists engaged with the 'difference' discourse, as already noted, leading to a lively and sometimes heated debate about some of the central issues at stake in trying to understand and represent the histories, lives and experiences of black and white women, especially in relation to each other.

Thus, although debate about what 'intersectionality' actually means has been rife (Brah and Phoenix 2004; Browne and Misra 2003), feminist scholars generally agree on its principal tenets. First, and fundamentally, intersectionality is the theory that categories such as 'race', gender, class and sexuality are socially defined whose meanings are historically contingent. Second, specific locations in this matrix of intersecting hierarchies create a unique set of experiences that are more significant than the sum of their parts, and reflect the 'multiplicative' nature of intersecting oppressions (Crenshaw 1991). Third, intersecting forms of discrimination create both oppression and opportunity (Collins 1990).[4] Fourth, because hierarchies of power are cross-cutting, it is likely that a person will be simultaneously advantaged by certain identities and disadvantaged by others. For example, a gay South Asian male may experience privilege because of his maleness, but be marginalised because of his race and sexuality. Fifth, and finally, these hierarchies intersect at all levels of social life, both through social structure and social interaction (Zin and Dill 1996). The most important implication of intersectionality is that theorising about 'race', class and gender is always both historicised and contextualised.

The essence of intersectionality, then, is that in a society marked by multiple systems of domination (based on 'race', gender and class, among others), individuals' experiences are not shaped by single identities or locations (as a woman or a black person), but that the experience of each is also marked by other social divisions. Crucially, it recognises that some women's experiences are marked by multiple forms of oppression, and that single categories can be further broken down so that 'women' (for example) can be situated in powerful/less ways to one another. This involves looking at how power is inscribed within individual systems of oppression (such as between women and men in South Asian communities) and between them (such as between white women and South Asian women as well as white and South Asian men). By rejecting meta-narratives or theories, intersectionality foregrounds the multiple aspects of women's social dis/location and identities and emphasises the intersecting forms of oppression that shape women's lives and multiple subject positions (Razack 1998). Intersectionality or intersectional analysis has been used to examine VAW in the US and Canada (see Sokoloff with Pratt 2005), although debate about whether some of this reproduces additive notions of oppression, especially when used in a limited way within political mobilisation, is still rife (Yuval-Davis 2006).

Indeed, the UK state policy of multiculturalism ignores some of the 'warnings' which have been flagged by feminist writers, and the very pitfalls identified have often been reinforced in practice. This has led some South Asian women's organisations to assert that multiculturalism has enabled the state to construct minorities in homogenised ways,[5] where women's voices are marginalised (see Chapter 2 by Wilson, Chapter 4 by Patel and Siddiqui, and Chapter 5 by Gill and Mitra-Kahn).

How to analyse the different social divisions inscribed within intersectionality is a problem that has preoccupied many scholars. Yuval-Davis (2006) highlights the 'conflation or separation of the different analytic levels in which intersectionality is located', arguing that the analytical separation of different social divisions, such as 'race', gender and class, is needed while looking at how each intersects in the lived reality of particular groups of women at particular times and in particular contexts (Yuval-Davis 2006, p.195). At the heart of the argument is the idea that since different social divisions are 'differently framed', resting on different ontological claims, they cannot be reduced to each other. Thus, it is the interrelationship of these elements in concrete settings that enable us to fully understand their impact on particular women at specific historical moments, because 'being oppressed.... is always constructed and inter-meshed in other social divisions' (Yuval-Davis 2006, p.195; see also Verloo 2006). Although there has been much debate in the UK about the *basis* for an analytical differentiation between social divisions, many writers have also drawn attention to the inadequacy of separating different oppressions and social divisions, structure (material) and culture (representation), and everyday experience and social structure (see Anthias 2001; Anthias and Yuval-Davis 1983; Brah 1996; Maynard 1994). In this way, the usefulness of giving primacy to unitary subject identities was debunked similarly to additive approaches to oppression.[6]

Although the use of the term intersectionality has become increasingly widespread, this has resulted for some in a lack of analytic clarity, espe-cially since the term seemingly implies different things depending on those using it. Thus Crenshaw (2001) speaks of 'a many layered blanket of oppression' or 'intersectional subordination'. For Yuval-Davis (2006) this is reminiscent of additive approaches, though Crenshaw (2001) makes a useful distinction between political and structural intersectionality which is often overlooked. The complexities of intersectionality have led writers to emphasise different points: some emphasise oppression identities – everyday life, culture, subjectivity – whereas others lay greater stress on social structural disadvantage (and the ways in which inequalities shape the relative positions of different groups). Certainly, Crenshaw's (2001) dis-tinction between structural and political intersectionality is useful in explaining the situation of South Asian women and their experience of VAW in the UK. Not only does the intersection of various social divisions define the experiences of domestic violence for South Asian women (struc-tural) but also in Crenshaw's words, both 'feminist and anti-racist politics have functioned in tandem to marginalise the issue of violence against women of color' (political) (Crenshaw 1993, p.3). This is clearly exempli-fied by the struggles of autonomous South Asian women's organisations in the UK (see Chapter 2 by Wilson).

Another useful distinction between these two different approaches to intersectionality has been made by Yuval-Davis (2006). She distinguishes between the *additive* model (which she criticises for failing to move beyond the experiential – social identities) and the *constitutive* model, advocated by feminist scholars in the UK, which guards against separating different levels of analysis because they need to be understood separately as well as in interaction with each other (Anthias and Yuval-Davis 1992; Brah 1996). A key difference between the two models of intersectionality is that while the former is focused on developing explanations for the dis/location of 'marginal' women, the latter has been developed to be applicable to any group, whether in a position of power or powerlessness (Yuval-Davis 2006). The *constitutive* model, thus, enables intersectionality to be used as 'a major analytical tool that challenges hegemonic approaches to the study of stratification as well as reified forms of identity politics' (Yuval-Davis 2006, p.201), though the question of which and how many social divisions should be included remains contested (Bradley 1996; Lutz 2002). Used as a tool for analysis then, this model of intersectionality helps to uncover the relation of different identity groups to power, their relationship to each other, as well as power relations within these groups at specific historical moments. This further allows us to recognise the 'contested nature of the boundaries of these identity groups and the possibly contested political claims for representation of people located in the same social positions' (Yuval-Davis 2006, p.204).

South Asian women, 'difference' and violence against women

A body of literature has emerged in the UK since the mid-1990s challenging the unidimensional view of South Asian women as passive victims of their cultures, communities and menfolk, a historical trajectory begun during colonialism when the obsession with *sati* (widow burning) defined the Westerner's views about the family and marriage systems of the 'natives'. Since the late 1990s, the multiplicity of their subjectivity and identity has been foregrounded along with the transforming, fragmentary, and contested nature of cultures in transition (Brah 1996; Puwar and Raghuram 2003; Thiara 2003; Wilson 2006). The multiple, complex and contradictory location of South Asian women in resistance politics in the UK has also been highlighted (Thiara 2002; Wilson 2006) along with the error of speaking about '*the* South Asian woman', because of its homogenising and naturalising impact on this category, itself a product of the West (Thiara 2003, p.79). However, in practice, these insights have failed to inform policy and practice responses to South Asian women generally, and within VAW discourse in particular. Instead, there appears to be an even greater 'fixing' of this category (South Asian woman) within the area of VAW, as the current policy/political preoccupation with practices such as forced marriage and 'honour'-related violence illustrate, practices which are not uncontested among South Asian women themselves (see Gill 2009).

Although two discernible strands have been identified elsewhere in the VAW literature and its treatment of ethnicity (Sokoloff and Dupont 2005, p.39), in the UK, most of the work on VAW and BME still predominantly seeks to highlight the experiences of different groups of women (mainly South Asian) affected by VAW (mainly DV) without a substantive exploration of the structural underpinnings of this in diverse communities. While broader theoretical developments around the concept of intersectionality have been pioneering, their impact on the VAW literature has been limited, and intersectional scholarship is in its infancy in the UK (Horvath and Kelly 2007). This is partly due to the fact that much of the VAW and BME literature has had a particular motivation – to emphasise the specificity of experience to help in the fight for greater recognition and redistribution. This may also be due to the way these studies have been funded, so that most of the existing research has largely been financed by government departments or organisations seeking to improve responsiveness, rather than independently determined. It is only since about 2002 that writing on VAW has begun to draw on intersectional conceptualisations (Batsleer *et al.* 2002; Horvath and Kelly 2007; Thiara 2005a). An intersectional approach is necessary, not only in providing an understanding of the ways in which different social divisions impact on and differentiate experiences of VAW among diverse groups of women, but also for challenging the problematic unidimensional articulation of cultures and communities reflected in recent policy and legal developments.

It is worth restating the point that the ways in which women experience violence, the options open to them in dealing with that violence and the extent to which they have access to services to help them are all profoundly shaped by the intersection of gender with other dimensions, such as 'race', ethnicity, class, 'culture' and nationality. Intersectionality, therefore, has much to offer in exposing women's diverse experiences of violence and their different needs in response to it, and can inform the development of policy and service delivery so that they are better targeted to meet those needs. However, it is not sufficient to use intersectionality to merely highlight women's different experiences across the major dimensions of power, as there also needs to be an interrogation of systems of power that re/produce subordination. Thus, scholarship and policy must move beyond the mere multiculturalist flagging of diversity, aimed at enhancing understanding of cultural differences and practices, an approach that is typical of *additive* intersectionality, towards deploying the *constitutive* model of intersectionality, which emphasises 'recognising and analysing the hierarchies and systems of domination that permeate society and that systematically exploit and control people' (Anderson and Collins 2001, pp.5–6). Of course, this shift has been of major concern to many feminists in the UK, as highlighted by our discussion of 'difference'. In practice, the two approaches lead to somewhat different types of practice, with the first being marked by the 'cultural differences' response and the second by the anti-racist, 'racial equality' approach. While these approaches are not mutually exclusive, in practice political advocacy has tended to highlight the first at the expense of the second.

'Collective victimhood'

Mainstream literature on VAW in the UK has generally reiterated the assertion that violence against women, and especially domestic violence, affects women across all sections of society irrespective of 'race', ethnicity, class and other characteristics (Hanmer and Itzen 2000; Walby and Allen 2004). This is a part of what has been termed the construction of 'collective victimhood' by some (Thiara 2008). Although research is sparse in the UK, elsewhere – in Canada, the US and Germany for instance – there are data to suggest that minority ethnic women are at greater risk of violence, particularly domestic violence, and that the most severe and lethal violence is more prevalent among low-income women of colour (Brownridge 2008; Johnson 2006; Rennison and Planty 2001; Schroettle and Khelaifat 2007; Sokoloff and Dupont 2005). Some writers have also indicated that South Asian women in the UK are likely to experience more severe abuse, and over a longer period of time (see Chapter 6 in this volume; Gupta 2003; Thiara 2005b) than white women. Furthermore, statistics show that

59 per cent of all homicides in London in 2005–06 were of BME women (see Thiara 2006).

However, very little mainstream research has sought to explore what the data tell us about the situations of different groups of women, or what the failures are in practice that result in their deaths. An important part of examining VAW is also recognising that racialised women experience additional forms of violence and control at the hands of state agencies, such as social services, housing authorities, the police and the criminal justice system, a process dubbed 'double victimisation' by some writers (Gill 2004; Razack 1998; Stark 1995). Thus, the construction of this 'collective victimhood' in the UK has led to a silence at worst and scant attention at best to the issues of BME women and VAW within mainstream feminist literature. More precisely, these issues have been left for black feminist activists and researchers to address. This failure either to address 'difference', or to leave it untheorised, has led to an elision of the ways in which inequality and discrimination continue to mark the lives of these women and further compound their experiences of violence and abuse.

The assertion that DV affects all women, irrespective of 'race', class and ethnicity, has been criticised by many in the US, who challenge the notion of 'universal risk' (Richie 2000), seeing it as a 'token attempt at inclusion of diverse perspectives but also evidence of sloppy research and theory building' (Kanuha 1996, p.40). In particular, this claim that women share a universal experience – 'collective victimhood' – is a limited way of understanding both the particularity and complexity of the abuse experiences of South Asian women, offering little for exploring the nature, prevalence and impact of violence on them.

As already noted, despite the silence of feminist literature, a tradition of black feminist research and activism has sought to give visibility to the experiences of VAW within particular BME communities. Although much of this literature is limited in scope, it has highlighted the ways in which 'race'/racism, ethnicity and culture help to construct particular experiences for BME women, a process described as 'minoritisation' by some writers, and not dissimilar to the 'racialisation' concept developed in the late 1980s (Miles 1989). Amina Mama's *Hidden Struggle* (1989), the first study of domestic violence in African, Asian and Caribbean communities in London, represents an examination of the subject within an international framework, and was the first work to utilise a theoretical position based on intersecting notions of power. Critiquing radical and socialist feminists, and their analysis of patriarchy, class and international capital respectively, Mama (1989) joined other black feminists in calling for 'race', ethnicity, culture and religion to be incorporated into any analysis of VAW, in a bid to 'develop a feminist praxis that takes the various social divisions more fully into account' and thus to challenge the inherent ethnocentrism and essentialism in dominant analyses (Mama 1989, p.4).

Mama's (1989) work was followed by other studies – based on local research – by black researchers and activists, who pointed out that the lives of BME women are varied because 'race'/racism, ethnicity, class, religion and nationality all impact both on their experiences of violence and abuse and the responses they receive from support agencies. Most of this literature, however, focuses on particular groups of women (South Asian women) and often only their experiences of domestic violence. While accepting some commonalities in experience with white women, these studies point to the specificity of BME women's experiences, both in the nature of abuse experienced and the barriers encountered when seeking help and support. As a consequence of this work, it is now widely recognised that South Asian women face the same problems as white women, while they also face additional difficulties in the context of domestic violence, based on 'race'/racism, ethnicity, culture, religion, nationality, immigration status, language, and community dynamics, all of which increase their vulnerability and limit their ability to leave abusive contexts and seek professional help (Anitha 2008; Izzidien 2008; Rai and Thiara 1997; Sen 1997). Furthermore, evidence shows that the marginalisation of women's abuse experiences within their communities by community leaders along with the discriminatory responses by support agencies compound their problems and result in greater victimisation (Gill 2004; Rai and Thiara 1997; Sen 1997).

The issue is further complicated by questions raised by several writers about the accepted ways of defining and measuring DV, because these definitions fail to take account of the socio-cultural contexts and culturally specific forms of abuse (Sokoloff and Dupont 2005). Both activists and researchers stress the importance of recognising that abuse against South Asian women is often perpetrated by family members – commonly more than one – as well as intimate partners (Parmar, Sampson and Diamond 2005; Thiara 2005b; see also Chapter 6), that South Asian women are likely to experience severe abuse over a longer period than white women, and that it takes them longer to move on from violence and abuse

(Humphreys 2008; Humphreys and Thiara 2002). Research has further revealed the culturally specific nature of the abuse perpetrated against South Asian women, in the form of forced marriage (FM) and 'honour'-based violence (Anitha and Gill 2009).

However, this emphasis on culturally specific forms of harm, though important, does run the risk of totally separating the abuse experiences of South Asian women from those of other women, a disassociation that encourages those responsible for responding to abuse to focus only on the incidents deemed to be culturally specific or to explain South Asian women's abuse experiences only through the lens of culture (Gangoli *et al.* 2006; Gill 2009; Samad and Eade 2002). Seen in the context of racism, this promotes a tendency to 'blame the victims', thus reproducing earlier debates about the backwardness of cultures or communities that remain unassimilated into 'British' society. Although the current discourse on ethnicity, culture and VAW is presented as though it is sensitive to 'culture', without the pitfalls of 'cultural relativism', in fact, embedded as it is in current political debates about community cohesion, it becomes implicated in racist 'othering' discourses and therefore marks a continuation of familiar, long-standing debates. While it is important to incorporate specific forms of abuse into any analysis or understanding of VAW and BME women, we also need to be mindful of the potential for a disconnection to occur, leading to the abuse of South Asian women being seen as separate and different. VAW, in all its forms, is primarily about the assertion of power and control over women. Although differences often exist in the explanations used to justify acts of violence, so that for FM and HBV, notions of 'honour', shame, reputation and culture are deployed, these should not take precedence over an analysis of power and control.

Since VAW is rooted in power and control, this alone acts as a powerful deterrent for women coming forward to speak of the abuse they suffer. Given their dis/location in British society, it is even more unsurprising that South Asian women face personal and social barriers in disclosing abuse. They may be reluctant to disclose abuse for fear of bringing shame on their families within communities, and of reinforcing racist stereotypes (Gill 2004; Mama 1989; Thiara 2005b). In particular, notions of honour and shame are so significant for some South Asian women that to talk about their experiences of abuse constitutes 'a violation of the social hierarchy and entails putting self above the family' (Gill 2004, p.474). Furthermore, women with uncertain or dependent immigration status are especially vulnerable to poverty and extreme isolation, and so refrain from disclosing abuse for fear of reprisals from the state (Roy 2008). Some groups of South Asian women are also more likely than others to live below the poverty line (Anitha 2008). It is the multiplicity and complexity which determine their situations that, we argue, need to be grappled with and understood, without recourse to 'comfortable' assumptions about South Asian 'culture' treating South Asian women in oppressive ways. Indeed, policy makers seeing VAW as something culturally specific to South Asian women has resulted in an essentialising of South Asian women's experiences and cultures, and has consequently marked their communities in negative ways. This represents a second layer of 'collective victimhood', which, in homogenising all South Asian women's abuse experiences, further serves to deny women the positive responses needed from support agencies. Although stemming from very different impulses, the two layers of 'collective victimhood' together obscure the complexity of the abuse experiences of South Asian women and compound their subordination.

What the preceding discussion reveals is that violence against South Asian women needs to be understood in relation to the broader social context, whereby the interplay of multiple sites of oppression shape the experiences of abused women and define their responses to their situations and problems. As we have stated, South Asian women's experiences of violence and abuse cannot simply be reduced to issues of gender inequality, and neither are they simply reducible to religion and culture. Instead, they must be seen in terms of the *intersection* of these and other elements. As Bograd (1999) states: 'intersections color the meaning and nature of domestic violence, how it is experienced by self and responded to by others, how personal and social consequences are represented and how and whether escape and safety can be obtained' (cited in Sokoloff and Dupont 2005, p.43). If we accept that social divisions are constructed and intermeshed, this suggests that the intersection of gender with other systems of domination needs to be analysed and understood to explain violence against South Asian women. Similarly, we need to examine how gender oppression itself may be defined by other social divisions or systems of oppression, and how these shape the responses women receive from support agencies and define their responses to their situations. This also impacts on the construction of their subjectivity (as victims or survivors, for example). If priority is given to family or community over the individual, then women will be reluctant to disclose their problems; where women are constructed as victims of cultural practices, this is likely to shape service responses as well as making it less likely that women will pursue criminal prosecutions. Thus whether women remain silent or speak out is likely to be shaped by complex factors – personal, social, representational, cultural and institutional – emphasising the need for an intersectional approach.

Implications for practice

Intersectionality ultimately indicates the need for practitioners and researchers to take account of the complex interplay of major social divisions and systems of domination in shaping the lives and experiences of individuals and groups. In relation to South Asian women and VAW, it suggests that an overemphasis on culture as the primary tool for explaining such violence risks obscuring the dimensions of 'race'/racism, ethnicity, class and nationality, which are integral to understanding the abuse experiences of South Asian women in the British context. This privileging of culture is often illustrated by the 'adding on' of South Asian women to conference and policy agendas as examples of additional cultural issues in relation to domestic violence. There is often a marked absence of other BME women from such agendas, as culture is equated with only particular groups within the dominant racialised discourse in the UK. Collins (1998) notes in this regard that the focus on cultural differences must not 'erase [the need to look at] structural power' (cited in Sokoloff and Dupont 2005, p.45), as to do so can reduce the potential for change. The issue is complicated as the spectre of South Asian women abused by 'backward men' who follow 'backward cultural traditions' has also been uncritically reinforced by some South Asian women practitioners, and is often more palatable to policy makers and practitioners.

Of course, focusing on culture as a way of understanding and responding to domestic violence can be extremely valuable and helpful. However, we must guard against reproducing essentialist notions of culture (Thiara 2003) and challenge such notions where they are deployed within policy and practice – whenever they combine to assert the 'collective victimhood' of all South Asian women, for instance. This reduction of domestic violence to culture has been challenged by some writers (Burman, Smailes and Chantler 2004). This point has also been made by Dasgupta (1998) in the US, who highlights the readiness of white Americans to accept that 'other' cultures are more readily accepting of woman abuse than white American society (Dasgupta 1998). Thus, intersectionality suggests that the ways in which cultural experiences of violence and abuse are mediated through other structures of domination need to be emphasised and understood.

Above all, to simply link culture with domestic violence is to deny culture the protective role that it plays in many women's lives, and to accept the assertions of those that use culture to justify VAW. In the US, for example, there is some evidence to suggest that cultural defence has been used effectively to reduce the sentences of men who kill their partners (Maguigan 1995; Sokoloff and Dupont 2005). As Sokoloff and Dupont (2005, p.47) argue, this form of defence deflects attention away from individual behaviour and results in cultural determinism (where the dominant group is seen to have a universal culture of civilisation). Razack (1998, p.57) also states that this fails to recognise that VAW is not a cultural attribute but a product of male domination inextricably linked to racism. Moreover, in focusing on and responding to violence against South Asian women, we must be wary of disempowering women still further by reinforcing negative stereotypes. This is easier said than done, as South Asian activists have discovered since the late 1970s. The absence of quality, grounded and well-funded research can lead to unwitting assertions of the 'collective victimhood' of South Asian women. Clearly, the challenge for researchers, activists and practitioners is to recognise the intersecting dimensions of power and oppression, thus enabling us to move our focus away from cultural factors to also consider issues of marginality and exclusion.

Intersectionality thus offers the best hope for a nuanced approach to VAW, as it allows us to examine issues of VAW in relation to South Asian women in the UK in all its complexity. The question that emerges, then, is how can the complexities exposed by intersectionality be understood by practitioners to effectively respond to South Asian women they may encounter? This is not an easy task, as dealing with 'difference' can be a scary business for practitioners. As a starting point in doing this, it is important for all to undergo self-reflection and ask, for instance:

- How am I located in the context of social divisions and systems of oppression and discrimination? What is my 'relationality' to South Asian women?

- How am I influenced by the wider construction and representation of South Asian women affected by violence and abuse in my responses to them?

- How do I contribute to the reinforcement of such representations and oppressions and how can I contribute towards challenging these?

Inevitably, the ways in which we understand and explain violence against South Asian women will shape the service responses that are developed to respond to their needs. As we have seen, it is important to take a broader view of VAW and to guard against cultural determinism. Intersectionality is crucial for understanding VAW and ethnicity in this way, enabling as it does an interrogation of the ways in which different social divisions and dominatory systems intersect, to produce particular experiences for particular groups of women at particular historical moments. Moreover, intersectionality enables an insight into the ways in which those *within* particular groups are situated in relation to power, as well as the ways in which power is inscribed in relations *between* groups.

If we accept that oppression is constructed through and intermeshed with other social divisions and systems of domination and discrimination, then the example of a South Asian woman affected by domestic violence with no recourse to public funds (because of her immigration status) encapsulates the ways in which diverse systems of domination ('race'/racism, ethnicity, gender, nationality, class, culture) produce a particular experience of oppression and lead to her dis/location. This shows us that an understanding both of the complex ways in which each system operates independently and the ways in which each one intersects with the others is necessary to understand such a woman's situation in its entirety. Such an intersectional understanding should then shape the support responses crucial to addressing her situation.

In conclusion, as we have demonstrated, the utility of analysing social divisions as separate and internally homogenous has been widely questioned within feminist discourse. Yet, although intersectional analysis is now widely used and focused upon by feminist and 'race' and ethnicity scholars in the US and UK, it has thus far not been employed to study VAW in the UK. We have argued for the need to revisit and draw upon these valuable insights to better understand VAW within diverse groups in the UK, and especially South Asian women. It is widely recognised that women from South Asian communities in the UK occupy a position marked by multiple marginality. In relation to VAW this means that they may face violence in their homes, discrimination in the public domain, and insensitivity at the hands of criminal justice and other public agencies. However, despite warnings from writers against essentialising the 'South Asian woman', in relation to VAW, we have shown that dominant responses continue to be marked by the construction of a 'collective victimhood' of South Asian women. This leads to a position where 'different experiences' are highlighted at the expense of conceptualising VAW in relation to 'difference', which enables an exploration of how women and communities are implicated in power relations. In advocating for the utilisation of the concept of intersectionality, we argue that it represents a powerful conceptual framework which can assist us to enhance our understanding of violence against South Asian women in all its complexity, contradiction and diversity, and inform our responses to it.

Notes

1. We use 'difference' as a conceptual term, not as a descriptive one; where this is done we use 'differences'.

2. Indeed, the theoretical debate around 'race' and ethnicity has been prolific and though not aired here, it is important in informing theorising on 'difference'.

3. As already noted, much of the earlier debate around intersections has been retained and further redeveloped within postmodern discussions of 'difference' and feminist theory and practice, especially that which has sought to conceive newer ways of organising around 'difference' – Yuval-Davis's (1997) transversal politics and Fraser's (1997) politics of difference.

4. Patricia Collins' (1990) contribution to this new feminist epistemology has had a profound effect on feminist thought. She has been instrumental in developing a social constructionist view of knowledge that links identities, standpoints and social locations in a matrix of domination (Collins 1990, pp.234–5).

5. Multiculturalism shifts emphasis away from racism as institutionalised inequality to cultural differences (mutually exclusive) or heterogeneity and the need to preserve, affirm and celebrate the traditions and cultures of different groups especially minorities.

6. Additive approaches were critiqued for conflating identity politics and positionality.

References

Afshar, H. and Maynard, M. (eds) (1994) The Dynamics of 'Race' and Gender. London: Taylor & Francis.

Anderson, M. and Collins, P.H. (2001) 'Introduction.' In M. Anderson and P.H. Collins (eds) *Race, Class and Gender: An Anthology.* Belmont, CA: Wadsworth.

Anitha, S. (2008) *Forgotten Women: Domestic Violence, Poverty and South Asian Women with No Recourse to Public Funds.* Manchester: Oxfam Publishing.

Anitha, S. and Gill, A. (2009) 'Coercion, consent and the forced marriage debate in the UK.' *Feminist Legal Studies 17*, 2.

Anthias, F. (2001) 'The material and the symbolic in theorizing social stratification.' *British Journal of Sociology 52*, 3, 367–90.

Anthias, F. and Yuval-Davis, N. (1983) 'Contextualising feminism: Gender, ethnic and class divisions.' *Feminist Review 15*, 62–75.

Anthias, F. and Yuval-Davis, N. (1992) *Racialized Boundaries: Race, Nation, Gender, Colour and Class and the Anti-Racist Struggle.* London: Routledge.

Barrett, M. (1987) 'The concept of "difference".' *Feminist Review, 26*, 29–41.

Batsleer, J., Burman, E., Chantler, K., McIntosh, H.S., *et al.* (2002) *Domestic Violence and Minoritisation: Supporting Women to Independence.* Manchester: Women's Studies Research Centre, Manchester Metropolitan University.

Bogard, M. (1999) 'Strengthening domestic violence theories: Intersections of race, class, sexual orientation and gender.' *Journal of Marital and Family Theory 25*, 275–289.

Bradley, H. (1996) *Fractured Identities: The Changing Patterns of Inequality.* Cambridge: Polity Press.

Brah, A. (1992) 'Difference, Diversity, Differentiation.' In J. Donald and A. Rattansi (eds) *'Race', Culture and Difference.* London: Sage and the Open University.

Brah, A. (1996) *Cartographies of Diaspora: Contesting Identities.* London: Routledge.

Brah, A. and Phoenix, A. (2004) 'Ain't I a woman? Revisiting intersectionality.' *Journal of International Women's Studies 5*, 3, 74–87.

Browne, I. and Misra, J. (2003) 'The intersection of race and gender in the labour market.' *Annual Review of Sociology 29*, 1, 487–514.

Brownridge, D.A. (2008) 'Understanding the elevated risk of partner violence against Aboriginal women: A comparison of two nationally representative surveys of Canada.' *Journal of Family Violence 23*, 353–367.

Burman, E., Smailes, S. and Chantler, K. (2004) 'Culture as a barrier to service provision and delivery: Domestic violence services for minoritised women.' *Critical Social Policy 24*, 3, 332–357.

Centre for Contemporary Cultural Studies (CCCS) (1982) *The Empire Strikes Back.* London: Routledge.

Collins, P.H. (1990) *Black Feminist Thought.* London: Unwin Hyman.

Collins, P.H. (1998) 'The tie that binds: Race, gender and U.S. violence.' *Ethnic and Racial Studies 21*, 917–938.

Crenshaw, K. (1989) 'Demarginalizing the intersection of race and sex: A Black feminist critique of antidiscrimination doctrine, feminist theory and antiracist politics.' *University of Chicago Legal Forum 1989*, 139–67.

Crenshaw, K. (1991) 'Mapping the Margins: Intersectionality, Identity Politics and Violence Against Women of Color.' *Stanford Law Review 43*, 1241–1245.

Crenshaw, K. (1993) 'Beyond Racism and Misogyny.' In M. Matsuda, C. Lawrence and K. Crenshaw (eds) *Words that Wound.* Boulder, CO: Westview Press.

Crenshaw, K. (2001) 'Mapping the Margins: Intersectionality, Identity Politics and Violence against Women of Color.' Paper presented at the World Conference on Racism, Durban, South Africa. Available at www.hsph.harvard.edu/grhf/WoC/feminisms/crenshaw.html, accessed on 29 June 2009.

Dasgupta, S.D. (1998) 'Women's Realities: Defining Violence against Women by Immigration, Race and Class.' In R.K. Bergen (ed.) *Issues in Intimate Violence.* Thousand Oaks, CA: Sage.

Davis, A. (1981) *Women, Race and Class.* London: The Women's Press.

Feminist Review (1984) 'Many Voices One Chant: Black Feminist Perspectives.' *Feminist Review 17* (special issue).

Fraser, N. (1997) *Justice Interruptus.* New York: Routledge.

Gangoli, G., Razack, A. and McCarry, M. (2006) *Forced Marriage and Domestic Violence among South Asian Communities in North East England.* For Northern Rock Foundation. Bristol: University of Bristol.

Gill, A. (2009) '"Honour" killings and the quest for justice in Black and minority ethnic communities in the UK.' *Criminal Justice Policy Review,* November.

Gill, A. (2004) 'Voicing the silent fear: South Asian women's experiences of domestic violence.' *Howard Journal of Criminal Justice 43,* 5, 465–83.

Gupta, R. (ed.) (2003) *From Homebreakers to Jailbreakers: Southall Black Sisters.* London: Zed Books.

Hanmer, J. and Itzen, C. (eds) (2000) *Home Truths about Domestic Violence.* London: Routledge.

hooks, b. (1981) *Ain't I A Woman?* London: Pluto Press.

hooks, b. (1984) *Feminist Theory: From Margin to Centre.* Boston, MA: South End Press.

hooks, b. (1989) *Talking Back: Thinking Feminist, Thinking Black.* London: Sheba Feminist Publishers.

hooks, b. (1991) *Yearning.* London: Turnaround.

Horvath, M. and Kelly, L. (2007) *From the Outset: Why Violence Should be a Core Cross-strand Priority Theme for the Commission for Equality and Human Rights.* London: End Violence Against Women Campaign.

Humphreys, C. (2008) 'Responding to the individual trauma of domestic violence: Challenges for mental health professionals.' *Social Work in Mental Health 7,* 1–3, 186–2003.

Humphreys, C. and Thiara, R.K. (2002) *Routes to Safety: Protection Issues Facing Abused Women and Children and the Role of Outreach Services.* Bristol: Women's Aid Publications.

Izzidien, S. (2008) *'I can't tell people what is happening at home': Domestic Abuse within South Asian Communities – The Specific Needs of Women, Children and Young People.* London: NSPCC.

Johnson, H. (2006) *Measuring Violence Against Women: Statistical Trends 2006.* Ottawa: Statistics Canada.

Kanuha, V. (1996) 'Domestic Violence, Racism and the Battered Women's Movement in the United States.' In J.L. Edelson and Z.C. Eisikovits (eds) *Future Interventions with Battered Women and their Families.* Thousand Oaks, CA: Sage.

Lorde, A. (1984) *Sister Outsider.* New York: Crossing Press.

Lutz, H. (2002) 'Intersectional Analysis: A Way Out of Multiple Dilemmas?' Paper presented at the International Sociological Association Conference, Brisbane, July.

Mackinnon, K. (1987) *Feminist Unmodified.* Cambridge, MA: Harvard University Press.

Maguigan, H. (1995) 'Cultural evidence and male violence: Are feminist and multi-culturalist reformers on a collision course in criminal courts?' *New York University Law Review 70,* 36–99.

Mama, A. (1989) *The Hidden Struggle: Statutory and Voluntary Sector Responses to Violence Against Black Women in the Home.* London: London Race and Housing Research Unit.

Maynard, M. (1994) ' "Race", Gender and the Concept of "Difference" in Feminist Thought.' In H. Afshar and M. Maynard (eds) *The Dynamics of 'Race' and Gender.* London: Taylor & Francis.

Miles, R. (1989) *Racism.* London: Routledge.

Mohanty, C. (1988) 'Under Western eyes: Feminist scholarship and colonial discourses.' *Feminist Review 30,* 60–88.

Parmar, A., Sampson, A. and Diamond, A. (2005) *Tackling Domestic Violence: Providing Advocacy and Support to Survivors from Black and Other Minority Ethnic Communities.* Development and Practice Report 35. London: Home Office.

Phoenix, A. and Pattynama, P. (2006) 'Intersectionality.' *European Journal of Women's Studies 13,* 3, 187–92.

Prins, B. (2006) 'Narrative accounts of origins: A blind spot in the intersectional approach?' *European Journal of Women's Studies 13,* 3, 277–90.

Puwar, N. and Raghuram, P. (eds) (2003) *South Asian Women in the Diaspora.* Oxford: Berg.

Rai, D. and Thiara, R.K. (1997) *Redefining Spaces: The Needs of Black Women and Children and Black Workers in Women's Aid.* Bristol: Women's Aid Federation England.

Razack, S. (1998) 'What is to be gained by Looking White people in the Eye? Race in Sexual Violence Cases.' In S. Razack (ed.) *Looking White People in the Eye: Gender, Race, and Culture in Courtrooms and Classrooms.* Toronto: University of Toronto Press.

Rennison, C. and Planty, M. (2003) 'Non-lethal intimate partner violence: Examining race, gender and income patterns.' *Violence and Victims 18,* 4, 433–43.

Richie, B. (2000) 'A Black feminist reflection on the antiviolence movement.' *Signs 25,* 1133–7.

Roy, S. (2008) *No Recourse – No Duty to Care? Experiences of BAMER Women and Children Affected by Domestic Violence and Insecure Immigration Status.* London: Imkaan.

Samad, Y. and Eade, J. (2002). *Community Perceptions of Forced Marriage.* London: Foreign and Commonwealth Office.

Schroettle, M. and Khelaifat, N. (2007) *Health-Violence-Migration: A Comparative Secondary Analysis of Health and Violence Related Situations of Women with and without Migration Backgrounds in Germany. A Summary of Main Results.* Bielefeld, Germany: Interdisciplinary Women and Gender Studies, Bielefeld University.

Sen, P. (1997) *Searching for Routes to Safety.* London: London Borough of Camden Equalities Unit.

Sokoloff, N.J. and Dupont, I. (2005) 'Domestic violence at the intersections of race, class and gender.' *Violence Against Women 11,* 1, 38–64.

Sokoloff, N. with Pratt, C. (ed.) (2005) *Domestic Violence at the Margins: Readings on Race, Class, Gender and Culture.* Piscataway, NJ: Rutgers University Press.

Spelman, E. (1988) *Inessential Woman.* London: The Women's Press.

Stark, E. (1995) 'Re-presenting woman battering: From a battered woman syndrome to coercive control.' *Albany Law Review 58,* 973–1026.

Thiara, R.K. (2003) 'South Asian Women and Collective Action in Britain.' In J. Andall (ed.) *Gender and Ethnicity in Contemporary Europe.* London: Berg.

Thiara, R.K. (2005a) 'Dilemmas of Diversity: Responses to Black and Minority Ethnic Women Experiencing Domestic Violence in the UK.' Paper presented to Co-ordination Action on Human Rights Violations (CAHRV) European Conference on Interpersonal Violence, Paris, 26–28 September.

Thiara, R.K. (2005b) *The Need for Specialist Domestic Violence Services for Asian Women and Children.* London: Imkaan.

Thiara, R.K. (2006) 'Black and Minority Ethnic Women Affected by Domestic Violence: Issues in the UK.' In International Planned Parenthood Federation (IPPF) *Choices: Sexual and Reproductive Health and Rights in Europe.* Belgium: IPPF European Network.

Thiara, R.K. (2008) 'Building Good Practice in Responses to Black and Minority Ethnic Women Affected by Domestic Violence: Issues from the United Kingdom.' *Ten Years of Austrian Anti-Violence Legislation.* Vienna: Federal Chancellery – Federal Minister for Women and Civil Service.

Verloo, M. (2006) 'Multiple inequalities, intersectionality and the European Union.' *European Journal of Women's Studies 13,* 3, 211–28.

Walby, S. and Allen, J. (2004) *Domestic Violence, Sexual Assault and Stalking: Findings from the British Crime Survey.* Home Office Research Study 276. London: Home Office.

Ware, V. (1992) *Beyond the Pale: White Women, Racism and History.* London: Verso.

Wilson, A. (2006) *Dreams, Questions, Struggles: South Asian Women in Britain.* London: Pluto Press.

Yuval-Davis, N. (2006) 'Intersectionality and feminist politics.' *European Journal of Women's Studies 13,* 3, 193–209.

Yuval-Davis, N. (1997) *Gender and Nation.* London: Sage.

Zin, M. and Dill, B. (1996) 'Theorizing Difference from Multiracial Feminism.' In M. Baca Zinn, P. Hondagneu-Sotelo and M.A. Messner (eds) *Through the Prism of Difference: Readings on Sex and Gender.* Needham Heights, MA: Allyn & Bacon.

Chapter 2

Charting South Asian Women's Struggles against Gender-based Violence

Amrit Wilson

In the late 1970s I had the opportunity to document the struggles of South Asian women in Britain through interviews and one-to-one discussions for my book *Finding a Voice: Asian Women in Britain* (Wilson 1978). I was struck not only by the courage and resilience of the women who spoke to me, but also, in many cases, by the stark isolation they faced in the newly established communities of Indians, Pakistanis and Bangladeshis in Britain. The majority of struggles of South Asian women against gender-based violence in that period were individual struggles fought alone without outside support and with very few routes to safety. However, even in the two years or so I spent researching and writing my book, a change had become perceptible. South Asian women were coming together to collectively confront this acute oppression. My book ended with the sentence: 'These are the early, early days of a conscious struggle' (Wilson 1978, p.171).

In the three decades or so since 1978, that struggle has become strong and highly organised and despite, or perhaps because of, the emergence of some differences in approach within it, that collectivity – a movement, a sector, call it what you will – has survived through dramatic changes in state policy. In this chapter, I trace that journey against gender-based violence from the late 1970s through the era of multiculturalism and

Thatcherism to present-day neoliberal policies and concerns with national security. In so doing, I also touch briefly on the changes in both the racialised patriarchy of the British state and the patriarchies of South Asian communities in Britain.

Some early experiences of organising as South Asian women

Britain's network of South Asian women's organisations working to combat domestic violence is unrivalled elsewhere in Europe or North America. Like all movements, it grew out of a variety of initiatives. Among these was one of the earliest South Asian women's group in Britain, a small organisation called Awaz (voice), which was set up in London in 1978. Awaz was an openly political organisation, not funded by the state or any charity. Many of the women in it had earlier belonged either to the pre-dominantly male Black movement or the predominantly white women's movement. By forming Awaz, in 1977, they had taken a stand against the sexism of the former and the racism of the latter. But these were not the reasons why this handful of mainly young South Asian women set up the group; rather, it was that they desperately needed a way of addressing their needs and those of other South Asian women (Wilson 2006, p.161).

South Asians in Britain, with few exceptions, were working class, doing some of the hardest and lowest paid jobs. Racist violence lurked in the streets while the attitudes of the educated English middle classes were often palpably colonialist and paternalistic. Within South Asian families, patriarchal relationships were shaped by their specific history in their country of origin. Often, as communities established themselves, these relationships became more intensely oppressive, reshaped by the experiences of racism and of being the most exploited section of the working class in Britain (Anthias and Yuval-Davis 1992; Brah 1996; Wilson 2006, pp.44–6).

Young South Asian women were drawn to Awaz and although there were only about 10 to 15 women who worked continuosly, hundreds participated in Awaz meetings and protests. As a political group, Awaz regarded its agitational work – pickets in solidarity against exploited workers, demonstrations against state violence and so on – as inseparable from its work supporting women who faced domestic violence and saw both of these as central to its efforts to understand and analyse the world.

What the women did in that short period, between 1977 and 1982, was remarkable. They set up the earliest campaigns against deportation and held the first demonstration at Heathrow Airport against the 'virginity tests' (Wilson 2006, pp.77, 172).[1] They supported South Asian women strikers at Grunwick and Futters in North London and at other workplaces.[2] In some instances, as in the Futters strike, they looked in depth at health and safety issues and campaigned to change conditions at work. They demonstrated in alliance with other Black groups against police racism. They regarded themselves as socialist feminists – but not content with simply using this as a term of political identity, they explored the routes of analysis it led them to. Patriarchy, for example, was seen as inextricably linked to and shaped by imperialism, 'race' and class; the struggle for 'equal rights' was regarded as useful only if accompanied by a struggle for changes in structures of power.

Throughout the late 1970s, Awaz's most consistent long-term project was the campaign to set up refuges for South Asian women facing domestic violence run by South Asian women. It involved various stages of negotiations with state agencies during which two questions persistently arose. The first, 'Why do you want separate refuges for Asian women?' which Awaz women answered by providing evidence of both cultural need and also the endemic racism of British society, which meant that women and children fleeing domestic violence were unlikely to feel at ease in a mainstream refuge. It was not easy to convince bureaucrats of these realities but it proved possible. The bureaucrats were far more resistant to Awaz's second demand – that the new refuges be run by (and only by) South Asian women. They appeared to feel personally accused – of sexism if they were men and of racism if they were white women – despite their concern for us. But after many meetings, Awaz secured funding for a refuge, and in the early 1980s were able, in collaboration with an organisation of South Asian women community workers, the Asian Women Community Workers Group, to set up a refuge in South London which was to be the precursor of what is now the Asha Project. Just one year before this an Asian women's refuge, Saheli, had also been established in Manchester (Anitha 2008).

That year, 1981, also saw the first major street battles in which young Black men confronted the police. These were essentially an explosion of anger over years of police brutality, racism and exclusion, and the refusal of a generation growing up in the UK to accept the humiliations which their parents had tolerated (Sivanandan 1990). They were followed immediately by a change in the strategy of the state. In fact, it was the dawn of the multicultural era because, while police powers and repression increased, with methods imported from Northern Ireland (Gilroy 1982, p.171), multicultural policies were brought in as the official response to the racism that had led to the riots (Sivanandan 1990).

Multiculturalism (or ethnicism) led throughout the 1980s to the funding of 'ethnic projects', the strengthening of what was regarded as 'ethnic cultures', and the setting up of 'community leaders' – usually patriarchal and almost always male and invariably willing to do the state's bidding. The new 'ethnic cultures' projected by the state in the multicultural era claimed to recognise ethnicity but denied internal differentials of gender, class and caste (Gupta 2003; Kundnani 2007; Wilson 2006). Oppressive gender relations were, therefore, implicitly accepted by the agencies of the state. Ethnicist policies originated and consolidated the notion that all struggles within the family were a result of 'western influence' or because Asian girls wanted to be 'like English girls' (Wilson 2006, p.74).

Such claims led to the widely accepted view in state agencies that women's struggles are not 'part of' South Asian culture and are, in fact, alien to it. South Asian women consistently tried to demystify this approach in their writings and campaigns (see, for example, Southall Black Sisters 1989; Wilson 1978). Through its establishment of reactionary, male community leaders, its definition and acceptance of South Asian culture as unchanging and patriarchal, multiculturalism strengthened patriarchal relations in the South Asian communities while, at the same time, portrayed South Asian women as victims without agency. It was very much a case of 'white men saving brown women from brown men' (Spivak 1988, p.296). And since ethnicist notions had also largely defined away racism and the power relationships which perpetuated it, gender and race could be portrayed by the state and state agencies as entirely separate elements of analysis and experience which never intersected.

The classification of 'ethnic cultures' had, in fact, allowed the consolidation of earlier racist images from a variety of historical periods: the crusades, the slave trade, the period of plantation slavery and colonialism. Multiculturalism used these images, though not in their original form, as Stuart Hall writes: 'These *particular* versions may have faded. But their *traces* are still to be observed, reworked in many of the modern and up-dated images' (Hall 1995, p.22). These racialised and gendered images have over time fed into the various constructions of South Asian women and men in Britain.

With the funding of specific 'ethnic' groups, many Black groups which had united the working-class South Asian, African and African Caribbean communities fragmented. Awaz survived that first round as it were though its days as an organisation were numbered. The refuge which had been set up was soon taken over by South Asian social workers for whom both feminism and anti-racism were anathema. These women, however, were the preferred 'representatives' of South Asian women within the emerging multiculturalist framework of the state. Awaz was not prepared for this blow and the organisation collapsed, though, of course, many of its members remained politically active.

In hindsight, it is clear that Awaz was a victim of its changing relationship with the state. Initially, its strategy had been two pronged – consisting of exposing and confronting the state's racism and violence against women (in the context of immigration, for example) and at the same time demanding that the state provide services to Asian women in the context of domestic violence. However, when its demands were partially met – to the extent that it was able to establish a refuge for Asian women – it had no clear strategy on how to handle this new situation which involved, inevitably, working within the framework of the state. Almost three decades later, because the South Asian women's movement against gender-based violence has succeeded in pressurising the state to meet some of our demands (for example, there are now specialist services and safe places for South Asian women facing domestic violence), our work in the context of domestic violence falls largely within the remit of the state-funded voluntary organisations and projects and statutory services. But as many of us are increasingly aware, this does not erase the state's patriarchal ideology, nor does it make it any less racist.

The 1980s and 1990s: South Asian women's refuges, funding and the state

While Awaz folded, a large number of other South Asian women's organisations established themselves all over Britain and grew in strength through the 1980s.[3]. Southall Black Sisters emerged in this period as a leading feminist organisation based in London helping women facing domestic violence through its advice centre, playing a campaigning role nationally, and mounting legal challenges over specific cases (Gupta 2003).

These refuges and resource centres were set up by women who had identified problems and then come together to solve them. As Anjona Roy, chair of Dostiyo, a small South Asian women's organisation in Northampton, explained, these women 'had ownership of the issues, and looked at them in depth and holistically. It was because of their own experiences that they integrated educational work (about women's oppression or about how to manage in a racist society) into service provision' (Wilson 2006, p.163). However, most of these organisations were perpetually financially insecure. The Thatcher era (1979–90), with its public service cuts and attacks on voluntary organisations, saw them constantly in fear of closure. Many South Asian women's organisations became registered charities, since, increasingly, this was the only way to raise the sort of money required to run a refuge. But as charities they had, under British Charity Law, to keep clear of anything which could be considered political. By the mid-1980s funders began, in the name of accountability, to demand hierarchal structures mirroring those of business organisations (with project officers answering to line managers and line managers answering to directors). Increasingly, funding organisations also made it clear that they required targets based on a market-orientated philosophy and language. The right outputs and 'performance indicators' were deemed essential and supporting traumatised women and children helping them gain control over their lives had now, absurdly, to be seen in terms of value for money (Inam 2003; Wilson 2006, p.164).

Like so many other women's groups, the structure and political approach of South Asian women's refuges were profoundly affected by these changes in the policies of the state and funders. These refuges had been set up in most cases by women who had themselves experienced domestic violence and had run as collectives, where in principle at least, power and decision-making were shared by management committees, workers and residents. Now many refuges abandoned these egalitarian methods; earlier they had considered themselves accountable to the women who came to them for help, now they found themselves accountable only to their funders.

In many organisations, open feminist debate diminished and collective discussions among residents of refuges were deprioritised. For example, although 'educational recovery' sessions had been incorporated into service provision, in many refuges these sessions were no longer collective discussions which highlighted the systemic nature of women's oppression, but were one-to-one sessions with case workers – suggesting by their very nature that domestic violence was a private and individual problems (Wilson 2006, p.164). In addition, given the restrictions of Charity Law, only in a minority of refuges were residents actively encouraged to inform themselves about current affairs or involve themselves in any political activity related to their own experiences. Inevitably, these developments led to divisions within the Asian women's movement against domestic violence with some organisations retaining their feminist and anti-racist politics while others became essentially 'service' organisations.

If the 1980s had brought the corporatisation of refuges, the 1990s brought a gradual transformation of the entire voluntary sector – including refuges – which continues to the present day.

Against a background of public service cuts and privatisation, quality assurance standards and managerialism have been used punitively to close down community organisations, whereby small organisations have been elbowed out of funding frameworks while big national charities and infra-structure organisations are strengthened and gradually drawn into deliver-ing what had earlier been provided by the state (Guardian 2008). This led to the silencing of independent organisations which seek to voice the needs of communities. As Andy Benson of the National Coalition for Independent Action (NCIA) puts it, small and medium-sized charities providing public services

> won't have the freedom to look downwards to their communities; they'll have to look up to their commissioners, who will be the ones deciding which services are the most appropriate. We're going to end up with a third sector that is expressly an arm's-length agency of the state'. (Guardian 2008)

Typical of the late 1990s was the takeover of the buildings of many Asian women's refuges by Housing Associations, gigantic organisations managed by the state and funded mainly by charities and state agencies.[4]

The 1990s: the rise of anti-Muslim racism

Despite some continuity, however, for South Asian women's struggles against violence, the 1990s were an entirely new phase which brought a reconfiguration of racism and almost simultaneously, a reshaping of multi-culturalism.

From the beginning of the decade the demonisation of Islam in the US global strategy began to feed into the British media, and into the ways in which minority ethnic communities were constructed, generating a specifically anti-Muslim racism. The construction of the 'Muslim' man as fanatical, fundamentalist, violent and owing allegiance to forces external – and hostile – to Europe came to the foreground in racist imagery (Fekete 2004; Mamdani 2008; Wilson and Wilson 2002). The Muslim woman continued to be seen as a victim oppressed by the men in her family, though increasingly she could also be seen as a threat – a terrorist who must be crushed (Abu-Lughod 2002). In this phase, too, culture and religion came to be conflated and populations which had earlier been categorised according to language or region of origin were identified by their religion above all else. 'Muslim' became the new 'ethnicity'. As Claire Alexander noted, in Britain, the term 'Muslim culture' increasingly started appearing in welfare state documents and in academia, despite the diversity of groups adhering to variants of the Muslim faith, which made the concept meaningless in practical terms as well as flawed on a theoretical level (Alexander 1998).

From the mid-1990s the government began to reshape multiculturalism by highlighting the notion of 'faith communities', and began to encourage organisations in the South Asian community that belonged to the religious Right; whether Hindu, Muslim or Sikh, they were all bolstered with local government funding. This made it possible to escalate anti-Muslim racism while categorising Muslim organisations as good and bad. Good Muslim organisations, and indeed Good Muslims, were those who in the state's discourses represented the acceptable face of Islam and kept order on behalf of the state. Bad Muslim organisations were those who were critical of the government's foreign policies (Mamdani 2008). At the same time, the first Gulf War with its ruthless attacks on Muslim populations, on the one hand, and the rise of right-wing 'Hindutva' in India (International Initiative for Justice 2003), on the other, meant that religious identities of a variety of political strands were being heightened in the South Asian communities in Britain.

South Asian women's organisations, however, with a very small number of exceptions, continued to be secular. South Asian women's refuges and other organisations combating violence against women emphasised that they continued to cater for and welcome women of all religions and none, and that they regarded South Asian women's oppression and the struggles against violence as a powerful and uniting collective experience (see, for example, Meera Syal's comment on the home page of the Newham Asian Women's Project: Syal 2003).

Muslim patriarchy and the 'knight in shining armour'

It was against this background that the state began to propose policies that appeared to confront 'Muslim' patriarchy. Multiculturalism had allowed the state to consolidate and strengthen both South Asian patriarchy and the construction of South Asian women as victims; at the same time, the state was under pressure from South Asian women's groups to respond to the sometimes extreme violence they faced. The state, having until then colluded with South Asian patriarchy, began to posture as confronting it, reacting with shock and horror as though patriarchy was a monster unknown to it, which had suddenly appeared from an 'alien' and 'backward' land. It began to undertake the first of a new type of intervention in South Asian culture.

A Forced Marriage Initiative was launched by a debate in the House of Commons in 1999, led by Ann Cryer, the MP for Keighley. In a speech laden with colonial overtones, she appealed to 'the leaders of the Asian Muslim community' to 'encourage their people to put their daughters' happiness, welfare and human rights first. If they do, their community will progress and prosper, in line with the Sikh and Hindu communities' (Hansard 1999). This suggested, therefore, not only that 'forced marriages' were the preserve of Muslims but also that Muslims were poor and working class as a result. In reality, of course, coercion of one sort or another can be a feature of family-arranged marriages across religious and class divisions.

Soon after this debate, the Home Office appointed a working group which, with the exception of representatives of two Asian women's groups, consisted of influential 'community leaders'. Within a few months, one of the Asian women's groups, Southall Black Sisters, left over disagreements about mediation, calling for the state to 'mainstream the issue of forced marriage by incorporating it in its national strategy on violence against women and children' (Wilson 2006, p.87). In June 2000, the report of the working group, entitled *A Choice by Right*, was launched by the Home Office with great fanfare (Home Office 2000). It led to a deluge of racist articles in the British press about brutal South Asian parents of girls who were far less mature than their white counterparts, and about horrendous experiences from which they must be rescued. Frequently, these articles were specifically anti-Muslim and the notion of women's agency was completely missing in these accounts. The report called for a debate around the issue and the debate was conducted by the media. Every tabloid now assumed the power to choose key spokespersons and bring selected victims as evidence into the public gaze, whetting the appetite of their readers with more and more salacious accounts of young women's suffering and brutal South Asian parents destroying their lives.

Forced marriages were defined by the Forced Marriage Initiative as marriages 'without the valid consent of both parties, where duress is a factor' (Home Office 2000, p.4). However, this was extremely problematic since, in this context, duress is a nebulous concept: family-arranged marriage is often an arena of struggle, which may be emotional or physical, and is affected by a complex set of interacting issues, from emotional blackmail and low self-esteem to isolation and exclusion as a result of racism. These issues, however, were never discussed – what was highlighted was 'choice'. Since the late 1980s, the focal point of the state's interventions has not been supporting women's attempts to resist violence and oppression. Instead, the state, in line with neoliberal ideology, has been concerned with the *right* of individuals to *choose* or, in the case of 'forced marriages', that young South Asian women are prevented from exercising their right to choose. This ignores the fact that power relations within the family and community undermine the neoliberal notion of choice and render it meaningless in practice (Wilson 2006, p.91).

Soon it became clear that the Home Office (and the Foreign and Commonwealth Office, which was also involved) was mainly concerned with the marriages of British South Asian women with men from South Asia who, by virtue of the marriage, then entered the UK (O'Brien *et al.* 2000). This linking of forced marriage (and soon the so-called 'honour killings') of South Asian women with immigration was an enormously significant step, because not only did it place the discourse on forced marriage squarely within the racist discourses on excluding New Commonwealth immigrants, but also it placed forced marriage within the remit of what the state saw as organised crime like the activities of a mafia, illegal immigration, trafficking and terrorism. This was to lead in time to attempts to make forced marriage a full-fledged criminal offence, despite the unanimous opposition of South Asian women's organisations (see Chapter 5).

Ushering in the era of 'Community Cohesion'

One of the media's many 'commonsense' views about Muslims is that hostility to them started after 9/11. However, as I have discussed earlier, this is not the case. While it is true that 9/11 led to an enormous escalation of racism, for the majority of Muslims of all communities (and other South Asian groups), deep-rooted racism had impacted on their lives throughout the era of multiculturalism, shaping immigration laws, welfare state policies, the attitudes of the police, causing discrimination in employment and spilling over into violent attacks on the streets; in the decade of the 1990s this racism had been reconfigured into a specifically anti-Muslim racism (Alexander 1998; Fekete 2004).

It was these experiences which led to ghettoisation and also strengthened patriarchy – South Asian women activists' struggles against violence and oppression were made far harder by the collusion of statutory and voluntary organisations in upholding patriarchal stipulations. They were hampered too by the extreme racism of media reportage of gender violence and the way newspapers often saw 'forced marriages', brutal parents and victimised daughters where in fact there were none (Gill 2006; Siddiqui 2006). Working-class South Asian communities in the north of England, most of them Pakistani and Bangladeshi, which had faced the worst effects of deindustrialisation in the 1980s, remained locked in the 1990s in a limbo of poor educational opportunities and unemployment. In the north of England, in towns such as Burnley, Accrington, Oldham, Blackburn and Bradford, a generation had grown up in communities, white and South Asian, which were among Britain's most impoverished 1 per cent. Not only were these communities kept apart by racism but also encounters with the state within South Asian communities too were shaped by racism (Kundnani 2007).

Racist gangs routinely invaded Asian areas and the police not only sided with the racists but also targeted these areas themselves. By the mid-1990s, the local media and police began to sensationalise Asian crimes against whites and interpret them as 'racially motivated' (Kundnani 2007, p.53, 196). In the summer of 2001, a series of violent confrontations in these northern towns led to the worst riots in England since 1981. In every case the violence was begun by racist gangs either going on a rampage or attempting to march through Asian areas and the police responding by donning riot gear and invading these areas themselves. The riots in Bradford resulted in injuries to hundreds of police officers and the destruction of many buildings. The press and a variety of New Labour commentators, like Trevor Phillips, spoke of Britain 'sleepwalking to seg- regation' (Phillips 2005; see also Guardian 2005) that over-tolerance of diversity had encouraged Muslims to live by their own values, that the riots were the result of the innate separateness of Islamic culture and that these communities had 'self-segregated'.

Ann Cryer, MP for Bradford and Keighley, continuing her crusade against 'foreign spouses', told Parliament that the principal cause of the disturbances was the practice of arranging marriages with foreign spouses because it led, she thought, to poor levels of English and consequent under-achievement (Hansard 2001). Within a few months of the riots, 9/11 happened, providing the ideal launching pad for government policies which were already in the making – policies which would justify a more authoritarian state and implement systematic exclusion in line with a neoliberal economic agenda.

The government's White Paper, *Secure Borders, Safe Haven: Integration with Diversity in Modern Britain*, published in early 2002 (Home Office 2002) and the government declarations which followed made it plain that the concept of institutional racism, acknowledged in February 1999 (Macpherson 1999), was now to be abandoned in favour of integration. In fact, racism was now regarded as a prejudice coming from unfamiliarity – the outcome of segregation not its cause (Kundnani 2007, p.131). As in the 1970s, integration was to be the new framework of race and immigration policies, and this time its goals were managed migration and 'Community Cohesion'.

Community Cohesion, despite its name, can best be understood as an essentially racist framework of policies based on the politics of fear and the state's concern with national security. It urges the closure of certain services and organisations – whose very existence, it rules, undermines the 'glue' (Department of Communities and Local Government 2008a) (of Britishness) which holds the UK together, and by doing so, it provides the state with a 'moral' justification for its neoliberal economic policies of cuts in public expenditure. Community Cohesion erodes the idea of specialist services and organisations, and rules that funds be withdrawn from special- ist Black, Asian, minority ethnic and refugee (BAMER) projects or their merger with mainstream services. In fact, it tries to erase the concept of specific needs altogether (Worley 2005). At the same time, the funds allocated to combating domestic violence were curtailed, leading women to ask if under new definitions they were not part of the community and if cohesion meant that domestic violence was now acceptable (Gill 2008). And there was also a change in the way violence against women was now viewed by the state. Despite the fact that 90–95 per cent of those who experience domestic violence are women (US Bureau of Justice 1994), state policy began to emphasise that it was all a question of gender, because men too faced violence from their partners. The systemic nature of women's oppression was therefore now to be sidelined in state policy.

Supporting People policies: a cruel irony

Within this ideological and economic framework came the restructuring of a number of welfare services and, in April 2003, the implementation of the so-called Supporting People (SP) programme. SP policies claimed to offer 'vulnerable people the opportunity to improve their quality of life by providing a stable environment which enables greater independence' (Department of Communities and Local Government 2005). In reality, they are another cost-cutting exercise which in the name of 'best value' is closing down specialist refuges or merging them with mainstream organisations and drastically reducing specialist services. It is endangering the lives of South Asian women and children fleeing domestic violence by closing down the routes to and places of safety, and it is doing away with the very mechanisms which make women stronger – holistic treatment, counselling, education and well-being programmes, and outreach services (Thiara 2005; Thiara and Hussain 2005; Wilson 2006, p.170).

SP consultants show little recognition of the needs of South Asian or other BAMER women, brushing aside the ways of working which have been fought for and established over a considerable period. Their assessments of best value – on the basis of which refuges are asked to close or merge – ignore the well-established fact that BAMER women and children facing domestic violence need greater advocacy, and often need interpreters and outreach and therapeutic work. As a research report commissioned by Imkaan (a second-tier organisation which works for a national network of BAMER women's refuges) points out, because the additional costs of providing specialist services are ignored in SP's value for money Quality Assessment Framework and in the more recent National Outcomes, assessments have been biased against BAMER refuges (Thiara and Hussain 2005).

Despite the existence of a specialist sector carefully built up over the years and ample research to show its crucial importance in saving lives, many SP consultants are asking refuge managers questions similar to the ones the women in Awaz had to answer way back in the 1970s: 'Why in this day and age, do you need Asian women's refuges? Why don't you merge with generic refuges?' (Wilson 2006, p.167) The answer this time round is that South Asian women, and in fact all BAMER women, *choose* specialist support, for reasons of safety, to counter the total isolation from family and community networks, and because these organisations meet their cultural needs, such as the food which is familiar to their children and which their religion permits, or counselling in their mother tongue from a counsellor who understands culturally specific domestic violence issues.

And then there is the question of racism – can BAMER women and children really feel at ease in mainstream, essentially white refuges? Too often racism is regarded as a male experience but the reality is that South Asian women and particularly Muslim women have increasingly been targeted. In 2001, 9/11 raised the plateau for racist attacks. According to Arzu Merali, Director of Research at the Islamic Human Rights Commission, who has collated reports of these attacks, there were about 300 attacks on Muslims in the first month after 9/11, most of them on women (Guardian 2001). In the weeks after the bombing of London's transport system on 7 July 2005, attacks on Muslims increased sixfold. People who might 'look like a Muslim', and particularly Muslim women in headscarves and *hijabs*, continue to be targeted and, thanks to the media, there is now an enormous hostility to Muslims across British society. In this climate of racism, fear and insecurity, what are the experiences of women facing domestic violence who go to mainstream refuges? Racial abuse, both verbal and physical, in these refuges has been a long-term, acute and well-documented problem in these organisations (Cooke, Davis and Wilson 1999; Mouj 2008; Rai and Thiara 1997; Thiara 2005; Wilson 2006). But this was not considered relevant by policy makers.

In June 2007, the National Supporting People strategy published by the Department of Communities and Local Government (2007), revealed that Supporting People initiatives would be integrated into Local Area Agreements (LAAs) and must reflect the new National Indicators set by the government. Remarkably, of 198 National Indicators, only a couple related to domestic violence: one related to the prevention of 'Domestic Violence murders' and the other related to 'repeat violence'. Now the first of these has been abandoned, with only the one, on repeat violence, retained. Also none of the National Indicators has a role for the voluntary sector; all are geared to the statutory or private sector. In addition, the ring-fencing of funds within specific themes, such as Safer Communities, has been abandoned. These funds will now be pooled with the intention of streamlining commissioning processes.

South Asian women's experiences of domestic violence services in this era of Community Cohesion and SP highlight the deep contradictions between the state's proclamations and the policies it implements. As many in the South Asian women's refuge movement are asking, if the state is concerned about South Asian women's lives being endangered by forced marriage and honour killings (singling out South Asian and Middle Eastern women in this respect), why is it closing down the very organisations and services which support and strengthen South Asian women (Gill 2008)? And these organisations are shockingly few and far between anyway: according to a Fawcett Society investigation, for example, Black women facing domestic violence have to contact an average of 17 agencies before finding help (for white women the number is 11) (Brittain *et al.* 2005).

However, whatever the contradictions, the underlying rationale of these policies is clear enough: vulnerable people are costing the state too much and they will be increasingly abandoned as the UK moves towards US-style welfare provision. The ideological message is that the withdrawal of the state from all responsibility is actually empowering for the individual, even if their survival is threatened.

The struggle for survival

Coordinating the struggle of BAMER refuges to survive, Imkaan set up a national campaign in February 2008 and released further two research reports (Mouj 2008; Roy 2008). Roy (2008) examined the situation of women with No Recourse to Justice, focusing specifically on the attitudes of local authorities (see Chapter 8). Mouj (2008) identified the arenas of struggles for BAMER refuges, highlighting the closure of essential services, the lack of consultation with long-established BAMER refuges, the reduction in safe spaces for women and children as a consequence and the lack of recognition of the refuge and other service needs of BAMER women and children within LAAs, which will, in the future, dictate local authority targets and funding allocations.

Imkaan's publications also pointed out a remarkable contradiction between these proposals for the future funding and delivery of domestic violence services and the government's own Gender and Race Equality Legislation:

> The Race Relations (Amendment) Act 2000 Section 2(2) was introduced in order to hold public authorities to account where they are charged to rebuild trust and demonstrate fairness by eliminating racial discrimination and promoting equality of opportunity and good race relations...
> The Gender Equality Duty [requires that] public bodies... take pro-active steps to promote equality between women and men [and] take account of the different needs of women and men in policy and service planning rather than react to complaints when things go wrong. (Mouj 2008, p.3)

In other words, SP and other neoliberal economic policies are in sharp contradiction with neoliberalism's own rights and duties and most significantly the laws which are based on these rights and duties.

Five months later (September 2008) this contradiction led to a remarkable victory for the BAMER women's sector. Southall Black Sisters, facing cuts in their core funding from Ealing Council, took the local authority to court and won (see Chapter 4 for a more detailed discussion of the case). The judge Lord Justice Moses commented on the UK government's approach to cohesion, stating that it seemed contrary to what it was trying to achieve, and that grassroots BAMER organisations needed to exist to help vulnerable and marginalised women and children contribute to, and benefit from, wider mainstream society. The case established an important precedent which some refuges may well be able to use to fight back. However, unless there is a change in government policy it will not help those organisations which are already tied into local service agreements and are not in a position to challenge local decision-making processes. At the time of writing this chapter, Imkaan's campaign to change policy continues, with 109 MPs signing an Early Day Motion, tabled by John McDonnell MP on 14 January 2008, against the closure of specialist services and the closure and merger of specialist refuges among other related issues.[5]

Domestic violence, the criminal justice system and the 'War on Terror'

Like so many neoliberal 'rights', the right to safety in the context of domestic violence is now being accompanied by 'responsibilities', and not fulfilling these could provide women with some typically neoliberal 'choices'. According to the Crown Prosecution Service (CPS 2005) *Guidance for Prosecuting Cases of Domestic Violence 2005*, they may well find themselves choosing between a prison sentence and supporting a prosecution against their will. The *Guidance* discusses cases 'where the victim indicates a wish to withdraw support for the prosecution and/or consideration is being given to investigating whether the victim will proceed if special measures such as screens and separate entrances could be provided' (CPS 2005, p.15). In addition, and most crucially, the victim can be compelled to give evidence through the use of a witness summons. If a witness refuses to attend as a result of a summons, the CPS document continues,

> we must go on to consider whether a warrant is appropriate. It is a difficult decision but one that must not be avoided…A witness before the court can be compelled to give evidence under the threat of being in contempt of court and subject to imprisonment. (CPS 2005, p.16)

Clearly women, and particularly South Asian women, are under pressure to withdraw support for prosecutions but these new punitive laws will make it harder for them to speak out at all against domestic violence. The Domestic Violence, Crime and Victims Act 2004 institutionalises this punitive approach. This law has its own infrastructure which is to receive priority funding and, as is now clear, will replace earlier structures of support. The infrastructure (Gill and Banga 2008) is essentially three pronged. First, MARACs (Multi-Agency Risk Assessment Conferences) are police-led multi-agency panels which discuss high risk cases of inter-personal or intra-familial abuse, drug-related problems, repeat victimisation etc. Secondly, Independent Domestic Violence Advocates (IDVAs) are direct employees of the state and who are so far being preferentially placed in statutory sector organisations or in giant voluntary sector organisations. Third, there are Specialist Domestic Violence Courts. As Gill and Banga (2008, p.12) write in an article based on the work of Newham Asian Women's Project:

Our experience shows that to date MARACs have not been effective in responding to these problems or offering solutions to them. In reviewing cases that remain low or medium risk and so do not reach a MARAC stage, it is most evident that early intervention and prevention, and direct support work provided by specialist agencies have been reasonably effective and these comprise the majority of cases in the Borough.

They point out that in the London Borough of Newham, the Domestic Violence Forum has made it clear that the services which will be considered for funding are those which provide 'increased rates of third party reporting and reporting of i) domestic violence to the police, ii) domestic violence incidents resulting in sanctions/detections, iii) sanctions/detections connected to sentencing' (Gill and Banga 2008, p.12). There is a danger, they say, that the outreach work done by women's organisations in Newham will be replaced by IDVAs and Specialist Courts functioning together (Gill and Banga 2008).

This is not unique to Newham, in Lambeth, as Ila Patel, the director of the Asha refuge told me in an interview in May 2008:

> Private consultants are also drafting the domestic violence strategy, the LAA is largely about leaving the voluntary sector out...Safety and support for women as priorities are being replaced by strategies which are about engaging women in the criminal justice system...despite the fact that statistics show that only 24 per cent of survivors report to the police and only one-third of those go to Court.

The government's National Indicators (or in fact its sole National Indicator) on domestic violence also locks into the criminal justice system. The way this operates in practice is clear from this experience of a worker at a mainstream West London women's centre:

> The only training on offer on issues affecting BME women is led by the community safety officer, who is based at the local police station and whose whole focus with reference to forced marriages and honour killings is not on what rights and resources the woman can access but on profiling the perpetrators. (BubblieKang 2008)

This profiling of perpetrators suggests that domestic violence and 'repeat violence' are in fact unusual events and not systemic to society; at the same time, given the climate of racism and the intensifying surveillance of

Muslim communities, which is part of the 'War on Terror', this profiling will inevitably target Muslim men.

While the state is profiling whole communities in the name of the War on Terror, in the name of protecting South Asian women from domestic violence, it is profiling perpetrators who we are increasingly being told come from the same communities of 'organised criminals'. Nazir Afzal, a director of the CPS, for example, speaks enthusiastically of 'hotspots' of radicalism and 'hotspots' of honour-based violence:

> the Forced Marriage Unit have a lovely map on their wall and it basically identifies where most of their referrals are from and, if you went in the Special Branch of the Terrorist Unit and looked at their map, you would see significant links, significant correlation... There was one case where I could actually evidence it, so how many others are there ... I have been talking to ministers for the last few months. I mentioned radicalism hotspots and the map of honour-based violence hotspots – then they really listened! (Afzal 2006)

And bringing the interventions into culture and religion full circle, a new so-called Muslim agenda focused around women and the War on Terror is being implemented by the state. This is happening on a local level by setting up and funding Muslim women's groups whose role, in the words of the Department of Communities and Local Government, will be to empower Muslim women by giving them 'a stronger voice, increased confidence and the knowledge to challenge and tackle violent extremism' (Department of Communities and Local Government 2008b). These groups funded by the government's Preventing Violent Extremism (PVE) Pathfinder Fund are being set up in local authorities where services for women facing domestic violence are being abolished. In Ealing, for example, two Muslim women's groups were being set up while Southall Black Sisters faced cuts. When members of Southall Black Sisters questioned this, they were told by Ealing Council that these Muslim women's organisations were in a different funding stream under which they must

> link to the overarching objective of creating a situation where Muslim communities reject and actively condemn violent extremism and seek to undermine and isolate violent extremists. A condition of the grant is that it is not used for the furtherance or propagation of a faith. (Ealing Council 2008)

Thus it would appear that in the new state and media discourses, the measure of Muslim women's 'empowerment' is not whether they are able to confront or escape domestic violence but whether they can be involved as the state's allies in the surveillance which is central to the 'War on Terror' (Da Costa and Dubey 2008). Meanwhile questions from Imkaan to the Metropolitan Police under the Freedom of Information Act 2000 about the numbers of women killed in so-called honour killings brought the response: 'we have had a nil return for data on Honour Killings'. However, homicide figures of the numbers of women killed in England and Wales for 2007–08 as a result of domestic violence were available: nine women were murdered in total, of whom five were white women and one was Asian (Middle Eastern women were not listed separately) – quite different from the number (twelve women a year) which the media claim originate from the Home Office (see, for example, Craig 2007).[6]

Looking ahead

The South Asian women's movement against violence has entered its thirtieth year fighting for survival in its present form. This is a far more complex battle than ever before because it has to confront too the state's attempts to mystify and co-opt it – through its 'choices' and its carefully engineered 'moral panics'. It faces also that most established of strategies of social control – the grooming of individuals from within the movement to be the 'authentic' voice of the BAMER women's sector. Like the 'community leaders' of the multicultural era these women are ready to do the state's bidding, eager, for example, to support criminalisation even when it comes at the cost of strengthening and supporting women.

The movement has responded to these challenges with enormous energy, with calls for a more political and analytical approach, and the forging of new alliances across gender and racial divisions. The history of the South Asian women's movement against gender-based violence not only reveals its own changing dynamics and ways of organising, but also throws into focus the changing policies of the British state – racialised policies on gender, gendered policies on race and policies which try to manage and control South Asian communities. The lessons one can draw from this history must depend inevitably on one's location in the structure of British society. For service providers, perhaps, it demonstrates most clearly the importance of always questioning one's assumptions about

South Asian women and South Asian patriarchy and being aware that race and gender are inseparable factors which shape the South Asian experience in Britain.

Notes

1. So-called 'virginity tests', were in fact humiliating internal examinations carried out by immigration authorities, on South Asian women entering Britain in the 1970s and early 1980s, as the wives or fiancées of men who were settled in the UK. Women who were wives and ruled to be virgins, or fiancées and ruled not to be virgins, were told they were lying about their identity and deported.

2. Strikes at Grunwick and Futters were two of a series of historic strikes by Asian women workers in the late 1970s and 1980s. The Grunwick strike received support from trade unionists across the UK but was ultimately betrayed by the Trades Union Congress (TUC). The Thatcher government used the strike as an excuse to pass a raft of anti-trade union laws. (For a more detailed account, see Wilson 1978.)

3. The eighties also saw the establishment of a few non-feminist, often religion-based South Asian women's organisations.

4. In 2006, 7 per cent of Housing Associations – those with 2500 plus homes – owned 78 per cent of all homes provided under 'social housing', which not only pay for themselves out of rent they charge to homeless and vulnerable people – and many housing associations charge market rents to these 'customers' – but actually make a surplus out of this which then masquerades as new state funding for housing (Wilson 2006, p.176). Small South Asian women's refuges taken over by these organisations clearly lost much of their independence.

5. The text of the Early Day Motion (EDM 693) is as follows:

   That this House notes that the Government has brought forward new legislation on domestic violence; draws attention to the acute under-funding of black, minority ethnic and refugee (BMER) women's services; further notes that research conducted by BMER women's organisations such as IMKAAN reveals that many BMER services are facing closure, takeover by mainstream organisations and reductions in funding, thereby dangerously reducing BMER women's access to places of safety; considers that women suffering from abuse and violence, who do not have settled immigration status in the UK, are prevented from seeking protection due to the no recourse to public funds requirement; believes that securing alternative safe housing, benefits and specialist services are often prerequisites to leaving an abusive relationship; calls upon the Government to acknowledge the value of small-sized grassroots specialist BMER women's projects and sustain investment in them; urges the Government to meet the demands made by IMKAAN and its network of over 40 BMER refuges across the UK, Saheli Ltd., Southall Black Sisters, Newham Asian Women's Project, Asian Women's Resource Centre and African Women's Care to abolish the no recourse to public funds requirement for all women with insecure status who are subject to violence and abuse in the contexts of marriage, domestic work and trafficking; and further calls upon the Government to set up a national cross-governmental violence against women strategy and, within that, a strategy around the needs of BMER women and children.

6   The Metropolitan Police's response to Imkaan's Freedom of Information Act request
     for data on Honour Killings was 'we have had a nil return for data on Honour Kill-
     ings'. According to the homicide statistics, 1 oriental, 3 Asian, 2 Afro-Caribbean and
     3 dark European women were murdered through acts of domestic violence between
     2006 and 2008, as well as 10 white women. They sent Imkaan the following data:

Victim Gender	Victim Ethnicity	2006–2007	2007–2008
Male	White European	6	6
	Dark European	0	3
	Afro-Caribbean	4	0
	Asian	1	2
	Oriental	0	0
Male Total		11	11
Female	White European	5	5
	Dark European	1	2
	Afro-Caribbean	1	1
	Asian	2	1
	Oriental	1	0
Female Total		10	9
Total		21	20

The above data table was produced using the MPS Crime Recording Information System (CRIS). When an offence occurs it is recorded on CRIS with any additional features of the offence, such as in the present case, where domestic violence was present.

References

Abu-Lughod, L. (2002) 'Do Muslim women need saving? Reflections on cultural relativism and its Others.' *American Anthropologist 104*, 3, 783–90.

Afzal, N. (2006) Extract from a speech given at Imkaan's roundtable discussion, *Responding to Violence against Women in the Name of 'Honour.'* London: Law Society, 22 November.

Alexander, C. (1998) 'Re-imagining the Muslim community.' *Innovation 11*, 4, 439–50.

Anitha, S. (2008) *Forgotten Women: Domestic Violence, Poverty and South Asian Women with No Recourse to Public Funds.* Manchester: Oxfam Publishing.

Anthias, F. and Yuval-Davis, N. (1992) *Racialised Boundaries: Race, Nation, Gender, Colour and Class and the Anti-Racist Struggle.* London: Routledge.

Brah, A (1996) *Cartographies of Diaspora: Contesting Identities.* London: Routledge.

Brittain, E., Dustin, H., Pearce, H., Rake, K., Siyunyi-Siluwe, M. and Sullivan, F. (2005) *Black & Minority Ethnic Women in the UK.* London: Fawcett Society.

BubblieKang (2008) *Guardian*, 16 February. Available at http://blogs.guardian.co.uk/ joepublic/2008/02/refuges_for_black_asian_and_mi.html, accessed on 6 August 2008.

Cooke, V., Davis, S. and Wilson, A. (1999) *Domestic Violence Service Provision: Black Women's Perspectives.* A Report Commissioned by the Domestic Violence Black

Perspective Task Group and supported by Northampton County Council, Race Consultative Panel. Northamptonshire: Northampton County Council.

Craig, O. (2007) 'Revealed: Rising toll of deaths before dishonour.' *The Telegraph*, 18 June 2007. Available at www.telegraph.co.uk/news/uknews/1554764/ Revealed-rising- toll-of-deaths-before-dishonour.html, accessed on 28 April 2009.

Crown Prosecution Service (2005) *Guidance for prosecution of cases of domestic violence.* London: Crown Prosecution Service Publications.

Da Costa, A. and Dubey, S. (2008) 'Britain targets Muslim women to fight extremists.' Reuters. Available at www.reuters.com/article/latestCrisis/idUSL19739136, accessed on 28 April 2009.

Department of Communities and Local Government (2005) *Supporting People.* Available at www.spkweb.org.uk, accessed on 28 April 2009.

Department of Communities and Local Government (2007) *Independence and Opportunity: Our Strategy for Supporting People.* Available at www.spkweb.org.uk/NR/rdonlyres/ 4E92E1E2-B5EF42B4-ADOC-FE5BG8C4330B/12855/6m070204supportingp eoplestrategy.pdf, accessed on 10 July 2009.

Department of Communities and Local Government (2008a) *Cohesion Guidance for Funders: Consultation.* Available at www.communities.gov.uk/publications/ communities/cohesionfundersconsultation, accessed on 28 April 2009.

Department of Communities and Local Government (2008b) *Empowering Muslim Women: Case Studies.* Available at www.communities.gov.uk/publications/ empowering muslimwomen, accessed on 28 April 2009.

Ealing Council (2008) *Minutes 26 February.* Available at www.ealing.gov.uk/ealing3/ export/sites/ealingweb/services/council/committees/agendas_minutes_reports/ cabinet/15may2007-19may2008/_26_feb_2008/_26_feb_2008/Item_4b_- _Appendix_E1.doc, accessed on 28 April 2009.

Fekete, L. (2004) 'Anti-Muslim racism and the European security state.' *Race & Class 46*, 1, 3–29.

Gill, A. (2006) 'Patriarchal violence in the name of "Honour".' *International Journal of Criminal Justice Sciences 1*, 1, 1–12.

Gill, A. (2008) 'Police are key to ending the deaths.' Letter to *The Independent.* Available at www.independent.co.uk/opinion/commnetators/aisha-gill-police- are-the-key-to- ending-the-deaths-780509.html, accessed on 28 April 2009.

Gill, A. and Banga, B. (2008) 'The reality and impact of the Domestic Violence, Crime and Victims Act 2004 on BMER women experiencing gender-based violence.' *Safe Journal of Domestic Abuse UK 25*, spring.

Gilroy, P. (1982) 'Police and Thieves.' In Centre for Contemporary Cultural Studies. *The Empire Strikes Back.* London: Routledge.

Guardian (2001) 'Under siege', *Guardian*, 8 December, p.11.

Guardian (2005) 'Why Trevor is right.' *Guardian*, 7 April, p.5.

Guardian (2008) 'It's nothing short of vandalism.' *Guardian*, 19 March, p.18.

Gupta, R. (ed.) (2003) *Homebreakers to Jailbreakers: Southall Black Sisters.* London: Zed Press.

Hall, S. (1995) 'The Whites of their Eyes: Racist Ideologies and the Media.' In G. Dines and J. Humez (eds) *Gender, Race and Class in Media.* Thousand Oaks, CA: Sage.

Hansard (1999) House of Commons, *Hansard*, 10 February 1999, Column 259.

Hansard (2001) House of Commons, *Hansard*, 17 July 2001, Column 8WH.

Home Office (2000) *A Choice by Right: The Report of the Working Group on Forced Marriage*. London: Home Office Communications Directive.

Home Office (2002) *Secure Borders, Safe Havens: Integration with Diversity in Modern Britain*. Cm 5387. London: Home Office.

Inam, M. (2003) 'Taking or Giving Refuge: The Asian Women's Refuge Movement.' In R. Gupta (ed.) *Homebreakers to Jailbreakers: Southall Black Sisters*. London: Zed Press.

International Initiative for Justice (2003) *Threatened Existence: A Feminist Analysis of Genocide in Gujarat*. Mumbai: International Initiative for Justice.

Kundnani, A. (2007) *The End of Tolerance: Racism in 21ˢᵗ Century Britain*. London: Pluto Press.

Macpherson, W. (1999) *The Stephen Lawrence Inquiry: A Report of an Inquiry by Sir William Macpherson to Parliament February 1999 (summary)*. Available at www.law.cf.ac.uk/tlru/Lawrence.pdf, accessed 28 April 2009.

Mamdani, M. (2008) 'Good Muslim, Bad Muslim: A political perspective on culture and terrorism.' *American Anthropologist 104*, 3, 766–75.

Mouj, A. (2008) *A Right to Exist: A Paper Looking at the Eradication of Specialist Services to BAMER Women and Children Fleeing Violence*. London: Imkaan.

O'Brien, M., Roche, B., Vaz, K. and Scotland, P. (2000) *Forced Marriage – the Overseas Dimension – Our Commitment*.' Statement by Mike O'Brien (Home Office), Barbara Roche (Home Office), Keith Vaz (Foreign and Commonwealth Office) and Patricia Scotland (Foreign and Commonwealth Office), 4 August. Available at http://collections.europarchive.org/tna/20080205132101/www.fco.gov.uk/servlet/Front?pagename=OpenMarket/Xcelerate/ShowPage&c=Page&cid=1007029395717, accessed on 3 November 2004.

Phillips, T. (2005) Speech to Manchester Community Relations Council, 22 September.

Rai, D. and Thiara, R.K. (1997) *Re-defining Spaces: The Needs of Black Women and Children and Black Workers in Women's Aid*. London: Women's Aid Federation England.

Roy, S. (2008) *No Recourse – No Duty to Care – Experiences of BAMER Women and Children affected by Domestic Violence and Insecure Immigration Status in the UK*. London: Imkaan.

Siddiqui, H. (2006) 'There is No "Honour" in Domestic Violence Only Shame: Women's Struggles against Honour Crimes in the UK.' In L. Welchman and S. Hossain (eds) *'Honour' Crimes, Paradigms, and Violence Against Women*. New Delhi: Zubaan.

Sivanandan, A. (1990) *Communities of Resistance: Writings on Black Struggles for Socialism*. London: Verso.

Southall Black Sisters (1989) *Against the Grain: A Celebration of Survival and Struggle, Southall Black Sisters*. Southall, UK: Southall Black Sisters.

Spivak, G.C. (1988) 'Can the Subaltern Speak?' In C. Nelson and L. Grossberg (eds) *Marxism and the Interpretation of Culture*. Urbana, IL: University of Illinois Press.

Syal, M. (2003) Comment on the home page of Newham Asian Women's Project. Available at www.nawp.org, accessed on 28 April 2009.

Thiara, R.K. (2005) *The Need for Specialist Domestic Violence Services for Asian Women and their Children.* London: Imkaan.

Thiara, R.K. and Hussain, S. (2005) *Supporting Some People: Supporting People and Services for Asian Women and Children Affected by Domestic Violence.* London: Imkaan.

US Bureau of Justice (1994) *Selected Findings: Violence between Intimates (NCJ 149259).* Available at www1.umn.edu/aurora/pdf/StatisticsHandout.pdf, accessed on 28 April 2009.

Wilson, A. (1978) *Finding a Voice: Asian Women in Britain.* London: Virago Press.

Wilson, A. (2006) *Dreams, Questions, Struggles: South Asian Women in Britain.* London: Pluto Press.

Wilson, A. and Wilson, K. (2002) '"Ethnicity", "Race" and Racism.' In G. Blakeley and V. Bryson (eds) *Contemporary Political Concepts: A Critical Introduction.* London: Pluto Press.

Worley, C. (2005). '"It's not about Race, it's about the Community": New Labour and Community Cohesion.' *Critical Social Policy 25*, 4, 483–96.

Chapter 3

Masculinities and Violence against Women in South Asian Communities

Transnational Perspectives

Marzia Balzani

This chapter examines how some South Asians living in Britain conceptualise and embody masculinity. Attitudes towards masculinity have not
simply been transplanted without modification; they are better understood
as responses to and the product of local social relations shaped by structures of educational disadvantage and economic and ethnic discrimination.
These different forms of discrimination and disadvantage need to be
analysed within the larger context of migration networks, the rise of
nationalism and the increased flows of information, goods and people
made possible by globalisation. Within this context the chapter examines
instances of violence by South Asian males against women, with the aim of
questioning the assumptions that lie behind policies aimed at tackling the
problem of gendered violence. Chief among them is the assumption that
Asian men are inherently more prone to violent behaviour than men from
the majority ethnic community. Above all, this chapter is about models of
masculinity – how they are created and sustained, and how they need to
change if women are to be protected.

This chapter brings together recent discussions of masculinities and globalisation in the social sciences to develop a framework for understanding gendered violence perpetrated by South Asian men in Britain. Since the 1980s, the concept of hegemonic masculinity, first proposed by Kessler, Ashenden, Cowell and Fowsett in 1982 and then developed by Connell (1987), has shaped analyses of masculinities across several disciplines.[1] In this formulation, the dominance or hegemony of masculinity may be established through force, but its supremacy is more effectively achieved through cultural and social institutions which shape behaviour and belief:

> hegemonic masculinities can be constructed that do not correspond closely to the lives of any actual men. Yet, these models do, in various ways, express widespread ideals, fantasies and desires. They provide models of relations with women and solutions to problems of gender relations. Furthermore, they articulate loosely with the practical constitution of masculinities as ways of living in everyday local circumstances. To the extent they do this, they contribute to hegemony in the society-wide gender order as a whole. (Connell and Messerschmidt 2005, p.838)

Clearly, although not all men actually embody such masculinities, many benefit from them, particularly in relation to their position of power and control over women. In addition, women themselves may be complicit in supporting and maintaining such hegemonic masculinities, which are seen as being part of the 'natural order' of things. This 'naturalising' of masculinities serves to obliterate historical memory and to block the development of understandings, practical and conceptual, of the relationships of gender, power and violence in which change can be imagined and implemented.

In the light of emerging scholarship and debate, Connell and Messerschmidt (2005) proposed a necessary expansion of the analytical frameworks that define hegemonic masculinity. They argued that 'regional and local constructions of hegemonic masculinity are shaped by the articulation of these gender systems with global processes' (p.849). Local realities can no longer be considered in isolation from international or transnational ones. 'Global institutions pressure regional and local gender orders; while regional gender orders provide cultural materials adopted or reworked in global arenas and provide models of masculinity that may be important in local gender dynamics' (p.849). This is not to say that the global always determines the local: the resistance of the regional must also be recognised (p.850).

This dialectic between the local and global provides the framework for discussion in this chapter. As embodied practices, masculinities are so enmeshed within local, regional and global structures and histories that one cannot make sense of them without locating them in their wider contexts, whether legal, geographical, social and/or gendered. Making sense of South Asian masculinities in contemporary Britain necessarily involves understanding them in relation to migration networks, legislation relating to immigration, youth identity, the rise of ethno-nationalisms in India and Pakistan, forced marriage, honour-related crimes, the treatment of South Asians by the criminal justice system, and the presence of religious-ethnic minorities in the UK as legacies of an imperial past.

South Asian male violence against women has too often been explained in both the popular media and the legal and political spheres with reference to cultural and social traditions. At its crudest, the argument runs: what Asian men do here and now in Britain is merely a remanifestation of what they have always done back 'home'. This specious argument creates the false impression that such violence is somehow uniquely endemic to these traditions, and also potentially characterises this violence as an essential trait that is embedded in the ethnic or 'racial' make-up of the men. Tradition is always an invention; as a response to the present, it is always a product of the modernity it appears to oppose (Hobsbawm and Ranger 1983). What happens here and now may look like what happens or has happened over there, but appearances can be deceptive. Gendered violence perpetrated by South Asian men in contemporary Britain can be properly understood only if we see it as a reaction to the current situation and as a response to new social, cultural and economic realities, both local and global, which shape present-day masculinities; realities which are in part a product of Western modernity itself. The complexity of these issues is real, but it should not prevent us from tackling them. If those working with the effects of gendered violence – in government, the judicial system, social services and education – are to develop meaningful responses to these new masculinities, it is imperative that the right questions be asked.

After a brief examination of the concept of hegemonic masculinity, this chapter considers specific issues relating to South Asians and gendered violence in the UK. The examples, placed within comparative frameworks, are drawn primarily from fieldwork with Hindu and Muslim South Asian communities in the UK and the South Asian subcontinent, and from expert reports for the asylum and immigration tribunals. In drawing on this material I have merged salient aspects of different cases and altered personal details to safeguard individual identities. The attempt to make sense, and locate forms, of masculine violence within national and international contexts here is not intended to explain away or excuse this violence. Nor is it my intention to imply that identical or similar forms of gendered violence do not occur within other communities, including the majority white population. Thus, although the examples presented relate largely to Muslims, the conclusions offered are broadly applicable to the experiences of other communities from the subcontinent.

Hegemonic masculinities

As already noted, masculinities are not static but relational, and so are cross-cut by other projects – political, religious, educational. Individuals demonstrate complex relationships with hegemonic masculinities; these are context specific and may lead individuals to embody the masculinities in some situations and to distance themselves from them in others. Purkayastha (2000) provides examples of South Asian American youths struggling to cope with Asian parental gender expectations differing from those of their peer groups. Asian youth are expected to be respectful, reserved and accommodating, but this pits them against white American mainstream scripts of maleness, where such traits are considered effeminate.

> Thus, the distress does not arise because the ethnic culture is 'traditional' compared to the 'modern' U.S. culture. The stigmatization arises from the current American norms of youth masculinity that favor aggressiveness, competitiveness, and physical prowess over politeness, compassion, or preference for non sports-related pursuits. (Purkayastha 2000, pp.210–11)

In this situation, Purkayastha notes that Asian youths may adopt 'alternate forms of resilient maleness' (p.211), such as in the fields of technology or science, or may even become traumatised: she tells of one young man who felt so stigmatised and unable to relate to the masculine expectations of his peers that he 'refused to go to college, and took up body building' (p.211).

Here is one case study detailing the emergence of new forms of South Asian masculinities in reaction to contemporary white Western norms, and not as an essentialised cultural trait transposed without modification from a 'traditional' context to the 'modern' world.

It is also perfectly possible for women to embody and perform hegemonic masculinity in support of a patriarchal gender order, and this goes some way to explaining why some South Asian women can, in certain circumstances, perpetrate crimes against other women in the name of honour, and why it is that women can actively support religious and political positions that serve to disempower and subordinate all women, as happens in right-wing nationalist movements (Rouse 2004; Sarkar 2001; Sarkar and Butalia 1995). This is more than women acting to preserve their own position within community or family – once they embody hegemonic masculinity they position themselves as powerful, and may enforce hegemony through violence. Women are also central to the project of gender construction among men – in this respect the work of women (as mothers, for example) is a crucial area for future research.

However, hegemonic masculinity does not only manifest itself in action; it is also a discursive phenomenon, and consequently discourse analysis can reveal how identities are constructed and negotiated in relation to others (Edley 2001; Edley and Wetherell 1996). The ways both dominant and subordinate groups stereotype others in order to justify their own actions and behaviours, creating an artificial divide between 'us' and 'them', help us to understand the ways in which some individuals may find themselves enabled or constrained, depending on the context in which they find themselves and how they construct their own identities (Tarlo 2005). Identity construction may serve to promote self-respect but may leave the same individuals in marginalised positions, with little room for manoeuvre.

Protest masculinities

Some young Asian men seek respect through aggressive masculine behaviour and yet find that such behaviour reinforces their exclusion from mainstream success. These are the 'protest masculinities' found in contexts where men are themselves disempowered and marginalised (Connell and Messerschmidt 2005, pp.847–8). They embody 'the claims to power typical of regional hegemonic masculinities in Western countries' but reflect a lack of 'the economic resources and institutional authority that underpins the regional and global patterns' (Connell and Messerschmidt 2005, pp.847–8).

Archer's work with young Asian-British Muslim men reveals the discursive aspects of protest masculinity, while others have considered a religiously informed protest masculinity to be instrumental in the formation of extremist groups (Archer 2001; Kimmel 2005; Toth 2005). Such protest masculinities may also be viewed as a remnant of the colonial subjection of South Asians which continues to express itself today in the UK in the form of social discrimination and exclusionary practices. What Stoller (1991) refers to as 'the salience of sexual symbols as graphic representations of colonial dominance' is relevant here because sexuality can become the site on which these complex cultural and historical forces are negotiated. 'Sexuality...serves as a loaded metaphor for domination... Sexual asymmetries and visions convey what is "really" going on elsewhere, at another political epicentre. They are tropes to depict other centres of power' (Stoller 1991, p.54). Protest masculinity is a dynamic reassertion of power and to the extent that it takes the shape of gendered or sexual aggression, it too can be said to obscure from view other social and political forces or 'centres'.

Thus the forcible control of South Asian women's sexuality by South Asian men may be viewed, on one level, as a reassertion of ownership and a rejection of the colonial enterprise whereby South Asian women were once 'possessed' by European men. This politics is further played out when South Asian men 'acquire' white girlfriends or wives to demonstrate their potency and the failure of white males to keep their own women for themselves. The contest here is always between Asian men and white British men, where the winners and losers are determined by the women they are able to possess and 'take' from their competitors. The primary data show men discussing women in precisely these competitive and ethnically charged ways, revealing that the structures of patriarchy are transferable across state borders and involve, at some level, men competing with men to the disadvantage of all women. As individuals cross international borders, they take with them the forms of patriarchy they have internalised and rework these in the new social situations in which they find themselves in the increasingly globalised context discussed below.

Globalisation

Mass movements of people and goods across the world means an increase in encounters between cultures and the possibility for social imaginations to develop in hitherto unforeseen ways. Present day society, no longer based on rigid hierarchies and structures, is in a state of flow, with criss-crossing, overlapping and intersecting networks, a world where imagination and access to communications media can change the course of events across the globe. Experience is no longer conceived of as unitary and coherent; rather, we are living in a fractured time, able to experience multiple places and be a part of multiple worlds simultaneously. Appadurai (1996) understands such contemporary experiences of disjuncture in terms of global flows, which he labels 'scapes' (a suffix taken from the concept of landscape): ethnoscapes, technoscapes, financescapes, mediascapes and ideoscapes. Each refers to one aspect of globalisation; each can be analytically isolated from the others for the purpose of study, but each inevitably and necessarily interects with the others in actual lived experience. Of particular relevance here are Appadurai's (1996) understandings of ethnoscapes and ideoscapes. The former refer to social groups and their movements across space, and the latter are those ideas, ideologies and conceptual systems that in a global world may begin in one place then spread, metamorphosing as they go, to manifest themselves in localised ways but always with reference to an actual or imagined point of origin.

This is not, however, a world in which all are able to benefit from the changes wrought by globalisation. Social inequalities may be exacerbated just as much as they may be rendered irrelevant. One of the consequences of the fracturing of old orders by globalisation is an apparent rise in the levels of violence of all types around the world, including an intensification and spread of violence against women (Appadurai 2001). The targeting of marginalised members of society or groups is itself linked to new patterns of violence resulting from globalisation.

An abstract force such as globalisation cannot be easily attacked, but the anxiety and rage caused by globalisation can be directed onto concrete individuals or groups that can then become scapegoats because of their socially constructed marginal or minority status. Within such groups, which are never homogeneous, subgroups, the marginalised among the marginalised, may find themselves at risk not only from the wider community but also from more powerful subgroups within their own communities. Minority women regularly constitute such a minority within the minority. Viewed in this light, South Asian women – particularly those who are 'outsiders', such as brides brought into their husbands' homes – are multiple minorities, as ethnic minority members in a majority white country, as women in a patriarchal state, and as possessions owned by the family. They are outsiders who are required to ensure the future of the family but who cannot be trusted because of their outsider status. For the family she marries into, the wife is necessary for her domestic and reproductive labours, but a constant threat to the integrity of the family because she is always, at one level, an outsider.

As the world stands on the verge of recession, itself a consequence of the globalised money markets and movements of resources, we may expect domestic violence to increase; unfortunately, it is typically at times of economic hardship that governments cut funding to organisations seeking to help those fleeing violence. The most recent UK government figures on domestic violence show a marked increase compared with the previous few years, and at the same time the government has chosen to make 'recourse to public funds' virtually impossible for some Asian women escaping domestic violence (Womensphere 2008).

This violence needs to be understood, not as a typical feature of the life of Asian women, but as a recent phenomenon. This does not mean that there was ever a time when violence against women did not occur, merely that we are living through a period when there have been significant increases in such violence. That this is a social phenomenon, and not linked to any supposedly 'natural' trait of the Asian male, is clear from research which show that in times of particular stress for populations levels of domestic violence increase. This happens in refugee camps and when social and economic factors make survival harder (Hasan 2002; Martin 2004).

Hasan (2002), for example, argues that the increase in violence against women, including honour killings, among Palestinians within Israel is a recent phenomenon in which the state is complicit. The immediate impetus for this increase in violence is the lack of stability in the social, economic and political situation of the Palestinians. Sexual politics and gendered violence thus becomes emblematic of a larger political picture where the battles between Palestinians and Israelis are fought out through individual domestic acts of violence against women perpetrated by Palestinian men on Palestinian women. As Hasan (2002) writes:

> we are witnessing a new pattern in the murder of women for the sake of family honour – one in which men who enjoy significant privileges under patriarchal rule attempt, through violent means, to bring stability to a world that is continually changing before their eyes, seeking more and more fervently to defend their traditional status vis-à-vis women. In this pattern sexual relations and the ideology of control are so intermingled as to become confused with one another, thus exposing the connection between them. (Hasan 2002, p.31)

That this violence is not intrinsic to Palestinian culture is made clear by Israeli state integration policies with regard to the Jewish Arab immigrants, which have undermined the cultural norms that once gave family heads customary authority to punish women for actual or assumed moral transgressions (Hasan 2002, pp.32–3). This clearly shows that change is possible and that the state can help to end gendered violence. If it chooses not to, as in the case of the Palestinians in Israel, it is because such violence serves a political agenda, one of providing 'evidence' that the Arabs cannot be assimilated, are incapable of 'civilised' behaviour and therefore require political domination by Israel.[2]

The same, with due regard for local context, applies wherever the state is complicit in perpetuating the myth of the unavoidability of male violence against women as in the UK today with regards to Asian men. This is particularly harmful to women from minorities who find themselves targeted as members of 'problematic' communities. Women from these minorities then find themselves at increasing risk of male violence from within their own communities. At the same time, they find the states in which they live failing to deal with this violence because it is projected as a cultural or religious problem that distinguishes the majority community from the minority and serves the political agenda of a government that may seek to marginalise some communities for its own ends, while publicly arguing that cohesive communities are the goal of government policies.[3] At the present time, Muslims living in the West are in just such a position:

> Recognisably racist, the figure of the unassimilable and diseased migrant masks the material relations that structure this encounter between the West and non-West, obscuring in particular the West's complicity in placing those populations under siege both before they leave their homelands and once within Europe's borders. Acknowledging little or no responsibility for the conditions in which Muslim migrants in the West

live, and indulging in the fantasy of a superior nation [that] must disci-pline and instruct culturally inferior peoples, Western states pursue policies of surveillance and control that heighten the level of racism those communities experience and that exacerbate the conditions under which Muslim communities become even more patriarchal and violent towards women. (Razack 2004, p.132)[4]

Asian male violence against women provides the ammunition that govern-ments need to curb immigration and pass increasingly draconian legisla-tion against minorities, all justified in the name of protecting women.

In this respect, although the recent attempt by the British government to tackle the issue of forced marriages is necessary, the decision to criminalise it is counter-productive, making it much harder for women at risk of such marriages to come forward and seek help for fear of criminalising their own families (McAlpine, Gill and Hegarty 2007, p.16). In some Western countries the issue of forced marriages has been dealt with by limiting immigration: problematic outsiders can be kept out through selective immigration, while states deny that such acts are in any way racially or religiously motivated because they are presented as measures to protect women. While a minority of all women do need pro-tection from violent males, this may not be the best way to ensure such pro-tection for South Asian women in the longer term. Despite increasing measures put in place by Western governments to control immigration, it is clear that such measures will not protect women from male violence. Only changes in male behaviour and attitudes towards violence against women will eliminate the violence South Asian women currently suffer.

Gender and violence

Male violence against women is perpetrated by younger and older men alike and by men from all class, ethnic and religious backgrounds. However, in this chapter I focus on younger men and consider some of the religious and/or cultural forces that may lead to violence. The conception of youth as a stage on the journey from childhood to adulthood has been undermined by the disappearance of the industrial society and the rela-tively stable class system that it upheld. The possibility of constructing a positive identity based on class and work is not an option for many young South Asians in the UK where rates of unemployment are high. Older men are not in a position to guide or understand younger men in a world that has left them behind, and so both class and generational structures have become disconnected from each other, and youth culture has become radically fractured as a consequence.

McDonald (1999) describes this situation in post-industrial states as a process of 'demodernisation': 'the culture of this emerging social model...juxtaposes the incongruous and explores the dissociation of once-coherent spaces, times and societies. The corresponding social model is shaped...by two processes – deinstitutionalisation and desocialisation' (McDonald 1999, p.5). Desocialisation occurs when the roles, values and norms through which the social and life worlds are constructed disappear, and the family, school and other key social institutions are no longer able to perform their roles of transmitting norms – including the social definitions of right and wrong. In this destabilised world:

> individuals are increasingly called upon to be 'entrepreneurs of the self'...at the centre of contemporary social transformation lies the rise of a new 'uncertain individual', characterised by greater responsibility and greater vulnerability, and a blurring of boundaries between self and the world, between private and public. Here...we encounter the shift from a culture of socialisation and institutions to a culture that is increasingly shaped by an imperative of self-esteem. Identity resources are increasingly critical to social actors in a society of risk and uncertainty as opposed to a society of reproduction and roles. (McDonald 1999, p.6)

The existence of this new product of desocialisation and deinstitutionalisation, the 'uncertain individual' who lacks boundaries between himself and the world, but who seeks self-esteem in self-fashioned identities, may help to explain some of the violence directed against women by some young men. In Bradford in the mid-1990s, for example, a small minority of young men chose to harass women – to whom they were not even related – in order to prevent them from, among other things, studying at tertiary level. Nor did this harassment take place only in public: it also included threatening telephone calls made to the fathers of the young women, berating them for their 'liberal' attitudes (Macey 1999a).

This example is just one of the forms of violence possible and merits closer consideration as a strategic use of religion and purported Islamic values expressed in forms of aggressive masculinity. More precisely, why do these young men identify so closely with highly conservative Muslim values? After all, they might have derived self-esteem through a youth identity that opposed such radical beliefs. To answer this, we have to consider the migration histories of the young men and their families, as well as their religious heritage, the global political context (at a time when the Taleban ruled in Afghanistan) and the local situation in Bradford, where young men of Pakistani heritage were failing in, and were failed by, the education system. These factors go some way towards explaining why this generation of young men, unlike their fathers and grandfathers, turned to Salafi-inspired Islam and attempted to bring this to the streets of Bradford.[5]

> Where demodernisation has taken place individuals may find them-
> selves…reduced to a mosaic of behaviours so diverse that they are inca-
> pable of generating any principle of unity of personality, or they seek this
> unity in a cultural heritage, a language, a memory, a religion or more so in
> libido just as impersonal as culture but which provides a principle of con-
> struction of the personality. We encounter here the central paradox of our
> society: just as the economy globalises and is transformed in an accelerat-
> ing way through new technologies, personality ceases to be projected
> towards the future, seeking support instead in the past or in ahistorical
> desire. (Touraine 1997, cited in McDonald 1999, p.7)

The minority of young men in Bradford who chose to fashion themselves as upholders of Muslim values did so by constructing an identity they considered based on their cultural and religious heritage, and designed to counter the Asian stereotype of the decadent West – a move that took them into an imagined past in order to find self-esteem in an aggressive South Asian masculine identity for the present.

It is ironic, therefore, that not only was the Islamic model chosen by these young men *not* a form of indigenous South Asian Islam, but also it was one that was partly rooted in Western political theories derived from both the radical left and the radical right (Gray 2003, p.3). Particularly relevant for the present discussion is the knowledge that the Islamic model of the more extreme Sunni Muslims has much in common with Western fascism from which it draws some of its intellectual inspiration (McDonald 2006, p.179).[6] This is especially so in relation to gender as the control of women and the enacting of alleged customary practices to limit their freedoms and to legitimise punishments if they are deemed to step out of the narrow confines of chaste wife, docile mother and economically dependent, intellectually stunted being were also features of the lives of women living under fascism in Europe in the mid-twentieth century. In this respect the impositions on women enacted by the Taleban rule in the late 1990s in Afghanistan could be viewed as a contemporary Islamised reworking of the fascist legislation passed in mid-twentieth-century Italy (Bettiga-Boukerbout 2005). This is just one of the ways in which neo-fundamentalist movements themselves are responses to the West, in dialogue with Western ideas, and are thus products of modernity, rather than returns to a pure, original Islam (Roy 2004; Ruthven 2004, pp.95ff.).[7]

This trend towards extreme conservatism among some young Muslim men can be seen from one perspective at least as a neo-fascist movement where beliefs in religious and racial purity and the strength of the nation are expressed in increased levels of surveillance and control. In Muslim communities these restrictions mostly target women through whom the future 'pure' Muslims will be produced. The control of women's sexuality is no longer merely a matter of safeguarding family honour; it is about the imagined future survival of community, nation and faith. In a land where educational success is denied, employment opportunities limited, where the institutions that made sense of the world for earlier generations are no longer viable and where self-esteem is undermined by discriminatory prac-tices, versions of strong South Asian masculinities expressed in these global ideoscapes offer some South Asian men a way of generating self-esteem through recourse to violence against women and against the West – a violence that ultimately also works against them, since '[a]ny strategy for the maintenance of power is likely to involve a dehumanising of other groups and a corresponding withering of empathy and emotional relatedness within the self' (Connell and Messerschmidt 2005, p.852). Violence perpetrated by young Asian men seeking a new identity for them-selves is destined to fail, as this violence does not lead to any integrated sense of self, or allow the expression of identities capable of transformation into a creative social movement to mobilise communities and produce a viable future.

The case of a young Pakistani man who was subsequently convicted of rape will help draw together some of the issues outlined so far. This man was from a small-town background in Pakistan and raised in a conservative environment within an education system that reinforced negative stereo-types about westerners. Arrival in the UK was culturally traumatic, and the school he went to failed to help him understand the local context for gender relations. As far as this young man was concerned, and because he could not adapt his Pakistani understandings to the new social world he found himself in, girls in the West were immoral. The young man also encountered models of aggressive white gang masculinity and responded by joining a Pakistani gang to assert an aggressive South Asian identity. Ethnic and racial boundaries and stereotypes were reinforced by a lack of positive interaction with people from other communities. Alcohol and drug abuse followed as did a non-South Asian Muslim girlfriend. Fearing for his long-term well-being, the young man's parents arranged for him and his girlfriend to marry so that the couple would settle down to a more responsible life. Homelessness followed, as did unemployment and continued substance abuse; ultimately the young man raped a white stranger.

This young man never understood the new world in which he found himself; indeed, he fell between two worlds – that of his parents and that of his peers. The models of masculinity of each were different and irreconcilable. The parents did what they could to help the son – hence the marriage that they encouraged and supported. Unable to deal with the difficult relationship the young man had with his confident and independent wife, unable to meet the ideals of a South Asian married man who – he had grown up to believe – was economically independent and able to command his household, and burdened with racist and sexist attitudes towards the majority white community, this young man committed a sexually violent crime. The ethnic background of the victim was significant, because this was an act of orientalism in reverse: he laid claim to a strong South Asian masculinity when he had nothing else left to identify with. These conflicting worlds and generational disjunctures were further exacerbated by anti-Muslim attitudes in the UK – attitudes which were themselves countered by the often stridently Islamic rhetoric expressed in the media from the subcontinent. The young man found a sense of self in a form of masculinity available to the young – one based on violence – and attempted to take control of himself by violently denying freedom of choice to another.

The prison rehabilitation programme treated him as an autonomous individual and tried to instil in him middle-class, liberal values based on a cognitive behavioural model designed in North America and developed on white American penal populations. Worryingly, the assumptions underpinning the...cognitive programmes...assume a general criminal personality that transcends gender, race, ethnicity and socioeconomic status...[where]...the realities of the lives of minority groups...are rendered not only unproblematic but also denigrated. They are seen as individuals with poor cognitive skills, intellectual ability or motivation to change.' (Shaw and Hannah-Moffat 2004, pp.108, 110)

In prison his ethnic and religious background were noted by the prison services as problematic as stereotypically Asian men, and particularly those of Muslim background, are viewed as holding inappropriate attitudes towards women. The crime was clear evidence of this.

While the circumstances of this young man's life, and the cultural stresses experienced by him are common, his decision to direct his aggression outside the domestic sphere was more unusual. Domestic violence is common in marriages, and in both Pakistan and India evidence shows that most women are subjected to some form of domestic violence during their marriages (United States State Department (USSD) 2006a; 2006b). For many women this is so normal they do not consider the violence aberrant and do not think to protest. Indeed, in some surveys a majority of women considered it acceptable for men to beat their wives in particular circumstances (USSD 2005). Therefore, from the perspective of a male arriving from the subcontinent, domestic violence may be seen as a prerogative of a husband, and from the perspective of a wife as something to be expected. Transnational marriages often have different gendered consequences and generally women come off worst in such marriages (Charsley 2005). Where the wife is British, the husband may not adapt easily to life in the UK and may not view his new wife's behaviour as acceptable given the norms in place in his country of origin. Violence is often the outcome. Where the husband is British and his wife enters the UK, he may view her as uncouth and mistreat her as a result. In both cases the woman is most likely to be left indoors with the housework while her new husband continues to enjoy the life he had prior to marriage. At best these wives are isolated and ignored.

Despite greater pressures on women to make marriages work, men too can come under considerable pressure to present their marriages as successful. In one case, a man killed his wife because she did not wish to divorce him and his family wanted the couple to remain married. Rather than divorce his wife, this man thought he could murder her in what became a poorly staged but grim 'accident', and thus divest himself of an unwanted wife without the stigma of a divorce to shame his family. Here the conflict was not simply that between a wife and husband over whether the marriage was to continue, but one that involved the parents of the husband, and where stigma related to how the rest of the community would view the wider family should a divorce take place. The man himself was not able to 'be a man' in his own terms and control his own life. His wife refused to divorce him and his own parents worked to keep the couple together. For this man in this situation, it appeared that the only way to be a man and to regain control was to commit a crime of violence against the woman he began to view as the 'problem' in his life. In family matters, men must face the fact that their lives as individuals, with some control of their own futures, will come into conflict with the requirements of the family, which may require them to deny or limit personal desires for the good of the family as a whole. In this case traditional models of masculinity embodying positive Asian values of family duty and responsibility conflicted with more individualistic contemporary models of masculinity, and when this conflict cannot be resolved the outcome is, more often than not, violence against women.

Conclusion

The goal must be to find ways in which reasonable expectations of individual autonomy can be negotiated with demands of family and community and without recourse to violence against women. No rehabilitation programme that does not deal with all these issues can ever hope to succeed in dealing with the specific issues raised by the position of South Asians in the UK and the very particular social, economic and familial causes of the violence directed towards South Asian women. This chapter has focused on some issues that impact local masculinities; the aim has been to generate greater understanding of these to tackle domestic violence when it arises and ideally prevent it from occurring at all. Only once this complex context is mapped out can we begin to challenge the negative masculinities that are conceived of as natural or traditional. I conclude with some broad suggestions for tackling gendered violence working from the pragmatic assumption that it is already too late to change the attitudes of most men and youth but not those of children.

For men, education needs to start young. Many boys in primary schools have witnessed, been victims of, or know about domestic violence. It is never too early to begin to find age-appropriate ways to raise awareness of the damage that violence does to victims and perpetrators. Older boys can discuss violence and their attitudes to it in a range of contexts, including violence between individual boys and between gangs, when they choose to use violence, and when they feel they have no choice but to use violence. As it is impossible to discuss violence without also bringing in gender, religion, racism, discrimination, structural violence and other social issues, these too need to be incorporated into programmes of discussion. In order to deal with gender-based violence assumptions underlying notions of 'tradition', 'culture' and 'honour' as they relate to the control of women need to be unpicked, and revealed as the contingent political and historical constructs they are. Associations between gendered violence and the minority status of South Asians can be developed to bring out the strategic ways in which such violence is used to demonise South Asian minorities in the West.

In short, the politics of gendered violence, and the interrelations between what happens in the home and the wider social, economic, political and cultural domains in a global context, need to be made explicit. In this way, gendered violence in the UK will not be essentialised as an unavoidable feature of a traditional society, but will nonetheless be located in the practices of specific ethnic communities living in particular places, and dealing with specific sets of constraints and possibilities. And if and when boys and young men do discuss the need to discipline their sisters, partners and wives, then the discussion must be held in a way that acknowledges all of the social and cultural forces that inform the issue. Models of masculinity are needed that do not lead to the victimisation of others.[8]

Such meetings need to happen in spaces where trust can be developed between participants and where boundaries of acceptable behaviour are clear. It might be necessary to encourage attendance at such meetings by offering some locally valued pursuit or activity which can be accessed only if discussions on gendered violence are attended with active participation. The aim of these discussion groups – which should be designed to avoid the impression that they are part of the education system which is itself implicated in forms of violence against minority populations – would be to prevent gendered violence from being a part of the lives of young men when they reach adulthood. Schemes and models for such work already exist, and models of good practice could be drawn upon to develop programmes for use among South Asians in the UK.

To continue to use models of the social world that assume the social order of the industrial age with the type of individual such an age produced, and that do not find the means to deal with the radically shifting and unstable worlds young people are growing up in, and further, to fail to recognise that the use of terms such as 'tradition', 'culture' and 'honour' may be no more than modern attempts to try to find fixity and stability in a world of flux will result in yet another generation of women suffering unnecessary domestic violence. To do nothing is to fail not only South Asian women but also South Asian men.

Acknowledgements

I wish to thank the editors, Aisha Gill and Ravi Thiara, for their generous advice, patience and good grace during the preparation of this chapter.

Notes

1. These include studies on interrelationships between gender and power, and how ethnicity, 'race', religion, imperialism and masculinities intertwine (Back 1994; Cornwall and Lindisfarne 1994; Kanitkar 1994). Many ethnographies and studies dealing with South Asians discuss masculinities in terms of domestic violence, ethnicity, educational performance, the construction of Asian 'criminality' in the subcontinent and the Western diaspora (Alexander 2000; Archer 2001; Chopra, Osella and Osella 2004; Gilborn 1997; Gutman 1997; Jeganathan, 2000; Macey 1999a, 1999b; Purkayastha 2000; Webster 1997).

2. Cf. Ammar (2007) on US assumptions that Islam is supportive of wife beating.

3. In 2008 the case of Southall Black Sisters (SBS) against Ealing Council served as one example of such a situation. Ealing Council sought to withdraw funding from SBS by arguing that social cohesion could best be served by eliminating specialist services and providing a 'one-service-fits-all' alternative. Lord Justice Moses' judgment of 29 July 2008 found in favour of SBS and made clear that social cohesion is not served but rather undermined by policies which have disproportionate impact on ethnic and minority communities. See www.southallblacksisters.org.uk/downloads/ LordJustice Moses_JUDGMENT.rtf, accessed on 28 April 2009.

4. This 'cultural' excuse for violence against women is also played out in the courts. Whenever cultural legal defences work, it is women who lose because they are subject not only to the sexism within their own communities but also the sexism and racism found in the majority community reinforcing the very patriarchal norms that

resulted in the violence the women are subject to from their own communities (Chiu 1994; Phillips 2003).

5. On conservative Islam as a religious revival to counter European imperialism, and as a form of Appadurai's ethnoscape, see McDonald (2006, pp.175–7), and on the different ways in which education discriminates among minorities based on ethnicity and gender, see Gilborn (1997).

6. This shared European political heritage also helps to explain some of the rise in contemporary violence against women in Hindu communities: the right-wing nationalist movements in India – which have their localised counterparts in the UK – are also, in part, inspired by the fascist ideologies of Eastern and Western Europe from the 1930s and 1940s (Bhatt 2001, pp.105ff.).

7. This is not to suggest that men who draw misguided justification and rationale for their gendered violence from very conservative forms of Islam (or Hinduism) are thereby more likely to become involved in acts of terrorism or violence beyond the domestic or local spheres. Links the Home Office makes between forced marriage, gendered violence and terrorism may result in fewer women escaping violence because of fears that family members may be labelled potential terrorists as a consequence. There are links between the rise of violence against women and the turn towards neo-fundamentalist religious movements, but these are not direct or simple links.

8. In this respect there is a need for historical knowledge and for a continued reminder of how things were. The advances made by women since the 1960s are in some places under threat. Rouse (2004) for example notes how women have been increasingly denied access to public spaces, including religious spaces that they were formerly permitted to enter in contemporary Pakistan. This geographical imposition, because of the increasing masculinisation of public space, is paralleled by a series of laws which have been passed in Pakistan, and which have lessened the rights and freedoms of all women in Pakistan. If a generation now grows up in this context, they may never realise that their mothers and grandmothers had greater freedom of movement and legal freedoms than they themselves do (Rouse 2004, pp.125ff.).

References

Alexander, C. (2000) *The Asian Gang: Ethnicity, Identity, Masculinity.* Oxford: Berg.

Ammar, N.H. (2007) 'Wife battery in Islam: A comprehensive understanding of interpretations.' *Violence Against Women 13*, 5, 516–26.

Appadurai, A. (1996) *Modernity at Large: Cultural Dimensions of Globalization.* Minneapolis, MN: University of Minnesota Press.

Appadurai, A. (2001) *New Logics of Violence.* Available at www.india-seminar.com/2001/ 503/503%20arjun%20apadurai.htm, accessed on 28 April 2009.

Archer, L. (2001) '"Muslim Brothers, Black Lads, Traditional Asians": British Muslim young men's constructions of race, religion and masculinity.' *Feminism and Psychology 11*, 1, 79–105.

Back, L. (1994) 'The "White Negro" Revisited: Race and Masculinities in South London.' In A. Cornwall and N. Lindisfarne (eds) *Dislocating Masculinity: Comparative Ethnographies.* London: Routledge.

Bettiga-Boukerbout, M.G. (2005) '"Crimes of Honour" in the Italian Penal Code: An Analysis of History and Reform.' In L. Welchmann and S. Hossain (eds) *'Honour': Crimes, Paradigms, and Violence Against Women.* London: Zed Books.

Bhatt, C. (2001) *Hindu Nationalism: Origins, Ideologies and Modern Myths.* Oxford: Berg.

Charsley, K. (2005) 'Unhappy husbands: Masculinity and migration in transnational Pakistani marriages.' *Journal of the Royal Anthropological Institute 11*, 85–105.

Chiu, D. (1994) 'The cultural defense: Beyond exclusion, assimilation, and guilty liberalism.' *California Law Review 82*, 4, 1053–125.

Chopra, R., Osella, F. and Osella C. (eds) (2004) *South Asian Masculinities: Contexts of Change, Sites of Continuity.* New Delhi: Kali for Women.

Connell, R.W. (1987) *Gender and Power.* Sydney: Allen and Unwin.

Connell, R.W. and Messerschmidt, J. (2005) 'Hegemonic masculinity: Rethinking the concept.' *Gender and Society 19*, 6, 829–59.

Cornwall, A. and Lindisfarne, N. (eds) (1994) *Dislocating Masculinity: Comparative Ethnographies.* London: Routledge.

Edley, N. (2001) 'Analysing Masculinity: Interpretive Repertoires, Ideological Dilemmas and Subject Positions.' In M. Wetherell, S. Taylor and S. Yates (eds) *Discourse as Data: A Guide for Analysis.* London: Sage.

Edley, N. and Wetherell, M. (1996) 'Masculinity, Power and Identity.' In Mac An Ghaill (ed.) *Understanding Masculinities: Social Relations and Cultural Arenas.* Buckingham: Open University Press.

Gilborn, D. (1997) 'Ethnicity and educational performance in the United Kingdom: Racism, ethnicity and variability in achievement.' *Anthropology of Education Quarterly 28*, 3, 375–93.

Gray, J. (2003) *Al Qaeda and What It Means to be Modern.* London: Faber & Faber.

Gutman, M. (1997) 'Trafficking in men: The anthropology of masculinity.' *Annual Review of Anthropology 26*, 385–409.

Hasan, M. (2002) 'The politics of honour: Patriarchy, the state and the murder of women in the name of family honour.' *Journal of Israeli History 21*, 1–2, 1–37.

Hobsbawm, E. and Ranger, T. (eds) (1983) *The Invention of Tradition.* Cambridge: Cambridge University Press.

Jeganathan, P. (2000) 'A Space for Violence: Anthropology, Politics and the Location of a Sinhala Practice of Masculinity.' In P. Chatterjee and P. Jeganathan (eds) *Community, Gender and Violence.* London: Hurst.

Kanitkar, H. (1994) '"Real true boys": Moulding the Cadets of Imperialism.' In A. Cornwall and N. Lindisfarne (eds) *Dislocating Masculinity: Comparative Ethnographies.* London: Routledge.

Kessler, S.J., Ashenden, D.J.; Connell, R.W. and Dowsett, G.W. (1982) *Ockers and Disco-maniacs.* Sydney: Inner City Education Center.

Kimmel, M.S. (2005) 'Globalization and its Mal(e)contents: The Gendered Moral and Political Economy of Terrorism.' In M.S. Kimmel, J. Hearn and R.W. Connell (eds) *Handbook of Studies on Men and Masculinities.* Thousand Oaks, CA: Sage.

McAlpine, C., Gill, A. and Hegarty, P. (2007) 'Why criminalise forced marriage? Islamophobia – and assimilation-based justifications.' *Psychology of Women Section Review 9*, 2, 15–28.

McDonald, K. (1999) *Struggles for Subjectivity: Identity, Action and Youth Experience.* Cambridge: Cambridge University Press.

McDonald, K. (2006) *Global Movements: Action and Culture.* Oxford: Blackwell.

Macey, M. (1999a) 'Class, gender and religious influences on changing patterns of Pakistani Muslim male violence in Bradford.' *Ethnic and Racial Studies 22*, 5, 845–66.

Macey, M. (1999b) 'Religion, male violence, and the control of women: Pakistani Muslim men in Bradford, UK.' *Gender and Development 7*, 1, 48–55.

Martin, S.F. (2004) *Refugee Women.* Lanham, MD: Lexington Books.

Moses, Lord Justice (2008) Judgment promulgated at the Royal Courts of Justice on 29 July 2008. Available at www.southallblacksisters.org.uk/downloads/LordJusticeMoses_ JUDGMENT.rtf, accessed on 28 April 2009.

Phillips, A. (2003) 'When Culture means gender: Issues of cultural defence in English courts.' *Modern Law Review 66*, 4, 510–31.

Purkayastha, B. (2000) 'Liminal lives: South Asian youth and domestic violence.' *Journal of Social Distress and the Homeless 9*, 3, 201–19.

Razack, S.H. (2004) 'Imperilled Muslim women, dangerous Muslim men and civilised Europeans: Legal and social responses to forced marriages.' *Feminist Legal Studies 12*, 129–74.

Rouse, S. (2004) 'Militarisation, Nationalism and the Spaces of Gender.' In S. Rouse, *Shifting Body Politics: Gender, Nation, State in Pakistan.* New Delhi: Women Unlimited.

Roy, O. (2004) *Globalized Islam: The Search for a New Ummah.* New York: Columbia University Press.

Ruthven, M. (2002) *A Fury for God: The Islamist Attack on America.* London: Granta Books.

Sarkar, T. (2001) *Hindu Wife, Hindu Nation: Community, Religion and Cultural Nationalism.* London: Hurst.

Sarkar, T. and Butalia, U. (eds) (1995) *Women and Right-wing Movements: Indian Experiences.* London: Zed Books.

Shaw, M. and Hannah-Moffat, K. (2004) 'How Cognitive Skills Forgot about Gender and Diversity.' In G. Mair (ed.) *What Matters in Probation.* Uffcolme, Devon, UK: Willan.

Stoller, A.L. (1991) 'Carnal Knowledge and Imperial Power: Gender, Race, and Morality in Colonial Asia.' In M. di Leonardo (ed.) *Gender at the Crossroads of Knowledge: Feminist Anthropology in the Postmodern Era.* Berkeley, CA: University of California Press.

Tarlo, E. (2005) 'The Jilbab Controversy.' *Anthropology Today 21*, 6, 13–17.

Toth, J. (2005) 'Local Islam Gone Global: The Roots of Religious Militancy in Egypt and its Transnational Transformation.' In J. Nash (ed.) *Social Movements: An Anthropological Reader.* Oxford: Blackwell.

United States State Department (USSD) (2005) *India Country Report*. Available at www.state.gov/g/drl/hrrpt/2005/61707.htm, accessed on 15 June 2006.

United States State Department (USSD) (2006a) *Report India: Report on Human Rights Practices 2006*. Available at www.state.gov/g/drl/rls/hrrpt/2006/78871.htm

United States State Department (USSD) (2006b) *Pakistan Country Reports on Human Rights Practices for 2006*. Available at www.state.gov/g/drl/rls/hrrpt/2006/78874.htm, accessed on 28 April 2009.

Webster, C. (1997) 'The construction of British "Asian" Criminality.' *International Journal of the Sociology of Law 25*, 65–86.

Womensphere (2008) *Abolish No Recourse to Public Funds: End Violence Against Women! Support the Day of Action: 23 April 2008*. Available at http://womensphere. wordpress.com/2008/03/14/abolish-no-recourse-to-public-funds-end-violence-against-women-support-the-day-of-action-23-april-2008, accessed on 28 April 2009.

Chapter 4

Shrinking Secular Spaces

Asian Women at the Intersect of Race, Religion and Gender

Pragna Patel and Hannana Siddiqui

This chapter looks at the struggles waged by South Asian women against domestic violence and other forms of gender-based violence within South Asian communities against the backdrop of the UK government's approach to multiculturalism since the late 1970s. By drawing on the authors' experience of Southall Black Sisters (SBS) (see Contributor Biographies for further details),[1] this chapter shows how early multiculturalism impacted negatively on the rights of minority women. By the late 1990s, for a brief period, it appeared as if our struggles against domestic violence was finally achieving results following recognition by the state of the need to develop 'mature multiculturalism', an approach which necessitates the recognition of the human rights of black and minority women. However, more recent developments have greatly undermined this position. The chapter then shows how since 9/11 and the London bombings in July 2005, the state's new approach to race relations involves the implementation of a 'faith' and 'cohesion' agenda which represents the 'softer' face of its counter terrorism measures. The shift from multiculturalism to 'multi-faithism' reveals a dual and contradictory approach to minority women. On the one hand, the state appears to be tackling gender-based violence, for example, forced marriage and honour crimes although it also uses these issues to tighten immigration controls. On the other hand, it actively encourages a 'faith'-based approach which reinforces unequal gender and other power relations within minority communities. We conclude that the consequent shrinking of secular spaces – a necessary precondition for women's struggle for freedom in the personal and public spheres – unless vigorously resisted, threatens the gains made by Asian women. This is clearly demonstrated by our campaign in 2008 against Ealing Council which sought to withdraw our funding and therefore essential services for abused minority women in the name of 'equality', 'diversity' and 'cohesion'. This experience marks a significant watershed in Asian women's struggles against those who use religion and racism to limit our freedoms.

Multiculturalism

In 1999, the Working Group on Forced Marriage set up by the Home Office,[2] of which SBS was a member, produced one of those seminal moments in the history of struggles by Asian and other minority women to compel the state to take account of our needs. The then junior Home Office minister, Mike O'Brien, made an announcement which went unnoticed in the wider society, but which was of immense significance to Asian and other minority women. He stated that 'multicultural sensitivities are no excuse for moral blindness' (Home Office 2000, p.10) and advocated a more 'mature' multicultural approach (Home Office 2000; see also Hansard 1999), which allowed for the recognition of gender-based violence and other harmful cultural practices within minority communities.

This was a historical and potentially liberating announcement for Asian and indeed other minority women who struggled for over two decades for the state to intervene in its protective capacity into the family affairs of minority communities.[3] Until that point, the needs of women affected by domestic violence and their demands for protection had been more or less ignored because the dominant multicultural approach adopted by the state accepted the need for 'tolerance' of different cultures within minority communities that were regarded as homogeneous, and lacked an understanding of how social identities are constructed within unequal power relations based on class, caste, gender and other divisions in these communities. Recent developments, however, including the rise of religious fundamentalism in all religions (the political use of religion to seek control over people, territories and resources), the push for a more 'cohesive' society, and the reconstruction of ethnic minorities as 'faith communities' (a contradictory process to 'cohesion' which recasts minority communities as faith communities and seeks to incorporate religion in the functions of public institutions) has now overshadowed the 'mature' multi-cultural approach and undermines anti-racist and black feminist struggles.

Early multiculturalism

Since the 1970s, multiculturalism has been the dominant social policy approach to race relations between the state and minority communities in the UK. It was first introduced in education but was quickly accepted as a tool of national policy across a range of issues at the local and national levels (Anthias and Yuval-Davis 1992; SBS 1989). Prior to the 1970s, the initial focus of British race relations policies was on assimilation into a 'British way of life' based on the notion that 'good' race relations can be achieved only if minority communities shed all aspects of their religious and cultural identity. This slowly gave way to a form of multiculturalism which valued the need for difference and to that extent was useful in the fight against racism. However, the problem with this notion of multicultur-alism is that it did not distinguish between valid cultural demands or fun-damental human rights such as the right to manifest different cultural and religious identities through dress, food and language or the right not to be subjected to discrimination, inhuman and degrading treatment and racism. Multiculturalism was seen as an end in itself – a way of simply recognising and 'tolerating' difference. The difficulty with the multicultural approach was that in practice it was stripped of its more progressive elements.

Perhaps the most significant critique of the early multicultural model is that ethnic difference was constructed in a stereotypical and essentialist manner, fixing and reifying boundaries of community affiliation. The more 'different' an identity was, the more authentic it became. In many respects, it drew on previous models of British colonial rule whereby the indigenous laws of the colonised country were codified with reference to religious texts but without reference to changing customs, practices and interpreta-tions (Sahgal 1992). Minorities were, therefore, viewed primarily as targets of social policy, rather than as actors in the democratic system (Ali 1992) and notions of citizenship were deemed not to apply except in a facile way – to demand allegiance to the state.

This notion of multiculturalism has since undergone a transformation following 9/11. The government has since attempted to revert back to aspects of previous (discredited) policies based on assimilation to promote 'cohesion'. It has also encouraged the creation of 'faith communities' – a construction borne out of community self-definition and state social policy. The result is that a complex web of political, social, economic and cultural factors, which helps to form a particular identity, is reduced to purely religious values which then become the overarching framework through which the needs of minorities are addressed.

Gender and multiculturalism

SBS and other minority feminists have been critical of the multicultural model for providing the space for unelected community representatives, usually male and from religious groups, but also from the business classes, to determine the needs of the community and to mediate between the community and the state. Although the interests of the community are often articulated in the name of anti-racism or even human rights, this very rarely includes recognition of the individual rights of women or other powerless subgroups within the community. In the process, the struggle for community representation at the political level becomes highly contested, but it has largely been won by predominantly fundamentalist and conservative male dominated groups who usually have exclusionary if not extremist political agendas. It is precisely these groups that have become more prominent under the new 'faith'-based approach.

Our starting point in tracing the impact and development of multiculturalism as it affects minority women, especially Asian women, is the case of 'Afia', a 13-year-old Bangladeshi girl from Tower Hamlets in East London, who in 1989 contacted SBS desperate for support in resisting a forced marriage. She was fearful that she would be taken to Bangladesh and forced into a marriage by her father in response to the actions of her older sister, who had previously run away from home to escape just such a fate.

Afia's only option was to be taken into care by social services. Even after she was informed of the harsh realties of care, she insisted that it was preferable to being married off in what would be, for her, a foreign country. But when the social services department was approached, its response was one of indifference to her fears. According to it, she was a 'typical' young

Asian adolescent experiencing a touch of the 'culture clash'. Asian and anti-racist experts within the social services department had declared that 'insensitive intervention' in families such as Afia's would be tantamount to racism. Social services refused to accept her into care without the consent of her father, which was, of course, withheld. Indeed, he denied all the allegations and said that he only wished to take his family on holiday.

Confronted with an inflexible attitude from social services, SBS was compelled to make an application for Afia to be made a ward of court and, pending a final hearing, the presiding judge ordered social services to find her a foster home. Unfortunately, the only homes that social services was willing to consider were other Muslim families. Afia protested strongly that she did not want to stay with another Muslim family for fear of being blamed for bringing dishonour on her father. Despite her protestations, social services proceeded to place her with a family whose attitude to her was far from supportive. While the policy to place children with families where their language and cultural heritage can flourish is laudable, it becomes dangerous when implemented as a blanket policy, irrespective of the child's other needs, especially when religion becomes the defining cultural and even racial criterion by which ethnic minority families are chosen. The presiding judge, for his part, was prepared to accept the concerns expressed, but said that he could not presume to tell social services how to do its job. Not surprisingly, after a few weeks, she returned to her own home.

At the final court hearing on wardship, social services produced a report stating that 'normal relations had been restored and that no further intervention was needed'. Throughout the proceedings, Afia was never asked what she thought, so proper instructions could not be taken from her. Nevertheless, in court we argued that she should remain a ward of court temporarily as a measure of security and protection. In its report, social services described Afia's family as poor and victims of racial discrimination. Social services argued that her father, as head of the family, was merely trying to do his best to support and protect them from racism. Its portrayal of the family's environment is of course a reality for many Bangladeshi families, but by ignoring the father's abuse of power within his own family, it colluded in the other forms of oppression to which minority women are subjected.

The social worker recommended discontinuation of wardship proceedings, stating that there were no ongoing concerns about Afia's fears of being forced into marriage. The social worker stated:

> What is left are differences of opinion between Afia and her parents such as may arise in any family...those differences will need to be resolved within the context of the family, and the possibilities of resolving them successfully may be diminished if the balance of power within the family is artificially distorted...since I believe that it would seriously undermine the parent's confidence and authority.

The presiding judge agreed to remove the wardship from Afia, and added:

> I am satisfied that it is not appropriate for the court to take any further part. If one looks into any family there are bound to be stresses and strains but this does not mean that the State should intervene.

From the mid- to late 1980s, cases like that of Afia made it crystal clear that the struggle for female autonomy within minority communities is inextricably linked to the development of multiculturalism since the approach lends itself to collusion with patriarchal systems of control of female sexuality and lays the foundation for a cultural relativist approach to women's rights. SBS has therefore been compelled to challenge multicultural policies for their unintentional but also often intentional effect in reinforcing rather than challenging abusive practices.

Cases like that of Afia have shown us that there is a constant interplay between struggles against racism and multiculturalism, and for minority women's human rights, to which we must be alert, since it impacts profoundly on the goals that we set ourselves and the strategies that we adopt. This interplay is nowhere better exemplified than in the way that the state has since responded to the question of multiculturalism and forced marriage.

'Mature multiculturalism'

The trigger for the shift in the state's response to minority women began with the case of Rukhsana Naz in 1998. Her death drew widespread media attention to the problem of forced marriage and encouraged a shift in policy from the government. Rukhsana Naz was killed by her mother and brother for refusing to stay in a forced marriage and for becoming pregnant by her lover. They were convicted of her murder in 1999. At the same time, the case of 'Jack and Zena', a young couple on the run from Zena's family, who opposed their interracial relationship and wanted to force her into an arranged marriage, also received widespread attention. These cases prompted Mike O'Brien to establish the Home Office Working Group on Forced Marriage. However, some members of the Working Group, including representatives of religious organisations, did not share Mike O'Brien's vision of a 'mature multiculturalism'. They argued instead for a 'softer' approach to forced marriage. Their view was that the main focus should be on changing social and cultural attitudes through public education led by community and religious leaders. They also advocated that mediation between the victim and her family as a means of tackling forced marriage was also a legitimate option. SBS opposed this position, stating that mediation was a dangerous practice because it placed victims under pressure to reconcile with family members without any redress to immediate protection if things went wrong and because it did not ultimately challenge the practice of forced marriage. We pointed to the case of Vandana Patel, an abused Asian woman, who in 1991 had been stabbed to death by her husband at a mediation meeting organised by the police at the Domestic Violence Unit at Stoke Newington Police Station. The police facilitated the meeting on the grounds that in domestic violence cases, it is 'legitimate for a couple to talk through their difficulties.'

From casework experience, we know that Asian and other minority women face considerable pressure from extended families and community leaders to reconcile with abusive husbands and relatives in order to safeguard their family honour. Informal methods of mediation is the norm and, in almost all cases, attempted without much success by women who are fearful of being ostracised and even killed for seeking outside help. We argued that any attempt to institutionalise mediation as a valid option would exacerbate the pressures that black and minority women already face to remain silent when experiencing violence and abuse. Moreover, the step would also amount to state abrogation of responsibility for their protection, thus making it even more difficult to challenge the practice of various agencies which accept mediation in the name of 'cultural sensitivity'. However, the Working Group, dominated as it was by community and religious 'leaders', continued to advocate mediation as a solution.

The acceptance of mediation as a means by which to tackle forced marriage compelled SBS to resign from the Working Group, but not before we had successfully included the recognition in the final report, *A Choice by Right* (Home Office 2000), that forced marriage is an abuse of human rights. SBS was later able to ensure that the guidelines on forced marriage issued by the Foreign and Commonwealth Office Community Liaison Unit (later to become the joint Home Office and Foreign Office Forced Marriage Unit) did not recommend mediation as best practice. However, implementing and enforcing these guidelines to prevent an indifferent or cultural relativist approach by agencies, such as the police, social services and others has proved more difficult.

Following the Working Group's report, sustained pressure from SBS and others has led to an improved response from the Forced Marriage Unit to those cases of forced marriage that have an overseas dimension. SBS and others have also supported the creation of the Forced Marriage (Civil Protection) Act 2007 initiated by Lord Lester, which enhance civil remedies for victims and place the forced marriage guidelines on a statutory footing. Both the Act and the guidelines are welcome additions to the protection available against forced marriage and abuse.

Post-multiculturalism: contradictory approaches

When viewed in the context of the emergence of the 'cohesion' and 'faith'-based approach', the state's current response to black and minority women's needs now reveals two contradictory approaches.

First, years of campaigning by SBS and others means that from time to time, black and minority women still retain some influence on state policy on issues affecting them, as highlighted by the introduction of policies and laws in relation to forced marriage, honour-based violence, female genital mutilation and to a limited extent, immigration and asylum matters.[4] Even here, however, there is a tendency for state institutions to 'exoticise' the more dramatic culturally specific practices such as forced marriage and honour killings and to isolate them from wider debates on violence against women and state accountability. This creates a parallel universe where domestic violence against minority women is considered 'different' from that experienced by white women, requiring 'different' analysis and solutions based on their racial and religious identities. Needless to say, this often results in further constrictions on the lives of women.

The response of the police to the case of Banaz Mahmod, a young Kurdish Iraqi woman, is a case in point. Banaz Mahmod, a married woman, was killed for seeking a divorce from her violent husband so that she could marry her boyfriend, who was considered 'unsuitable' because he was from a different ethnic and tribal background. She was raped, strangled and buried in a suitcase by a group of men from her community at the instigation of her father and uncle, who were convicted of her murder in 2007. Banaz Mahmod's case received high profile media coverage as an 'honour' killing. However, its real significance was not that it was an honour killing, but the fact that, prior to her murder, the police knew about the danger to her life but failed to act to protect her. Before her death, Banaz and her boyfriend had been subjected to a number of death threats and an attempt by her father to kill her. On New Year's Eve in 2005, Banaz's father plied her with drink in order to reduce her ability to defend herself as he prepared to strangle her. However, before he could attack her, she managed to escape into their back garden and tried to alert her neighbour by banging on her neighbour's window, which she accidentally broke. Receiving no response from the neighbour, Banaz jumped over the garden fence and ran bleeding and bare footed into a coffee shop, where the police and an ambulance were called. Banaz told the police about her father's attempt to kill her and repeatedly asked for her boyfriend, fearing that he was also in danger. However, the police response was dismissive. Instead of investigating the incident as one of attempted murder, they considered charging her for criminal damage for breaking the neighbour's window! The police officer assumed either that Banaz was drunk and was merely seeking attention from her boyfriend or that she was simply 'rebelling' against her parents' cultural beliefs and practices and did not therefore take her allegation seriously.

The police response, or lack of it, demonstrates the need for an urgent public inquiry on the question why, after three decades of legislation and policies, the state continues to flout its obligations under the Human Rights Act 1998 and international human rights law to protect women from domestic violence in all its manifestations, including honour crimes. There continues to be little or no comprehensive investigation into continuing police failure in domestic violence cases, with the result that, with a few individual exceptions, there is insufficient and inconsistent progress among the rank and file, despite improvements at the policy level. Implementation of policies on domestic violence remains extremely poor and patchy and the same mistakes are repeated by police forces across the country within all communities. Banaz's case is one in a long line of deaths of women and children in circumstances where the dangers to their lives were known to the police.[5] However, either this issue is often obscured by the overemphasis that is placed on the 'exotic' contexts of the deaths of black and minority women or, as in the case of African and Caribbean women, there is still a propensity to criminalise the behaviour of women by arresting and charging them for violent assaults when they have called the police for protection.[6]

Secondly, although the state has begun to assert more clearly the view that harmful cultural practices will not be tolerated, the 'faith'-based approach contributes to a set of policies aimed at recognising and protecting religious identity, increasingly to the detriment of women's rights. In our experience, the accommodation of religious identity within state institutions, including the legal system, is undermining, albeit slowly and surreptitiously, the rights of minority women. This is illustrated by the ways in which the state appears to be toying with the demand to incorporate aspects of shariah laws (mainly in relation to the family) within the legal system, a move which is encouraged by leaders of the church and judiciary.[7]

Immigration and domestic violence

Another problem with the state's approach to harmful cultural practices is the focus on tighter immigration controls as a 'solution'. We welcome the fact that there is now greater recognition that the worst forms of oppression are often experienced at the point of the intersection of a number of factors that make a person vulnerable to abuse or exploitation – race, gender, age, sexuality and class. For example, racist nationality, immigration and asylum laws compound minority women's experiences of violence and increases their vulnerability, requiring changes to both domestic violence and immigration and asylum laws and policies. Yet it is in the area of immigration and asylum issues that we face some of our toughest challenges. If the state is to make good its promise to protect all women and children from domestic violence, and if it is to meet its obligations under international human rights law, it is essential to de-link the question of protection from immigration control.

Far from heading in a more compassionate direction, the government is determinedly pursuing a punitive and inhumane immigration and asylum agenda. Recent proposals on marriage to overseas partners, for example, have further strengthened the discriminatory and racist nature of the immigration system. The use of immigration controls to address the issue of forced marriage has been vigorously advocated by politicians like Ann Cryer MP and some Asian women's groups such as Karma Nirvana. Since 2000 onwards, the government has introduced a number of legal and policy measures, including raising the age at which an overseas spouse can join his or her British spouse. Initially the age was raised from 16 to 18 and more recently, from 18 to 21. Under the pretext of 'strengthening safe-guards against forced marriage' (Home Office and UK Border Agency 2008) and to prevent bogus marriages, the government has proposed a series of highly questionable solutions which will have a profound impact on the settlement rights of minority communities, particularly those from the Indian subcontinent (Home Office and UK Border Agency 2008).

Notwithstanding the fact that forced marriage is an abuse of women's fundamental human rights, the approach is not about addressing forced marriage but about controlling the flow of male migration from areas of the world considered 'backward'. This is the one of the central planks of the state's policy on forced marriage. Yet there is no concrete evidence to show that this policy works. Indeed, research commissioned by the Home Office, which has deliberately not been published, shows that raising the age of marriage has no impact on the incidence of forced marriage (Hester *et al.* 2008). SBS's own experience shows that those who are determined to take children abroad for the purpose of marriage, are doing so undeterred. Parents circumvent the law by taking children abroad at a younger age, forcing them into a marriage and then abandoning them until they are 18 years of age. Their actions expose adolescent women, in particular, to greater risk of violence, rape and sexual abuse, making it harder for them to return to the UK and mount an effective legal challenge in the civil or criminal courts. Their problems are compounded by the fact that by the time they can seek redress, they are usually pregnant or have young children.

The government's lack of transparency is also apparent in other ways. A purported consultation exercise was undertaken but opinion on raising the age limit was evenly divided and other substantive issues not taken into account, including the fact that the proposals are disproportionate and will have a substantially negative and discriminatory impact on those from Asia and Africa. The UK Border Agency's (previously known as the Border and Immigration Agency) own figures for 2006, for example, show that

41,560 applications for settlement as a spouse, civil partner or unmarried partner were granted, presumably on the basis that they were genuine (Border and Immigration Agency 2007). This can be compared to the 300–400 cases of forced marriage reported to the Forced Marriage Unit every year (Home Office and UK Border Agency 2008), although from these figures it is not clear as to how many of cases have an immigration dimension. In other words, over 99 per cent of all relationships or marriages with overseas dimension are not forced.

The government has also failed to disclose the fact that its proposals to tackle forced marriage follow, more or less exactly, immigration measures instituted in Denmark and other Western European countries which have been condemned by human rights commentators.[8] Clearly, in seeking to emulate the Danish and other European immigration models, the UK sends a sinister message to minorities that their rights will be constantly under scrutiny and as such they can never feel secure in exercising their right to freedom of movement and enjoyment of private and family life. This is exactly the form of state intervention that was opposed by anti-racist organisations in the 1970s and 1980s.[9]

SBS has consistently stated that it does not wish to see serious issues such as violence against women, forced marriages and 'honour killings' reduced to a question of immigration control, since such an approach simply compounds the discrimination faced by black and minority people and does not address the question of the safety of women who are subject to violence. Rather than pursue yet more draconian immigration controls, we have pointed out that the most effective measures of protection from forced marriage involve a series of legal, welfare and educational initiatives including the need for more specialist resources (refuges and advice centres) for black and minority women.

Black and minority women need to be afforded safety and protection in the UK in the same way that women are protected in the wider community. Issues of violence against minority women should therefore be addressed within a domestic violence or violence against women policy framework, which takes account of the impact of immigration controls rather than through an immigration control framework which justifies further restrictive practices in the name of protecting black and minority women from domestic violence. Paradoxically, our view is that it is the relaxation of the immigration controls which will help to address problems of forced marriage, since marriage will not be seen as a route to gaining entry to the UK!

The discriminatory nature of the government's approach has not escaped many women, who feel that those who advocate further immigration controls to deal with forced marriage never show the same interest to abused women who are seeking asylum or have insecure immigration status. For example, the operation of the 'no recourse' rule,[10] plus the failure to recognise gender-related persecution, ensures that such women are denied state protection and support. SBS and others have campaigned long and hard, without much success, for the government to lift the no recourse requirement so that 600 (and possibly more) abused women with insecure status are afforded proper protection.[11] These women cannot obtain emergency accommodation or financial support due to the bar on access to public funds, including housing. As a result, many face extreme violence, imprisonment, starvation and death.

The desecularisation of black feminist spaces

Despite significant flaws, the Home Office Working Group on Forced Marriage represented something of a seismic shift in relation to the state's response to minority women. Unfortunately, the progression towards 'mature multiculturalism' was stunted by the state's response to the rise of violent (Muslim) extremism with profoundly discriminatory and anti-civil liberties measures. This has also shaped a new approach to minorities which rejects multiculturalism in favour of 'cohesion' and 'integration'.

Partly as a result of these shifts in state policies, black and minority women have also had to contend with the resurgence of religious fundamentalism in their communities. This resurgence has been gathering pace since the late 1980s, following the Rushdie Affair, but has considerably heightened following the London bombings in 2005.

Since the late 1980s, the mood in all the various minority communities has been one of growing intolerance for all those who seek to challenge cultural and religious values and religious abuse of power. We have witnessed, with alarming frequency, fundamentalist and authoritarian protests to any form of dissent from an imposed religious identity. It would seem that orthodox leaders in all religions are vying for control over the representation of their communities. In the process, what is made transparent is the reinvention of essentialist notions of religion as a framework for high-lighting inequalities and demanding recognition (Yuval-Davis 1992).

More specifically, since 9/11, partly in response to the rise of anti-Muslim racism, many Muslims, including Muslim women, are becoming increasingly vigilant in their efforts to protect religious identity resulting in a series of demands for greater recognition, often articulated in the name of discrimination and human rights. In reality, however, such demands mask the real agenda, which is to perpetuate the control of women's hearts, minds and bodies. Demands made by Muslims to extend the blasphemy law, funding for religious schools, dress codes and the right to apply customary (religious) laws instead of civil law in the governance of family affairs are just some examples. Other minority groups, predominately Hindus and Sikhs, have followed suit, demanding that their educational, welfare and family needs also be addressed in accordance with their religious values.

In August 2000, for instance, the Islamic Human Rights Association (Awaaz 2006)[12] protested against a government-backed European directive, which, according to them, would force Muslim charities and schools to employ non-believers and homosexuals. This was considered to be an attack on religious freedom and would have exposed 'faith'-based organisations to infiltration by hostile campaign groups. Like the Christian charities that have opposed discrimination law applying to their children adoption services, the association argued that the duty not to discriminate undermined the religious ethos of their organisations.

In 2005, we witnessed protests by Sikhs against the play *Behzti* (Dishonour) which dealt with issues of rape and abuse of power within a Gurdwara (Sikh temple). While the protests led to intimidation and threats of violence from Sikh extremists, even so-called 'moderate' Sikhs, for example the so-called Sikh Human Rights Commission, felt that the play's author, Gurpreet Bhatti, had 'crossed the line' and caused extreme offence by setting her play in what is regarded by Sikhs as a 'sacred' place. Both extremist and moderate Sikhs were notably more preoccupied with the question of blasphemy than with the reality of women who are raped and assaulted on a daily basis, sometimes by or with the collusion of the very custodians of community morality.

Not to be outdone, the Hindus have followed the example set by the Muslim fundamentalist leadership in using the language and techniques of human rights. In 2006, we saw successful attempts by Hindu fundamentalists to stop an exhibition of paintings by a renowned Indian painter, M.F Hussain, on the grounds that his depiction of naked female deities offended Hindu religious sensibilities, irrespective of the fact that over the centuries, Hinduism has been littered with such images. The campaign was led by the so-called 'moderate' Hindu Forum of Britain and a shadowy Hindu Human Rights group,[13] both of whom took it upon themselves to represent all Hindus. More recently, the Forum, with the support of the Runnymede Trust, has been busy constructing a 'Hindu' voice and community in the UK (Hindu Forum of Great Britain and Runnymede Trust 2006).[14] Yet, while professing to uphold the rule of law, justice and democracy, the Forum has remained silent about the violent tactics employed by Hindu fundamentalists in India, who have threatened the painter and his property.[15] Indeed, despite his links with the Hindu extremist groups, the General Secretary of the Hindu Forum, Ramesh Kallidai, was appointed as a commissioner for the Commission on Integration and Cohesion. Elsewhere, so-called moderate Hindus have campaigned against the depiction of Hindu deities in consumer products and, more importantly, against the depiction of domestic violence and forced marriage, the existence of which is often vigorously denied by many Hindu 'leaders'.[16]

The growing climate of intolerance is not confined solely to minority communities. It is also reflected in the wider society, as shown by the protests against the *Jerry Springer Opera* broadcast by the BBC in December 2004, and in the campaigns to prevent discrimination law applying to gay adoptions or to teach creationism in science lessons in schools. The difference however, is that unlike minority communities, there is greater space and protection for those wishing to dissent in the wider society.

In minority communities, religious institutions are mainly dominated by a conservative and even misogynist and homophobic religious agenda, and although there are liberal strands, their voices are often marginal. For example, the Muslim Parliament of Great Britain published a report on the prevalence of child abuse within madrassas or religious schools (Muslim Parliament of Great Britain 2006), but it was overlooked by the state and all the key Muslim organisations; there remains a resounding silence as to its content and implications within all the Asian communities. Community leaders often fend off criticism by claiming that their religion does not condone abuses against women or children. However, the problem with such assertions is that issues such as forced marriages or honour crimes are simply seen as symptoms of malfunctioning cultures, and therefore nothing to do with religion per se. But such assertions are often disingenuous since they allow religious spokespersons to condemn the custom and practice of everyday life within minority communities, without having to admit that there are no neat distinctions between culture and religion. Nor do they take the responsibility to tackle abusive practices or, if they do, it is with the aim of keeping the family intact. Further, such denial and avoidance allows fundamentalists to argue even more forcefully that communities should return to the 'purity' of original religious teachings (Sahgal 2006).

The Behzti play is but one example of attempts to silence women's voices of dissent. We are aware of countless cases around the UK where South Asian and minority religious institutions have either been involved in or condoned domestic and sexual violence and child abuse. There have even been cases where religious leaders have sought to 'exorcise' women or children by beating them, sometimes to death, for nonconformist behaviour perceived as 'possession by evil spirits'.[17] While these cases represent the more dramatic end of the spectrum, women find their aspirations quashed by religious leaders on a day-to-day basis. They often find themselves trapped at home because of the stranglehold of culture, religion and enforced mediation by religious leaders. As minority women in the UK have no effective political representation and no power to challenge the hegemony of the religious establishment, they, along with other subgroups, have the most to lose (Brittain et al. 2005). Women have only their voices of dissent as a tool by which to demand more freedom. The suppression of dissent is, therefore, literally a matter of life and death for many. This is precisely why SBS opposed the creation of the new offence of Incitement to Religious Hatred in 2005. We perceived it as an attempt to introduce the outdated blasphemy laws through the back door,[18] and argued that the main targets would not be those engaged in fomenting hatred towards other religions but those who wished to dissent from within religion, in other words those representing a challenge to orthodox traditions as well as women, gays and lesbians. Our fears were confirmed by a spokesperson from the Sikh Human Rights Commission who, in response to the Behzti affair, stated on television that if the law had existed at the time, the group would have used it to prevent the play from being performed.

The emergence of 'faith communities'

For secular feminists within minority communities, the challenge of religious fundamentalism is only a part of the battle. A more difficult and invidious battle lies with mainstream religious leadership itself – the 'moderates' – who, with the demise of progressive secular institutions within minority communities,[19] are seen to be fulfilling a crucial role in mediating between state and community. This is of course a process that has always occurred under multiculturalism but what is different this time, is the acknowledgement by the state that religion is a vital part of public life which cannot be ignored.

Since the London bombings and civil unrest fuelled by racial tensions, black and ethnic minority communities, redrawn as 'faith communities', have been specifically identified by the state as important sources of social capital. That is the increasing recognition that the social networks, experiences and resources of the faith groups have been neglected for too long. They are deemed to be invaluable to urban regeneration and therefore full opportunity is given to faith groups to build capacity and to participate fully in civil society (Joseph Rowntree Foundation 2006).[20] Interestingly, however, it is only Muslim groups that are deemed to be relevant to stamping out extremism and achieving social cohesion.[21] But in the process, the work of secular groups, especially Asian women's projects that have worked across religious and ethnic divides, is not only being ignored but also increasingly left out of funding and policy initiatives. Another aspect of this development is that it also fits neatly into a wider neo-conservative agenda in which the privatisation of what were once considered to be vital state functions, such as schooling and welfare provision, is deemed essential.

Faith groups have therefore been placed at the heart of the regeneration of communities and as a direct result, religion is becoming increasingly entrenched within state institutions at central and local levels, and is reflected at all levels of state policy. Further, those faith groups or leaders that shout the loudest – overwhelmingly authoritarian, if not fundamentalists – are taken to be the representatives of their communities. This multi-faith approach has provided the space for the politics of identity based on religion to flourish.

The result is that the various religious leaderships within minority communities have gained in confidence and power. It has also brought into their domain areas which hitherto have been addressed by progressive secular anti-racist and feminist groups, including issues such as domestic violence, child protection, and the rights of black and minority offenders in the criminal justice system. Notions and models of citizenship based on respect for individual human rights are being replaced by notions of social cohesion and integration involving adherence to 'core British values'. However, adherence to core values does not result in the loss of religious identity. In fact the faith-based approach encourages adherence to religious autonomy as well as to a core set of values which are mostly about the maintenance of public order. The overarching aim of the state is to isolate religious extremists, and to provide the space for so-called religious 'moderates' to assert their version of religious identities. For example, the Islamic Human Rights Commission has made it clear that it sees no reason why Muslims cannot be guided by their personal religious laws since it does not impact on social cohesion. The 'faith-based' approach, therefore, substitutes the demand for equality with the demand for greater recognition of diversity and the need for 'religious literacy'. That is, the need to understand the theological values and traditions as espoused by religious leaders, but not recognition of the various liberal religious or cultural traditions within a community.

The creation in 2007 of the Muslim Arbitration Tribunal (MAT) for alternative dispute resolution in cases of domestic violence, forced marriage and marriage generally, is an example of how religious frameworks are being developed by so-called 'moderates' to contain the rights of minority women (Muslim Arbitration Panel 2008; Taher 2008). The MAT will enable arbitration (mediation by another name) of family disputes to take place in accordance with Islamic law. It will also allow for determinations to be enforced under the Arbitration Act 1996 in cases where both parties have agreed to be bound by the outcome. This development will allow unelected and unaccountable community elders to preside as judges and make determinations based on religious interpretations that have historically discriminated against women and legitimised their oppression within the family. The MAT is however presented as a viable way of accommodating religious personal laws within the secular civil legal system and is tempting to a state that is looking for ways of cutting legal aid and time-consuming litigation. In our view, however, such attempts to introduce shariah law either within the existing legal framework or as a parallel system is an extremely alarming development since it adds to the immense community pressures that minority women already face to agree to mediation and governance based on their religious identity. The MAT scheme effectively takes away the safety net of the secular legal system that is underpinned by human rights values to which minority women have contributed and fought for. What makes these initiatives doubly dangerous is that they are being supported by highly influential liberal establishment figures including the Archbishop of Canterbury and Lord Justice Phillips. In the rush to be tolerant or sensitive to religious difference, they create the space for the most reactionary and even fundamentalist religious leaders to take control of minority communities.

Funding and cohesion

The current drive towards 'cohesion' is also regressive because it provides the breeding ground for racists to confidently call for more 'rights for whites'. This is based on the view that the majority community has been neglected because of multiculturalism and 'political correctness'. At the heart of the cohesion agenda therefore lies the promotion of a notion of integration based on the assumption that organising around race and ethnicity encourages segregation. Yet as already noted, at the same time, the cohesion approach also encourages segregation on the basis of religious identity.

In 2008 SBS was forced to confront these contradictions in state policies towards minority communities head on when faced with funding cuts by Ealing Council. If unchallenged, the decision to withdraw our funding would have resulted in the demise of organisations like ours that have been set up not only to counter racism but also to provide minority women with real alternatives to community (religious and cultural based) mechanisms for dealing with disputes within the family. This in turn would set back the advances we have made to compel the state to recognise that the human rights of minority women are non-negotiable and that they cannot be subject to differential standards when seeking protection from gender based violence.

On 18 July 2008, at the High Court, Southall Black Sisters won an important legal challenge affirming its right to exist and continue its work. At stake was a decision by the London Borough of Ealing in West London to withdraw funding from SBS – the only specialist provider of domestic violence services to black and minority women in Ealing – under the guise of developing a single generic service for all women in the borough. The council sought to justify its decision on the grounds of 'equality', 'cohesion' and 'diversity'. It argued that the very existence of groups like SBS – the name and constitution – was unlawful under the Race Relations Act 1976 because it excluded white women and was therefore discriminatory and divisive! Yet at the same time, Ealing Council has also sought to encourage the creation of a wide variety of Muslim conferences and organisations to discuss scholarly interpretations of Islam; Muslim mentoring schemes; Muslim volunteer schemes for hospitals, schools and the police, and to set up Muslim women's groups as part of its 'cohesion' strategy (London Borough of Ealing 2007).

We argued that Ealing Council's policy in effect meant that the race equality legislation could not protect those who are historically disenfranchised and discriminated since it rejected the notion of positive action. The Equalities and Human Rights Commission (EHRC) which intervened in the legal case also criticised Ealing Council's interpretation and implementation of the race equality legislation.

Judge Moses, who presided over the case, agreed that Ealing Council had deliberately misconstrued and failed to have proper regard to its duties under the Race Relations Act and had taken a flawed approach to cohesion in reaching its decision:

> There is no dichotomy between the promotion of equality and cohesion and the provision of specialist services to an ethnic minority. Barriers cannot be broken down unless the victims themselves recognise that the source of help is coming from the same community and background as they do. Ealing's mistake was to believe that cohesion and equality precluded the provision of services from such a source. It seemed to believe that such services could only lawfully be provided by a single provider or consortium to victims of domestic violence throughout the borough. It appreciates that it was in error and that in certain circumstances the purposes of Section 71 and the relevant statutory code may only be met by specialist services from a specialist source. That is the importance of the name of the Southall Black Sisters. Its very name evokes home and family.[22]

Ealing Council was therefore forced to concede that it would have to reconsider its position afresh. The SBS case has created a legal precedent about the local authority approach to the funding of specialist organisations. The SBS challenge to Ealing Council represents a key moment for black and minority groups that have organised politically to counter racism and gender, caste, religion and ethnic divisions between and within communities in the UK. While successful in forcing the council to withdraw its decision and to rethink its policy on domestic violence services in Ealing, our experience has also sounded a warning bell to secular progressive groups in particular.

Ealing Council's cynical use of the government's confused 'cohesion' agenda to cut our funding has profound implications for the human rights of black and minority women in particular. Specialist secular services likes ours are needed not only for reasons to do with language difficulties and cultural and religious pressures on women but also because of our considerable experience in providing advice and advocacy in complex circumstances: where racism and religious fundamentalism is on the rise in the UK and worldwide; where legal aid is no longer easily available; where privatisation of what were once important state welfare functions is accelerating; and where draconian immigration and asylum measures are piling up. These developments cut off the route by which many minority women gain the knowledge and confidence they need to assert their rights and undermines their attempts to organise collectively across internal divisions. Secular spaces are literally being squeezed out of minority communities. This is precisely why SBS opposed the recent attempts by the state to extend the requirement to give due regard to the need to promote equality of opportunity to religion or belief.

For SBS, the case represents a particularly significant moment in our battle against racism, and the 'cohesion' and 'faith' agenda. The decision of the High Court has safeguarded a more progressive vision of equality. A vision which can be used not only to counter those who regard 'cohesion' as being contrary to notions of racial or gender equality but also to counter religious leaders who seek to impose their version of religious identity in order to trump the rights of women and other minorities. As Lord Justice Moses, quoting the chairman of the Equalities Review, said:

> An equal society protects and promotes equality real freedom and substantive opportunity to live in the ways people value and would choose so that everyone can flourish. An equal society recognises people's different needs, situations and goals and removes the barriers that limit what people can do and can be.[23]

Conclusion

The struggle against violence against Asian and indeed other minority women has now reached a crossroads where the issues of race, religion and gender intersect. The gains of 'mature multiculturalism' are overshadowed by 'multi-faithism' and an assimilationist social cohesion post-9/11 and post 7/7 agenda,[24] giving rise to a new confidence to fundamentalists and racists alike to limit the freedom of women and minority communities.

It is these political developments that have compelled groups like SBS to defend ever more vigorously the secular black anti-racist and feminist spaces that we have created. This is now our most important struggle in addressing gender-based violence, in the face of attempts by the state and religious leaders to corral us into specific reactionary religious identities in the name of 'cohesion', on the assumption that we live in a post-racist, post-feminist and classless society. This is the significance of our successful challenge to Ealing Council: it highlighted the urgent need to develop a politics of solidarity within and between communities which recognises that what is at stake is no less than the fight for secular, progressive, feminist and anti-racist values. Political self-determination may be supported by the courts from time to time, but the larger struggle can be won only through a more united campaign for justice and human rights.

Notes

1. Southall Black Sisters was founded in 1979 to address the needs of Asian and African Caribbean women. It provides advice and advocacy services, and campaigns and conducts policy work on gender-based violence in minority communities, particularly South Asian. Although locally based, the work of SBS has a national reach due to its work on domestic violence, suicide and harmful cultural practices such as forced marriage and 'honour' crimes, and related issues of racism, poverty, homelessness and immigration matters. Over the years, SBS has led the way in reforming the criminal justice system in relation to abused women who kill, as illustrated by the high profile case of Kiranjit Ahluwalia. It has also been at the forefront of reforming immigration and the 'no recourse to public funds' law for women who experience domestic violence and have insecure immigration status.

2. The Home Office Working Group on Forced Marriage was set up to address the problem of forced marriage following a series of high profile cases. Forced marriage is practised in all the various Asian and minority communities but was not addressed by the main frontline agencies, including the police, schools and social services, all of whom are legally responsible for the protection of vulnerable adults or children.

3. We emphasise the protective aspect of the state because historically the state has always intervened in black and minority families in a negative way through

oppressive immigration and policing measures. These have had the effect of dividing and criminalising families, causing considerable hardship and suffering. The oppressive nature of state intervention has been well documented in writings on racism in the UK. However, precisely because of this experience, until the 1990s, the state and various community groups, including progressive anti-racist campaigns, denied the need for the state to intervene even where women and children experienced domestic violence. They argued that such intervention was tantamount to racism. SBS and some other black feminist organisations challenged this view on the grounds that the state was accountable to women's needs and that struggles against domestic violence and racism had to be waged simultaneously. See, for instance, Southall Black Sisters (1989) for an account of the tensions that existed and the debates that ensued.

4. For example, following a campaign led by SBS, the Home Office introduced the immigration and domestic violence concession in 1999, which was incorporated into the immigration rules in 2002 and is known as the Domestic Violence Rule. It enables overseas spouses to stay in the UK indefinitely if their marriage or relationship to a British national or settled person breaks down due to domestic violence within a two-year probationary period. In such cases, the overseas spouse must meet the evidential criteria as set out in the immigration rules to demonstrate that she is a victim of domestic violence. The no recourse to public funds requirement is a condition attached to entry to the UK for persons with limited leave, such as those who arrive under a spousal visa. It means that they cannot claim most social security benefits or seek social housing. The effect of this is that abused women with insecure immigration status are trapped in violent marriages. SBS has led a long campaign to exempt victims of domestic violence, and more recently, trafficked women and overseas migrant workers, from the no recourse to public funds requirement so that they can escape abusive situations without fear of destitution.

5. See, for example, the case of Julia Pemberton who, along with her son, William Pemberton, was killed by her husband in 2003. Prior to the killings, Julia had made complaints to the police about her husband's violence and his threats to kill her. The police ignored her reports and pleas for protection. See www.guardian.co.uk/society/2006/jul/24/crime.penal (accessed on 28 April 2009). Another case is that of Hayley Jane Richards, who was murdered by her boyfriend, Hugo Quintas, from whom she had recently separated, on 11 June 2005, in her home in Wiltshire. Prior to her death, she had reported an assault and threats to kill her to the police, but they had failed to act to protect her. See http://news.bbc.co.uk/1/hi/england/wiltshire/4085018.stm (accessed on 28 April 2009).

6. Over the years, SBS has dealt with cases of African Caribbean women who have called the police in the face of domestic violence, but who have then been arrested and charged with serious offences such as grievous bodily harm.

7. See the section on 'The emergence of faith communities' in this chapter for details on how shariah laws are being accommodated within the legal system.

8. Commentators on the Danish situation for example have noted that the so-called forced marriage measures were introduced in the context of profound political developments within the Danish government and society which lurched to the right and legitimised the adoption of an extreme right-wing anti-immigration agenda aimed at targeting Muslim immigrants in particular and preventing family reunification within minority communities.

9. See Note 3 above.

10. See Note 4 on the Domestic Rule and the operation of the no recourse to public funds requirement.

11. In 1992, SBS raised the issue of 'no recourse' at the Home Affairs Select Committee's inquiry into domestic violence. As a result, in 1999, the government reformed the immigration law for victims of domestic violence but failed to address the problem of 'no recourse'. In 2004, SBS introduced an amendment to the Domestic Violence, Crime and Victims Bill, which received cross-party support. We sought an exemption for victims of domestic violence from the no recourse to public funds requirement. Although sympathetic, the government refused to adopt the amendment on the grounds that it would undermine the 'integrity of the immigration and benefit rules'. Under pressure, however, the government introduced temporary measures such as providing a one-off grant to Women's Aid to operate a 'Last Resort' scheme. However, as we predicted, the funds were soon depleted and not replaced. Following this, the Home Office issued a letter to all local authorities reminding them of their duty under the Children Act 1989 and various community care legislation to assist vulnerable people, which could include victims of domestic violence. In response to mounting criticism, in March 2008, the Home Office announced that it will introduce limited backdated payments to women subject to 'no recourse' if successful in their applications under the Domestic Violence Rule. While this proposal is welcome, it is still inadequate since it does not enable women to have emergency access to public housing and subsistence pending their application to remain in the UK. Women will continue to face destitution and as a result, many will still be prevented from leaving or will return to abusive marriages.

12. According to Awaaz, the Islamic Human Rights Commission (IHRC) in the UK is a radical Islamist organisation that uses the language of human rights to promote an extremist agenda including the adoption of shariah law.

13. There is very little detail available on this organisation or how it came to represent the views of all Hindus in the UK. Yet it was quoted in the press during the Hussain affair (see Hindu Forum of Britain and Department of Communities and Local Government 2006).

14. The joint report by the Hindu Forum of Great Britain and the Runnymede Trust (2006) purports to identify the nature of the British 'Hindu' community, yet there was no democratic consultation process involving Indians of Hindu origin to ascertain their concerns or indeed how they identified themselves.

15. The Hindu Forum and its leaders have been the subject of an investigation by the group Awaaz and also by Andrew Gilligan of the *Evening Standard*, who exposed the links between Ramesh Kallidai, the general secretary of the Hindu Forum of Britain, and Hindu fundamentalists and violent extremists in India who are responsible for the murder of thousands of Muslims. The links between the Hindu Forum and Hindu fundamentalism caused some concern among officials within the Commission on Integration and Cohesion, but these concerns do not appear to have been acted upon (see 'Revealed: the rise and rise of the fundamentalist father' by Andrew Gilligan, *Evening Standard*, 11 June 2007).

16. For instance, in 1994, a group of Hindu fundamentalists attempted to ban the film *Bhaji on the Beach*, a film depicting the lives of Asian women who survive domestic violence. A group of men surrounded a cinema in Nottingham to intimidate and prevent people from attending.

17. In 1992, a father and two Muslim clerics were involved in torturing a 20-year-old Asian woman, Kousar Bashir, to death during a ritual exorcism. At trial, Kousar's father claimed that he was acting on the instructions of the clerics but was found guilty of her murder. The clerics were found guilty of causing grievous bodily harm. See also the case of Victoria Climbié, who in 2000 was killed by her great-aunt and her great-aunt's boyfriend, who thought that she was 'possessed'. It was also significant for the multicultural assumptions that were made which led social workers, the police and health professionals to ignore the abuse she was subjected to.

18. Southall Black Sisters has repeatedly called for the blasphemy laws to be repealed on the grounds that they are outdated and privilege Christianity over other religions.

19. This history of black and minority communities in the UK is littered with examples of secular, anti-racist and feminist organisations that often led struggles against imperialism and racism (as manifested on the streets and in immigration and nationality laws, policing, schools and the workplace) and class and gender inequality. Many were inspired by nationalist, anti-imperialist and even socialist struggles waged in countries of origin and around the world including the civil rights and black liberation movements in the US.

20. This is a summary of a major study conducted by sociologists for the Joseph Rowntree Foundation, which examines the contribution that can be made by 'faith communities' increasingly viewed as 'social capital'. It is an example of the high level of academic activity that is now devoted to constructing notions of 'faith communities' and to look to ways to improve the participation of faith based groups in civil regeneration.

21. In July 2007, the government announced that it was making available £70 million to Muslim groups or activities aimed at fighting Muslim extremism under the Preventing Violent Extremism Fund.

22. Kaur and Shah (on the application of) vs. London Borough of Ealing [2008] EWHC 2062 (Admin).

23. Lord Justice Moses quoting from *Fairness and Freedom*, published in 2007. Kaur and Shah (on the application of) vs. London Borough of Ealing [2008] EWHC 2062 (Admin).

24. The London bombings by Muslim terrorists on 7 July 2005.

References

Ali, Y. (1992) 'Muslim Women and the Politics of Ethnicity and Culture in Northern England.' In N. Yuval-Davis and G. Sahgal (eds) *Refusing Holy Orders.* London: Virago Press.

Anthias, F. and Yuval-Davis, N. (1992) *Racialized Boundaries: Race, Nation, Gender, Colour and Class and the Anti-Racist Struggle.* London: Routledge.

Awaaz (2006) *The Islamic Right. Awaaz, South Asia Watch, June.* Available at www.awaaznews.com/0406/AWAAZ_April06_for_web.pdf, accessed on 28 April 2009.

Border and Immigration Agency (BIA) (2007) *Marriage Visas: Pre-Entry English Requirement for Spouses Consultation Paper.* London: BIA.

Brittain, E., Dustin, H., Pearce, C., Rake, K., Siyunyi-Siluwe, M. and Sullivan, F. (2005) *Black and Minority Ethnic Women in the UK*. Fawcett Society.

Equalities Review (2007) *Fairness and Freedom: The Final Report of the Equalities Review*. London: Crown Copyright. Available at http://archive.cabinetoffice.gov.uk/equalitiesreview/upload/assets/www.theequalitiesreview.org.uk/equality_review.pdf, accessed on 10 July 2009.

Forced Marriage Unit (2009) *Forced Marriage Statistics*. Available at www.fco.gov.uk/en/fco-in-action/nationals/forced-marriage-unit, accessed on 28 April 2009.

Hansard (1999) *Adjournment Debate on Human Rights (Women)*. In *Hansard*. London: House of Commons 325, 8 February to 16 February.

Hester, M., Chantler, K., Gangoli, G., Devgon, J., Sharma, S. and Singleton, A. (2008) *Forced Marriage: The Risk Factors and the Effects of Raising the Minimum Age for a Sponsor, and Leave to Enter the UK as a Sponsor or Fiancé(e)*. Available at www.bristol.ac.uk/ sps/downloads/FPCW/forcedmarriageresearchsummary08.pdf, accessed on 28 November 2008.

Hindu Forum of Britain and Department of Communities and Local Government. (2006) *Connecting British Hindus: An Enquiry into the Identity and Public Policy Engagement of British Hindus by the Runnymede Trust, Commissioned by the Hindu Forum of Britain*. London: Hindu Forum of Britain and Department of Communities and Local Government.

Hindu Forum of Great Britain and Runnymede Trust (2006) *Connecting British Hindus*. London, July.

Home Office (2000) *A Choice by Right: The Report of the Working Group on Forced Marriage*. London: Home Office Communications Directorate.

Home Office and UK Border Agency (2008) *Marriage Visas: The Way Forward*. London: UK Border Agency.

Joseph Rowntree Foundation (2006) *Faith as Social Capital*. Findings available at www.jrf.org.uk, accessed on 28 April 2009.

London Borough of Ealing (2007) *Ealing's Shared Future Integration and Community Cohesion Strategy 2007–2011*. London: London Borough of Ealing.

Muslim Arbitration Panel (2008) *Report: Liberation from Forced Marriages*. London: Muslim Arbitration Panel. Available at .matribunal.com, accessed on 28 April 2009.

Muslim Parliament of Great Britain (2006) *Child Protection in a Faith-Based Environment: A Guideline Report*. London: Muslim Parliament of Great Britain.

Sahgal, G. (1992) 'Secular Spaces: The Experience of Asian Women Organising.' In N. Yuval-Davis and G. Sahgal (eds) *Refusing Holy Orders*. London: Virago Press.

Sahgal, G. (2006) 'Legislating Utopia: Violence Against Women, Identities and Interventions.' In N. Yuval-Davis, K. Kannabiran and U. Vieten (eds) *The Situated Politics of Belonging*. London: Sage.

Southall Black Sisters (1989) *Against the Grain*. London: Southall Black Sisters.

Taher, A. (2008) *Revealed: UK's First Official Sharia Courts*. Times Online, 14 September. Available at www.timesonline.co.uk/tol/news/uk/crime/article4749183.ece, accessed on 18 November 2008.

Yuval-Davis, N. (1992) 'Fundamentalism, Multiculturalism and Women in Britain.' In J. Donald and A. Rattansi (eds) *Race, Culture and Difference*. London: Sage Publications.

Chapter 5

Moving toward a 'Multiculturalism without Culture'

Constructing a Victim-Friendly Human Rights Approach to Forced Marriage in the UK

Aisha K. Gill and Trishima Mitra-Kahn

Introduction

Since 1999 there has been an enormous surge in the level of public awareness in the UK of the issue of forced marriage (FM). Yet despite this rising
awareness, at least 400 cases of FM are reported to the Forced Marriage
Unit of the Foreign and Commonwealth Office every year (Forced
Marriage Unit 2008). The result has been an urgent national debate on the
problem, centred on the need to determine its precise nature as well as
attempts to provide viable and sustainable responses for addressing it. The
UK government has taken several bold steps towards tackling these issues,
promoting initiatives intended to protect the well-being of young people,
while still respecting the integrity of their families and communities.

While acknowledging the government's good intentions on this issue,
this chapter argues that its strategy for dealing with FM is deeply problematic and, moreover, that its desire to criminalise FM, or to counteract it with
civil penalties, is unlikely to have any real benefits as it is not victim
friendly. Instead, we argue that FM can be properly addressed only if government intervention facilitates the ability of minority women to fight for

gender equality as opposed to simply being given the 'right to exit' from their communities. At the heart of any such intervention, we argue, is the construction of a reworked theory of 'multiculturalism without culture' based on the work of Ann Phillips (2007) that centres equally on gender rights, is victim friendly, yet specific to the particular struggles of women within these communities. Such a 'multiculturalism without culture' advocated by Phillips (2007) would particularly avoid the racialised and assimilative overtones of the current community cohesion paradigm and instead be focused on reconciling gender equality with minority group identity – the two features of multiculturalism that have hitherto been framed by the state in opposition to one another, with disastrous consequences for efforts to reduce the problem of FM.

The chapter is organised as follows. First, we examine the history of FM as a policy concern. In doing so, we critically analyse the numerous government consultations which culminated in the introduction of the Forced Marriage Civil Protection Act 2007. Our aim is to show how each consultation document was clearly dissociated from a violence-against-women agenda, and was instead aligned with the issue of immigration, a vilification of multiculturalism, an unquestioning acceptance of the theory of community cohesion and the continual Othering of minority communities. Second, we reflect upon the discourse of multiculturalism and how gender relations are framed within it. Specifically we question whether a controversial aspect of multiculturalism – the 'right to exit' – can be useful for women within minority groups living in a multicultural society as a viable solution for fighting gender-based violence. On this point, we believe that the 'right to exit' is a fundamental aspect – and even the theoretical mainstay – of UK government policy, and one that we feel typifies the failings of a particular brand of multiculturalism which, in our view, is neither nuanced nor reflective of contemporary society. 'Right to exit' is a barrier for the achievement of a coherent recuperative strategy for FM; one which has its origins in an unsophisticated multicultural approach, and which leads away from the need to address FM from a violence against women or 'victim-friendly' perspective. Having established our case against this aspect of government policy that, we believe, provides the greatest obstacle to the creation of a new, forward-thinking, multicultural approach to FM.

We conclude the chapter by suggesting measures and policy recommendations for tackling the problem in a more unified, holistic way that addresses the complexity of the debate on FM by focusing the policy debate on the rights and conditions of women victims. We propose to do this by making two fundamental arguments. First, we contend that government intervention should be theoretically underpinned by values of 'multiculturalism without culture'. Secondly, more practically, we propose using a reworked human rights perspective for ameliorating FM. In adopting such a strategy, the UK government will necessarily avoid views of cultural essentialism, instead basing its strategy on the achievement of gender rights and gender equality as a necessary condition for women to wage more localised struggles (such as opposition to FM) against patriarchy in minority communities.

Settling the issue: forced marriage and the legislative response to forced marriage in the UK

Since 1978 violence against women (VAW) has become a matter of major public and academic interest. Investigative work has begun to reveal the extent to which various forms of violence, ranging from domestic violence to sexual violence and from culturally sanctioned forced marriages to female genital mutilation (FGM), are inflicted on women globally (Coy, Kelly and Foord 2009). Since 2003 in particular, the government has put in place a number of initiatives to combat domestic violence, culminating in the Domestic Violence, Crime and Victim's Bill in 2003. This Bill was targeted at protecting victims of domestic violence and their families living in the UK. However, the development and implementation of policies addressing specific harms against black and minority ethnic (BME) women has been slow in comparison to those responding to harms against women from all communities, such as violence by partners or former partners. As recently as the 1980s, women from minority religious and ethnic groups in Western European countries were not identified by policy makers as a demographic in need of particular protection. Consequently, the specificity of their needs was more likely to be ignored. Presently, the majority of countries in Europe have developed laws, plans of action and policies to tackle the abuses experienced by many women and girls in immigrant, refugee or minority communities.

The UK defines FM as a marriage into which people have been coerced against their will and under duress, thus setting it apart from other forms of marriages practised in ethnic minority communities (such as arranged marriages). With the establishment in 1999 of a Working Group on Forced

Marriage as well as the creation of a Community Liaison Unit in the Foreign and Commonwealth Office (FCO), charged with dealing with the so-called 'overseas dimension' of forced marriage, FM was firmly established as a policy concern in the UK. An initial criticism of this initiative was the fact that the Unit was based within the Foreign Office, as it was said that this placed undue emphasis on cases involving a foreign spouse. The danger, according to this line of thinking, was that cases of FM involving two UK citizens and/or residents were likely to be ignored. The unit was relaunched in 2003 as a joint Home Office/FCO unit, but remains nevertheless located in the Foreign Office rather than in the Home Office, where it could operate alongside the Home Office's work on domestic violence.

The next section will explore in more detail the issue of FM and official responses to it by the UK government.

The criminalisation debate, the Private Member's Bill and the merits of a civil remedy approach to forced marriage

In September 2005, the Joint Foreign and Commonwealth Office and Home Office (JFCO/HO) Forced Marriage Unit consulted on a proposal to create a specific criminal offence related to FM. They worked closely with women's organisations such as Newham Asian Women's Project (NAWP), Ashiana, Rights of Women, and Southall Black Sisters (SBS) as well as academics to assess the viability of this possible legislation (Gill 2006). A dominant argument against this proposal was that a criminal offence specifically targeting FM would not be an effective deterrent to this practice, nor would it provide adequate protection for its victims. Those against the measure contended that such legislation would, first, add little to the existing body of law on murder, kidnapping and offences against the person, secondly, that police intervention would be counter-productive for preventing such actions, and third, that it would be difficult to obtain sufficient evidence to satisfy the criminal burden of proof needed to prosecute this offence. Another concern regarding this potential criminal law was that it would ultimately deter victims of forced marriage from coming forward to seek help. In this respect any ensuing prosecution would be brought by the state against the suspect in the *public* interest, rather than being initiated by the victim in the *victim's* interest. The fear of many in the violence against women movement was that victims would hesitate to come forward out of fear that family members would be prosecuted as part of a state-run legal proceeding in which they themselves had very little input or control over. For this reason there was a general consensus that such legislation would be problematic. Detractors instead stressed the need to create early intervention and preventative mechanisms to combat forced marriages. As a result of this debate the UK government ultimately decided that it would not be helpful to introduce a criminalising statute, and in June 2006, the government decided against making forced marriage a crime.

However, despite widespread support for this decision, a number of participants and outside groups felt that this was a missed opportunity. They argued that criminalisation was the only way to stop this harmful practice or, at the very least, to 'send a clear message' to potential perpetrators of this crime (Klite 2007). In December 2006, Lord Lester of Herne Hill QC, in collaboration with the Southall Black Sisters, proposed a Private Member's Bill which set out civil remedies and once again called for a stand-alone law to address the problem of forced marriage. The Bill attracted a wide range of supporters, including those who favoured criminalisation, a coalition which he referred to as the 'enlightened British Asians and other minorities'.

Undeniably a civil law on FM such as this would promote a more 'victim-friendly' approach than a criminal law, since it would be the victim, or someone acting in the victim's interest, who would initiate legal action as opposed to the state. Nevertheless many women's organisations remained sceptical about the draft Bill. The reason for this scepticism was that in its original form, the Bill failed to integrate the discourse of FM into a wider discussion concerning issues of violence against women. In doing so it subtly reinforced popular media perceptions of forced marriage as a cultural rather than gender violence problem. These objections led to the January 2007 submission of an official critique of the draft Bill sponsored by Imkaan, NAWP and Equal Opportunities Commission highlighting the importance of establishing a civil response *within* the Family Law Act (FLA) 1996. They pointed out for example that the procedures for obtaining injunctive relief were similar to those currently existing in other domestic violence situations adjudicated under the FLA. Considering that in cases of domestic violence the courts, police and family lawyers were already familiar with the workings of the FLA it served to reason that, incorporating forced marriage within its remit would involve minimal disruption and costs – and, most importantly, ensure swifter redress for victims of this offence. This opposition to a stand-alone measure was presented at a subsequent reading of the Bill in the House of Lords.

Forced Marriage (Civil Protection) Act (Part 4 of the Family Law Act 1996)

On 26 July 2007 the Private Member's Bill received royal assent as the ·Forced Marriage (Civil Protection) Act. This sanction was given after the Act was first restructured to bring the major features of the Private Bill into law through a series of amendments and additions embedded within the Family Law Act Part 4A. The Forced Marriage (Civil Protection) Act expressly prohibits the practice, inducing or aiding of forced marriage defined according to the law as the (a) forcing or attempting to force another person to enter into a marriage or a purported marriage without that other person's free and full consent, or (b) practising a deception for the purpose of causing another person to enter into a marriage or a purported marriage without that other person's free and full consent. The Act provides civil remedies and protections for victims and potential victims, an issue previously unaddressed in existing legislation. In particular, the Act has replaced expensive and overly complex services available to victims of FM with a simplified process specifically tailored to the needs of these victims. In effect, it makes forced marriage (and related actions to procure it) an actionable and explicit civil wrong, with accompanying remedies (chiefly forced marriage protection orders) to protect those threatened with or subjected to these practices. In particular, the Act makes it easier to obtain applications prior to the event as well as clarifying the illegality for both immediate and extended family members to 'aid and abet' such action. It also forcefully condemns the use of deception for the purpose of causing a forced marriage. It provides for powers to arrest and, when appropriate, remand into custody those suspected of perpetrating this offence.

One area in which the measure is particularly significant is in its aforementioned targeting of the use of deception to cause another person to enter into a marriage (or purported marriage) without their free and full consent. Forced marriage is commonly achieved through deception, such as when a victim is removed from the UK to another country on the pretext of going on holiday, a scenario not previously covered by the law.

Additionally, the Act extends to those who aid and abet forced marriage, as well as those who induce others to undertake this Act. This section of the Act thus has a threefold purpose: first, to deter families and individuals from forcing young women into early marriages by increasing their fear of arrest and punishment, second, to reduce the number of women subjected to early marriage, particularly in South Asian communities, and third, to provide further moral regulation via the law through initiating new schemes creating specialist prosecutors trained to deal with forced marriage cases and 'honour'-based violence cases.

The civil remedies that would be available under the Act primarily focus on the protection of the victim and the prevention of forced marriage, rather than on the punishment of the perpetrator. The principal remedy in the Act for this purpose is the injunction – an order made by the Court prohibiting certain acts that may lead to a forced marriage. The importance of this measure, according to the Act's, is that it enables victims to attain swift and effective legal recourse to prevent their forced marriage from taking place. This may also mean that the victim later stands a greater chance of becoming reconciled with his or her family. The Act would not preclude the possibility for the criminal prosecution of a forced marriage offence. Indeed in certain instances the public interest may require it. This Act thus provides an important tool for tackling FM both on the civil and criminal level.

Preliminary data, published by the Ministry of Justice on the number of Forced Marriage Protection Orders (FMPOs), showed that by 14 May 2009 23 FMPOs had been issued across England and Wales since the introduction of the Act on 25 November 2008. Prior to the Act going live, the Ministry of Justice set up three consultations in 2008 designed to sequester opinions on the feasibility of third-party intervention, define the role of the third sector for this process, and assess the technical and legal aspects of the 'Rules of Court' in regards to FM. In the same year, the Home Office concluded two consultations: one on the issue of marriage to partners from overseas and one on the feasibility of introducing a pre-entry English language requirement for partners from overseas.

In the following sections we present a critique of the various consultation documents that have been produced as part of this strategy, particularly examining the gender and race politics that underpin each document.

Moving away from the victim: immigration and the problem of forced marriage

While criminalisation is no longer viewed as a legitimate option for dealing with FM, civil remedies recommended by the government such as visa regulation and entry denial have focused the public debate on this issue in terms of immigration as opposed to gender rights. The framing of FM as an immigration problem is perhaps not surprising given its context following the terrorist attacks of 11 September 2001, after which most Western European democracies came to believe that the movements of migrants throughout the 1990s actually 'concealed a potential for terror attacks, a threat of security' (Jordan, Strath and Triandafyllidou 2003, p.197). In light of this fact, the 2001 creation of a community cohesion review team to address the problem of racially motivated violence among white and Asian youths in Oldham, Burnley and Bradford, sent out a clear message that practices such as FM exist because multiculturalism has allowed Britain to 'sleepwalk towards segregation' (T. Phillips 2005). Lewis and Neal (2005) note that 'what has been particularly apparent has been a partial shift away from affirmations of British multiculture towards a (re)embracing of older notions of assimilationism within a newer, de-racialised, language of social cohesion' (Lewis and Neal 2005, p.437). This linking of the debate on FM with the politics of multiculturalism and the new 'community cohesion' paradigm has meant that the FM debate has become obscured and its status as a violence against women issue is in danger of becoming lost.

In this section, then, we look closely at how the issue of FM has become increasingly entwined with issues of immigration and border policing since the FM Act was announced in July 2007. By analysing data from the consultations held on key components of UK immigration policy – marriage visas and the English language requirement – we aim to show that the victim-centred approach of the FM Act is merely a rhetorical tool designed to efface what is, in reality, a measure designed to police borders and manage migration (Gupta 2008).

Whatever happened to multiculturalism: forced marriage and the politics of immigration

The community cohesion paradigm, which arose in particular from the events of 11 September 2001, the war in Iraq and the London bombings of 2005, has added an ethnic and religious dimension to how FM is constructed in policy discourse. The scrutiny of certain religions such as Hinduism, Sikhism and Islam under the rubric of community cohesion has led to an insinuation that these religions are incompatible with a liberal society, because of their continued ideological facilitation of honour crimes and FM. Viewed through the community cohesion lens, then, FM appears, not as a problem arising from patriarchal practices, but as an expression of 'bad' cultural attitudes originating in *Othered* places – predominantly the Indian subcontinent – and perpetrated by *Othered* men on British soil.

The characterising of this problem as something that stems from an *Othered* (or foreign Non-British) culture, has allowed the government to propose solutions centring on stricter immigration controls, following the lead of Denmark and Norway. The Danish Amendment to the Aliens Act 2002, which raised the age of the right to the reunification of migrant spouses to 25 years, caused a considerable furore among the third sector in Denmark, especially when the Danish prime minister called it 'firm and fair'.[1] At the time, many commentators felt that the new family reunification laws had little to do with ameliorating FM, and more to do with the tightening up of Danish immigration law. As a result of the amendment, according to one commentator, young women were

> now forced to migrate to other Scandinavian countries where it is not as difficult to obtain family reunification permits. Thus young women are still forced into marriages, but the difference is that now they have to leave their network and families and live in an entirely different country with a man that they have not chosen. (Nielsen, 2005, p.8)

It seems that the consultations on marriage visas and English language requirements currently underway in the UK bear a striking resemblance to Danish immigration policy, at least in theory. The Commission on Integration and Cohesion Report, published in June 2007, had already promoted the belief that a common language is necessary for achieving community integration and cohesion. Moreover, English fluency was heralded as fundamental to an individual's enjoyment of British society since, according to official documents, 'diversity can have a negative impact on cohesion' (Commission on Integration and Cohesion 2007, p.9). Equally, English 'would help spouses integrate more quickly into the community, and boost their confidence in participating in employment' (English for Spouses Consultation 2007, pp.1–2).

It was in this context that the government used the English language requirement consultation to sequester information on two questions: first, whether or not spouses should demonstrate a knowledge of English before they migrate to the UK; and second, whether spouses should be denied entry into the UK, or have their right to remain revoked, if they failed to show such language proficiency. While knowledge of English is certainly valuable for those living in the UK, and is especially valuable for the victims and survivors of FM as it allows easier access to service providers, the English language requirement proposed by the government is prejudiced and unfair to minority communities, and women in particular. Asking new spouses to demonstrate 'some level of proficiency' is an ambiguous demand at best (i.e. how would such proficiency be assessed?), and a violation of numerous human rights at worst (such as the enjoyment of the right to private or family life). Furthermore, even if the objectives (i.e. English language proficiency) and the measures held to promote those objectives were legitimate, there remains a crucial question – how can measures put in place to ensure compliance with the new rules be appropriately determined? For example, would the objective of attaining a level of English language proficiency *'justify limiting a fundamental right'*? (Immigration Law Practitioners' Association (ILPA) 2008, p.3, emphasis added). If spouses are not permitted to come to the UK because they have not passed an English language test, this could be considered a form of unjustifiable discrimination. Additionally, given that the Home Office already has the powers of removal under the Immigration and Asylum Act 1999 (ILPA 2008), it seems inappropriate that the consultation would concentrate so overwhelmingly on further limiting the indefinite leave to remain. This misplaced focus was especially problematic because it drew attention away from what should be its primary objective – how to best serve the victims of FM.

Two wrongs do not make a right: the inability of the 'community cohesion' paradigm to deal with FM

Since the London bombings of 2005, with a subsequent policy environment principally concerned with community cohesion, it is hardly surprising that immigration restrictions are being used to deal with FM. In this respect, the government has promoted the ideal of community cohesion for fighting the detrimental effects of past multiculturalism with its perceived naive emphasis on cultural respect and non-interference in minority practices which many scholars believe that have led to increased incidents of domestic violence such as FM (Beckett and Macey 2001).

In the previous section, we showed how based on the evidence provided by the consultation processes for formulating and implementing FM, present efforts to address this offence are primarily based on values of community cohesion. Here we would like to delve deeper into how this paradigm theoretically informs the UK government's intervention strategy. In our opinion, FM is officially understood as a problem for the UK in so far as the experiences of such 'victims' and the criminal (*Other*) men who facilitate such practices temporarily threaten the (moral) culture of the UK. FM is cast not as a problem of patriarchal practices but as the 'bad' cultural attitudes of certain forms of patriarchy – 'bad' cultural attitudes located in foreign places, predominantly the Indian subcontinent. Also of significance is the dominant assumption, as a result of this community cohesion paradigm, that FM is principally caused by inherent religious and cultural attitudes as opposed to other factors. However, a deeper examination of these issues, such as a more sustained investigation of the key religious texts of affected communities, reveals that the problem lies not only with the religious beliefs of Islam, Sikhism or Hinduism (for example), but by the socialisation of the women in such a way as to make them unaware that 'they have human rights'. Thus human rights laws designed to facilitate individual self-determination are lost on women victims of deviant cultures of patriarchy (Barzilai 2004; Innes 2003; Walby 1990).

Yet within current UK legislation on FM, this deviance is not located in the patriarchal relations of power per se, but in the fact that women are kept from an awareness of self-determination by culture. The casting of a deviant (culture) of patriarchy as the fundamental (and) unchanging problem leading to FM deploys (neo) colonial modern operations of power that naturalise the 'backward' state of the *Other* places (Treacher 2003;

Williams and Chrisman 1993). More recently in the debate of creating remedies for forced marriage in the UK, what has been evident is that relatives of 'future forced marriage victims' will be cast or characterised as 'knowing' and possibly 'willing' in the practice of FM, which suggests a deviant culture of patriarchy, one that extends beyond the 'wrong' decisions of any individual to characterise the culture as a whole.

We see such arguments stemming from the theoretical application of the community cohesion paradigm to the problem of FM. The basic premise in moving away from criminalisation to finding civil remedies to FM was that it would be more victim friendly. It is ironic then to note that all the consultative processes mentioned in this chapter and the new law itself is focused not on victims of FM per se, but on figuring out how marriage migration can be managed, how porous borders can be better secured, and how state machinery can be given greater powers of greater intervention. In such a policy environment it is hardly surprising that multiculturalism, a policy that celebrates diversity and rejects social cohesion is unwelcome. In fact, if we believe that multiculturalism facilitates the continuation of forms of domestic violence such as FM through calls for the respect for cultural differences, then it should not be alarming when community cohesion is framed as the panacea for the problems of 'parallel lives' brought about by the multicultural model of respect for difference.

However, such a theory of multiculturalism based solely on its emphasis of respect for difference is unfinished and ultimately counter-productive. Simultaneously, applying a community cohesion perspective while dealing with FM reeks of assimilative high-handedness and would further aid in the demonisation of minority communities as deviant cultures of patriarchy, one where individual violent acts could be seen as characteristic of the culture as a whole. In the next section therefore, we would like to reintroduce multiculturalism theoretically into the debate on how best to intervene in cases of FM. This reintroduction of multiculturalism, one 'without culture' it is hoped will focus policy attention back onto the victims of FM.

The easy target: has multiculturalism failed minority women?

In order to propose more adequate solutions for addressing FM, a more thorough investigation of the theoretical underpinning of such policies must first be formulated. To do so, it is imperative to assess the strengths and weaknesses of the theoretical paradigms informing past UK responses to FM. Specifically, given our already stated criticism of community cohesion values, we now turn to the problems of previously dominant principles of multiculturalism so that they may be improved and made applicable to the contemporary struggle for creating a 'victim-friendly' approach for dealing with FM.

Our intention is to analyse what we believe to be a very restrictive understanding of multiculturalism – one which has theoretically grounded the various consultations and the eventual Act itself. The community cohesion paradigm should not be the alternative theoretical leitmotif when dealing with practices such as FM, as we have argued before. Instead, we call for a reworked multicultural policy, grounded in feminist methodology and practice, that will allow the government to resolve the problems it faces in reconciling the claims of individual gender equality and minority group identities.

Our intention here is not to discuss all the various difficult questions raised by the reality of cultural diversity within liberal democracies, nor the ways in which these questions have been addressed in the vast literature about 'multiculturalism'. Neither are we interested in providing an overview of multiculturalism in Manichean terms of good or bad. Rather, we intend to focus on the specific problem of gender-related injustices within a group, injustices which may result from multicultural accommodation. More specifically, we intend to examine aspects of the 'multiculturalism' debate that are relevant to our discussion of women's challenges to those cultural and religious norms that discriminate against them. We want to show that it is the non-articulation of a clear social policy on multiculturalism, coupled with the wrongful application of multiculturalism through an ill-conceived idea of 'right to exit', that is at fault in the UK government's failure to deal with FM.

The 'right to exit', as we use it in this chapter, refers to the capacity of community members to choose to leave their communities, and so cease to be subject to their norms and practices; a choice that they can exercise if they do not agree with the majority beliefs and practices within these communities. The 'right to exit' has repeatedly been invoked by theorists in the context of discussions of gender-based issues, principally in order to advocate the importance of female community members being able to leave their communities and seek egalitarian alternatives outside of them.

Further, we argue that in vilifying multiculturalism as detrimental for women, the government has failed to differentiate between different types of multiculturalism: the multiculturalism that has a negative effect on gender equality (in terms of the cultural practices of ethnically framed groups) and the multiculturalism that, as a policy, imperfectly administers services to women through interventions that are theoretically framed keeping 'the right to exit' in mind. Thus it is our contention that if the failed policies of multiculturalism catalysed the community cohesion paradigm, then the deficiencies of community cohesion may hopefully give rise to a refashioned and improved multiculturalism.

Gender justice and multiculturalism

Multiculturalism is often blamed for legitimising situations of gender-based discrimination by representing certain practices, such as honour crimes and FM, in culturally essentialist terms. An example of this can be seen in Johann Hari's (2007) analysis of several legal cases involving crimes against women in Germany. Hari (2007) observes that in these cases, the German judges handed down reduced sentences to males convicted of these crimes – including perpetrators of 'honour' killings – on the grounds that both they and their women victims belonged to ethnic groups which, the judges believed, would consider domestic violence to be culturally expected, and therefore an acceptable part of family life. Hari (2007) cites the German magazine *Der Spiegel* on this issue, which argues that the German courts have been responsible for a 'chain of horrific rulings'.

Hari (2007) unfortunately attributes this to the role of multiculturalism in German law, a decision that fails to recognise the root causes of the problem: first, the racialised assumptions about Muslim culture made by non-Muslim German judges who had no expert background in shariah law, and second, the failure to uphold the rights of women, as equal individuals, to claim non-discriminatory justice under the German human rights code. The judges cited the belief that the accused males had a culturally defined expectation of a certain level of domestic discipline, and this was used as the rationale for imposing lower sentences. The judges made no mention of the fact that the act of migrating to Germany must involve a fully conscious expectation of being held accountable under German law. Thus, these rulings reinforced the men's 'right' to wield domestic authority, rather than in favour of the women's rights to expect nationally standardised justice. In effect, the judges made assumptions about the cultural space these families had immigrated from, and then proceeded to hand out sentences as though these men had never actually entered Germany, but had continued to be governed by the laws and customs of their prior home. Furthermore, these rulings reinscribed German borders, demonstrating that they extended only around the bodies of 'German' women and not around those who were seen as the cultural 'Other', i.e. the women whose status as outsiders within the national psyche was thus firmly reinforced.

But what about the UK, where a multicultural policy does exist, and where individuals may legitimately expect to have some degree of cultural retention, not only in daily life, but in legal matters as well? Does this mean the UK has left itself open to legitimising the same racialised, gendered inequalities in the justice system that were manifested in Germany in the guise of so-called multicultural sensitivity? Many of the discussions on multiculturalism in the UK have focused on the following question: when, and under what circumstances, must the state 'intervene' in the norms of minority groups (see Parekh 2000; Phillips and Dustin 2004)? More relevant to the case of FM in the UK are policy questions as to where and when the government may intervene based on these multicultural values. Most advocates of 'multiculturalist accommodation' agree that there are some cases where the state must intervene in group norms, and other cases where it should not intervene.

Shachar (2001) questions and criticises this line of thought, which assumes that one must choose between the two options: state 'intervention' in group norms through the enforcement of the principle of gender equality, and state 'non-intervention', which means letting the group maintain its cultural traditions even when the price is the continuation of sex discrimination within these groups. Shachar (2001) disagrees with Kymlicka's (1995) opinion that the state has no authority to intervene in the internal affairs of national minorities (Kymlicka 1995), even if such communities violate some of their members' individual rights. Shachar (2001) stresses that the state is not just an 'outside' third party that is clearly and neatly detached from the 'inside' group realm. Therefore, she argues that 'non-intervention' is a misleading term, as 'it re-enforces the myth that left to their own devices identity groups could exist as autonomous entities bearing little relation to the state' (Shachar 2001, pp.37–40). Shachar's (2001) critique, when applied practically to the problem of FM, is interesting because it shows how a particular brand of multiculturalism has been used to hitherto oversimplify FM to a simple ascription of an *Othered* culture. This ultimately trivialises FM and denies victims the potential to be thought of as resisting agents capable of drawing on the resources of a democratic society to better their lives, or as agents having recourse to a court system that will punish the perpetrators of violence (Sen 2008). Moreover, Shachar's (2001) critique is also very helpful, as it shifts the discussion from a focus on whether or not states *should* intervene in group norms to the question of *how* they should intervene.

Yet the question still remains: how should the government solve the specific problem of gender-related injustices within minority communities since traditionally Multiculturalism in the UK has been predicated on a respect for cultural difference?

In the next section we will problematise the 'right to exit' as a solution to deal with cases of FM. The stories for instance of Jack and Zena Briggs,[2] and the young Sikh girl ('KR'),[3] who was made a ward of court, demonstrate the government's making available of this right as an option for both victims and potential victims of FM (Philips and Dustin 2004). It is our opinion that the 'right to exit' acts as a roadblock to the reformulation of an effective policy on multiculturalism because as a form of multicultural justice it asks women to make an imperfect choice: either to live in the mainstream culture, and so have access to equality through the national system, or to retain a sense of cultural belonging by electing to remain an outsider to the nation, and so be unable to enjoy equal protection under the law. Before we can provide any concrete solutions to the problems facing the government's strategy for tackling FM, then, we must examine this final component of their policy in more detail.

The right to exit: derailing multiculturalism in the campaign against forced marriage

Through a closer look at the FM Act and the myriad consultations that have gone into its formulation, one can clearly see that the 'right to exit' underpins the government's response towards ameliorating the problem of FM. By giving courts the right to make forced marriage protection orders, it seems as though the theoretical structure underpinning efforts towards eradicating FM involves telling women that they have the ability to leave their communities. This solution to FM based on the 'right to exit' is, in our view, predicated on the continued construction of minority communities as the 'other'. As such the predominance of this solution within the FM Act reflects the government's view of minority citizens as 'other' and therefore not deserving of the right to protection within their community.

Kukathas (1992) has suggested that the right of groups to live according to their own cultural practices should depend, not on the culture's particular right to be preserved, but on individuals' freedom to associate with others, 'to form communities and to live by the terms of those associations' (Kukathas 1992, p.116). A corollary to this is that the individual should also be free to *dissociate* from such communities:

> If there are any fundamental rights, then there is at least one right which is of crucial importance: the right of the individual to leave a community or association by the terms of which he or she no longer wishes to live. (Kukathas 1992, p.116)

The problem with Kukathas's (1992) argument is that the most important condition enabling a substantive freedom to exit from a community is the existence of a wider society that is accessible and helps facilitate these wishes. The 'right to exit' can be credible only if the wider society functions with a considerable degree of individual independence (Kymlicka 1995). Furthermore, the right to exit is problematic because individuals disempowered within minority communities, such as women, in practice often are not aware or able to make this choice due to material factors such as economic dependence and a lack of resources preventing them from learning about alternative life options and criticising the norms of their communities. Kymlicka (1995), for example, argues that when people have been deprived of literacy, education or the freedom to learn about the outside world, they do not have the substantial freedom as promoted by Kukathas (Kymlicka, 1995).

Though we do not dispute the validity of both Kukathas's (1992) and Kymlicka's (1995) arguments our critique of the 'right to exit' comes from a different direction. 'Solutions' to the problem of cultural and religious norms that discriminate against women, and which are based on the notion that women must be 'free' to exit their particular communities, are meaningless in those cases where women critique the gender norms in their communities, but who nonetheless show no desire for leaving their community. A large number of minority women in the UK, based on our personal experience, desire to remain in their communities and transform them from within. In this respect, far from trying to 'break away', these women are struggling to become full members of their communities. For them the option of 'exit' is of less importance than the fight for gender equality. Therefore, telling women who are subject to particular harmful practices in their communities that they have the option to leave those communities not only would be inadequate, but also would actually be contrary to many of those women's demands to effect change from within. Forcing women to choose between individual rights or cultural belonging (promoted under the auspices of integrating law and multiculturalism or – to use the latest phrase – 'community cohesion') is to compel them to accept what is, at best, partial membership in the nation.

Irrespective of whether or not it is actually a viable alternative for most women, the right to exit is actually not something that most women from minority communities want. Data obtained by frontline, grassroots organisations suggest that these women have little or no desire to leave their communities, nor any desire to criminally prosecute their families (Derby City Council 2005). Similarly, they hold the belief that 'separation and divorce is not a victory, as in most cases women are ostracised from the community. It would deprive clients from support from family members' (Anchor Counselling Practice 2005, p.2). Furthermore, 'familial bonds and loyalties will deter many from using the law, and the law may create division and distress in the family unit if used' (Muslim Council of Britain 2005). This 'would make any future reconciliation, if desired, impossible' (Kent Police 2005, p.1).

In our opinion, the form of multiculturalism that promotes a policy solution for dealing with FM based on the 'right to exit' must be considered a failure because it ignores broader gender struggles and women's daily realities within these communities, thus creating a non-victim-friendly approach. This 'right to exit' is an incomplete concept, because it does not take into account two fundamental issues: first, that most victims of FM, as grassroots BME organisations have argued, have little desire to leave their communities, and second, that strategies based on the right to exit represent minority communities as harbingers of bad cultural practices, rather than seeing patriarchy as the culprit, an approach that ultimately derails the violence against women agenda. Clearly, this is not a failure of multiculturalism per se, but a failure of a certain brand of multiculturalism. If the right to exit is heralded as a solution to FM, then British multiculturalism offers an impartial solution to the problem of FM: either remain members of a collective or leave the collective as individuals, individuals in a liberal Western hegemonic manner. This solution is not a forceful legal mechanism for ensuring that people and institutions are held accountable for discriminatory acts and decisions.

Bringing back the victim-friendly approach: reworking multiculturalism and human rights in the struggle to end forced marriage in the UK

It should be clear from the preceding analysis that our critique focuses on the UK's ill-designed and fundamentally misconceived initiatives against FM. Importantly, these objections do not lead us to advocate a hands-off policy. By contrast, we espouse the belief that both 'arrogant assimilationalism and hands-off toleration carry risks' (Phillips and Dustin 2004, p.2). What we are advocating is that the government use a reworked multiculturalism paradigm which frames FM as fundamentally an issue of the abuse of women's human rights. Such a strategy will ensure that the primary focus of intervention vis-à-vis FM remains the victim thus focusing policy on improving the condition of women affected by this offence.

Reworking British multiculturalism: the feasibility of a 'multiculturalism without culture'

One of the core problems in the debate over the legal authority of British multicultural policy is the lack of a clear definition of what constitutes culture, and consequently ambiguity over what is meant and practically implied by the right to retain certain behaviours and beliefs. Cultural practice may, depending upon the individual, include things such as polygamy, refusal of medical intervention and extreme gender-based restrictions on behaviour. The government primarily treats these matters as falling under the jurisdiction of the legal system. Official multiculturalism, however, approaches cultural practice as though it were a simple matter of holidays, food and dress – items that Hage (1998) refers to as 'soft culture'. Thus if policy discourse and state are predicated upon a loose notion of 'soft culture' then multicultural policies will remain piecemeal and simply 'based on concessions, extensions and exemptions such as scheduling exams to avoid key festivals for various religious groups, Sikhs being exempt from wearing helmets' (Meetoo and Mirza 2007, p.190).

While it is not within the scope of this chapter to provide a definitive taxonomy of multiculturalism, we argue that any government policy based on multiculturalism dealing exclusively with problems between communities, but not problems within communities, is destined to fail as the gendered power divisions within groups will not fall within its ameliorative capacity. If problems between communities and not within communities remain its only concern, then multiculturalism will continue to privilege ethnicity over gender, cultural rights over human rights. Further an inability to recognise *different opinions within different groups* through an official discourse of multiculturalism reinforces previous types of government intervention against FM, despite their historically disastrous effect for reducing violence against women. In addition, the construction of multiculturalism only as an allegory of respect for difference will mean that initiatives to end violence against women in general, and FM in particular, remain linked to a narrative of 'Western progress' and a latent assumption that certain cultures must be 'shown the way' to Western enlightenment.

We are not alone in making this argument, in fact, the old Trudeau-era formulations of multiculturalism in terms of group-based inclusion has been challenged by the work of theorists such as Vertovec (2006), who contends that contemporary notions of diversity and hybridity have escalated to the point where a traditional, multicultural engagement with well-defined groups is both outdated and harmful. And the problem of multiculturalism's engagement with culture according to a group-based model is most clearly evident when considering the position of women who occupy either mainstream-migrant or non-mainstream communities. In her work, *Multiculturalism without Culture*, Anne Phillips (2007) has made the claim that 'a defensible multiculturalism will put notions of human agency much more at its centre, it will dispense with strong notions of culture'. Her basic contention is that multiculturalism can be made compatible with the pursuit of gender equality and women's rights so long as it dispenses with an essentialist understanding of culture (Phillips 2007, pp.8–9). Phillips (2007) calls for a strengthening, rather than a reduction, of multiculturalism, urging specifically for 'a multiculturalism that dispenses with reified notions of culture that feed those stereotypes to which so many feminists have objected, yet retains enough robustness to address inequalities between cultural groups' (pp.8–9). Phillips (2007) sees this as something that fundamentally begins with individual rather than group rights, and formulates her proposals for 'multiculturalism without culture' from this position. Indeed, this new conception of multiculturalism will ultimately be more effective in dealing with practices such as FM than retrograde calls to integrate disparate communities cohesively.

What we are advocating in terms of a coherent governmental policy for addressing FM is one based on a type of multiculturalism that dispenses with notions of *authentic* culture and instead places individuals at its core. Although Phillips (2007) speaks of a multiculturalism without culture, she does not stretch the argument far enough to show how such a scenario, at least policy wise, can be generated. In the next section, we hope to show how framing FM ultimately as a human rights abuse can engender the sort of 'multiculturalism without culture' that Phillips (2007) speaks of.

Using human rights to achieve 'multiculturalism without culture'

In our opinion, we strongly suggest that a rights-based approach towards FM should be defined and developed, and that this be done from a clear violence-against-women perspective in order to address the harms sustained by women so that an ideal of *multiculturalism without culture* is plausible and defensible. Such a clear violence-against-women policy would challenge the public/private distinction so that policy and interventions 'work to ensure that women's voices find a public audience, to reorient the boundaries of mainstream human rights law so that it incorporates an understanding of the world from the perspective of the socially subjugated' (Charlesworth 1994, p.76).

But is this possible? Can human rights law incorporate the subjective voices of the socially subjugated? Okin (1998) and others emphasise that the idea of rights as universal is problematic because this idea is specific to a 'Western' liberal context, and universalising it would thus impose (neo)colonial power relations. Yet, without some universal concept of 'human-ness', there would be no basis upon which to claim human rights and the human rights of women. This tension, which establishes some universal conception of human-ness, while also being careful not to flatten the differences between women, centrally informs feminist human rights literature. This feminist critique of human rights (re)produces the very concerns contained within mainstream feminist discourses regarding heterogeneity within the supposed homogenous category of 'woman' (Okin 1998; Phillips 2007).

The majority of feminist human rights literature acknowledges that what makes women's human rights a global concern is the universality of women's subordination – of patriarchy, or the cultural expression of male privilege – rather than any universal conception of rights. Thus, claims of cultural relativism in dealing with the idea of human rights and international law have led to critiques of (neo)colonial privilege informing definitions of human rights (Coomaraswamy 1994). Under the assumption that 'it would be wrong to assume that the values contained in the UDHR [Universal Declaration of Human Rights] are truly universal' (Coomaraswamy 1994, p.41), such advocates argue the necessity of 'Third World' involvement in identifying problematic aspects of culture, thus respecting relativism, while agreeing that the subordination of women, in its varied forms, exists universally.

As Coomaraswamy (2002) writes:

> What we need today is internal dialogue, first among women in third world societies and then between the women and the larger community. Outsiders must promote and aid this dialogue, giving their support so that such a dialogue is open, rich and transformative. (Coomaraswamy 2002, p.16)

The problem remains that the 'solution of dialogue' simply seeks to include 'Third World' subjects, but does not necessarily challenge the modern operations of power at work in producing human rights and universal principles. What such calls for translation miss is that the problem of universal human rights and the particularity of women's experiences that need to recognised/included within human rights law is a problem that exists *before* translation. That is, the problem of human rights as a claim to universality that both disavows and produces difference/particularity requires unpacking the epistemic conditions of the production of universality itself. Translation and dialogue – between the internal community of 'women in the third world' and the 'outsiders' of the larger community – does not interrogate the conditions of universality; translation simply (re)enacts those conditions through the inclusion of some particularity at the cost of others (Coomaraswamy 2002, p.16).

But a conception of universal human rights can accommodate cultural differences by including an account of intercultural dialogue and by not insisting that an agreement on human rights extends all the way to having the same reasons for the agreement. Reconciling human rights and cultural diversity cannot be done entirely at the theoretical level. That task must be left to participants in intra-cultural and intercultural dialogue: they can draw on their own traditions to make them consistent with human rights and to constructively engage with other traditions with the aim of mutual understanding and agreement. But that does not preclude the need for theoretical work. Philosophical conception of human rights should involve critical reflection on the intercultural dialogue and on the nature of the desired agreement of human rights. Furthermore, rethinking human rights for a global multicultural context means considering the perspectives of non-Western cultures (An-Na'im 1994).

To elucidate, at the practical level, FM breaches a number of articles of the European Convention of Human Rights to which the UK is a signatory. For example, FM clearly violates Article 12 of the convention, which declares that 'Men and women of marriageable age have the right to marry and to found a family, according to the national laws governing the exercise of that right'. The article demands that there is free and full consent to marriage by the intending spouses as mandated by the underlying principles of self-determination and human dignity required by the convention (Liberty 2005). These aspects of the right to marry (or not marry) are moreover recognised explicitly in a number of legal agreements to which the UK is party. FM also breaches the right to bodily integrity as guaranteed by a range of international human rights' instruments, and, in some respects, customary international law. It is likely that the practice of forced marriage would contravene Article 3 of the Convention prohibiting torture and inhumane or degrading treatment. The European Court of Human Rights (ECHR) has provided clear legal guidelines for determining whether Article 3 has been breached, particularly with regard to the age, sex and vulnerability of the victim. The ECHR has also stressed that this right applies to all mental and physical suffering experienced by a victim which exceeds a minimum level of severity. Further, FM may also involve the deprivation of personal liberty, namely, the arbitrary detention of victims by family members which is again a violation of human rights.

Moreover, international law has acknowledged that forced marriage constitutes a practice similar to slavery, which is of course prohibited by customary international law and a range of human rights treaties. Finally, some cases of forced marriage can result in the violation of an individual's right to life, where those who refuse to enter into a marriage are killed.

While these are just a few examples to show how the international human rights machine can be used to frame FM as a human right's abuse, it is clear that nonetheless women's international human rights must be further developed on a number of fronts. Certainly the relevance of the traditional canon of human rights to women is important to document. The potential of an individual complaints procedure under the Women's Convention should be seriously explored. At the same time, rights that focus on addressing the harms sustained by women, need to be identified and developed, challenging the public/private distinction by taking the rights discourse into the private sphere. But, most fundamentally and importantly, the boundaries of mainstream human rights law must incorporate an understanding of the world from the perspective of the socially subjugated.

What we are arguing for is that a rights-based approach to FM is not only normatively desirable but also practical. Given that the government continues to commission consultation reports on domestic violence (Home Office 2005), financially support 'independent domestic violence advisers' and formulate 'Together we can end violence against women' strategy plans, we wonder why the issue of FM is constantly and ironically ignored within this agenda. Instead, FM remains exoticised – treated as a separate entity marginalised from the broader struggle against gender-based violence. So, whereas official policy on domestic violence in the UK is allied with the Human Rights Act 1988 and the European Convention on Human Rights, FM continues to be delinked from a human rights abuse perspective, almost as if to insinuate that human rights laws designed to enable individual self-determination are lost on the women victims of 'deviant' patriarchal cultures (Wilson 2007).

In this respect, using a rights-based approach towards ameliorating FM puts the focus on victims and specifically on women who can use universal values of gender equality and rights to fight for more specific gender demands against patriarchal violence such as FM. Such a rights-based approach to FM will help victims achieve gender equality *within* community as opposed to merely the 'right to exit' these communities.

If FM is cast in such a reworked human rights abuse way, then ameliorative strategies will also move beyond the assumptions about the immutability of 'culture', and so facilitate more careful thinking about strategies for preventing violence in the future, as well as allowing us to define multiple forms of violence (racist violence, familial violence or intimate violence, for example) in relation to masculinity. Ultimately, framing FM as an abuse of women's human rights is a call for people to come together to address the tensions between cultural relativism and universal feminism, to support the possibility of working towards abolishing patriarchal privileges in all its forms.

It is after all very possible to acknowledge and confront violence against women within communities without descending into culturally deficit explanations that they are implicitly patriarchal. Is it possible to achieve *multiculturalism without culture*? Yes, if patriarchy and iniquitous gender relations are interrogated, challenged and ultimately held responsible for FM, not unsubstantiated essentialist explanations about the cultures that sanction it.

Acknowledgements

The authors wish to thank Professor Floya Anthias for her helpful comments and suggestions on an early draft of this chapter.

Notes

1. Prime Minister Anders Fogh Rasmussen's Opening Address to the Folketing (Danish Parliament) on 4 October 2005. Available at www.stm.dk/Index/dokumenter.asp?o=6&n=0&h=6&d=2402&s=2&str=stor, accessed on 9 September 2007.

2. Jack and Zena Briggs (not their real names) were married in March 1993, and Zena's family threatened to kill them both. Zena's parents had been planning who Zena would marry since her birth. Refusing to go along with their wishes caused violence and abuse, and the couple had to flee for their lives as they were hunted down by Zena's family. They spent over a decade on the run and lived in more than 30 homes.

3. 'KR', the youngest daughter of a Sikh family of Indian origin, left home at 16 to live with her sister, who had earlier moved in with a man against her parents' wishes. The father reported KR as a missing person, and the police returned her to the care of her father. When she was 17, KR was taken to India by her parents and placed in custody of her aunt. KR's sister instituted wardship proceedings and KR was made a ward of court, which was continued during her minority. KR persuaded her relatives to take her to the British High Commission in Delhi to establish whether her stay in India

was voluntary; when she stated that she was not in India voluntarily, she was flown back to the UK. The judge held that child abduction remains abduction, even when both parents are abductors and the child is nearly an adult (source: Re KR (A Child) (Abduction: Forcible Removal by Parents), [1999] 2 FLR 542).

References

Anchor Counselling Practice (2005) *Anchor's Response to the Forced Marriage Criminalisation Consultation*. London: Anchor Counselling Practice.

An-Na'im, A. (1994) 'State Responsibility Under International Human Rights Law to Change Religious and Customary Law.' in R. Cook (ed.) *Human Rights of Women: National and International Perspectives*. Philadelphia, PA: University of Pennsylvania Press.

Barzilai, G. (2004) 'Culture of patriarchy in law: Violence from antiquity to modernity.' *Law and Society Review 38*, 4, 867-84.

Beckett, C. and Macey, M. (2001) 'Race, gender and sexuality: The oppression of multiculturalism.' *Women's Studies International Forum 24*, 3-4, 309-19.

Charlesworth, H. (1994) 'What are "Women's International Human Rights"?' In R. Cook (ed.) *Human Rights of Women: National and International Perspectives*. Philadelphia, PA: University of Pennsylvania Press.

Commission on Integration and Cohesion (2007) *Our Shared Future*. Available at www.integrationandcohesion.org.uk/~/media/assets/www.integrationand cohesion.org.uk/our_shared_future%20pdf.ashx, accessed on 28 April 2009.

Coomaraswamy, R. (1994) 'Are women's right's universal? Re-engaging the local.' *Meridians 4*, 1, 1-18.

Coy, M., Kelly, L. and Foord, J. (2009) *Map of Gaps: The Postcode Lottery of Violence Against Women Support Services*. London: End Violence Against Women Campaign.

Derby City Council (2005) *Response to the Forced Marriage Criminalisation Consultation*. Derby: Derby City Council.

English for Spouses Consultation (2007) *English for Spouses New to the UK*. Available at www.ind.homeoffice.gov.uk/6353/6356/17715/englishforspouseconsultation .pdf, accessed on 31 December 2007.

Forced Marriage Unit (2008) *Information for Forced Marriage Victims*. Available at www.fco.gov.uk/en/travelling-and-living-overseas/things-go-wrong/forced-marriage, accessed on 28 April 2009.

Gill, A. (2006) 'Patriarchal violence in the name of "Honour".' *International Journal of Criminal Justice Sciences 1*, 1, 1-12.

Gupta, R (2008) 'This crackdown on forced marriage is not all it seems.' *Guardian*, 25 July. Available at www.guardian.co.uk/commentisfree/2008/jul/25/immigration.familyandrelation ships, accessed on 28 April 2009.

Hage, G. (1998) *White Nation: Fantasies of White Supremacy in a Multicultural Society*. Annandale, NSW: Pluto Press.

Hari, J. (2007) 'How multiculturalism is betraying women'. *The Independent*, 30 April. Available at www.independent.co.uk/opinion/commentators/johann-hari/johann-hari-how-multiculturalism-is-betraying-women-446806.html, accessed on 28 April 2009.

Home Office (2009) 'Together we can end violence against women and girls consultation.' Available at www.homeoffice.gov.uk/documents/cons-2009-vaw, accessed on 29 May 2009.

Immigration Law Practitioners' Association (ILPA) (2007) *Response to Consultation on Simplifying Immigration Law.* London: ILPA.

Innes, M. (2003) *Understanding Social Control Deviance, Crime and Social Order.* Maidenhead, UK: Open University.

Jordan, B., Strath, B. and Triandafyllidou, A. (2003) 'Contextualising immigration policy implementation in Europe.' *Journal of Ethnic and Migration Studies 29,* 2, 195-224

Kent Police (2005) *Response to the Forced Marriage Criminalisation Consultation.* Kent: Kent Police.

Klite, M. (2007) 'Multi-culturalism damages UK, says Cameron'. *The Telegraph,* 28 January. Available at www.telegraph.co.uk/news/uknews/1540790/Multi-culturalism-damages-UK-says-Cameron.html, accessed on 28 April 2009.

Kukathas, C. (1992) 'Are there any cultural rights?' *Political Theory 20,* 105-39.

Kymlicka, W. (1995) *Multicultural Citizenship.* Oxford: Oxford University Press.

Lewis, G. and Neal, S. (2005) 'Introduction: Contemporary political contexts, changing terrains and revisited discourses.' *Ethnic and Racial Studies 28,* 3, 423–44.

Liberty (2005) *Liberty's response to the Joint Home Office and Foreign Commonwealth Office consultation on forced marriage.* London: Liberty.

Meetoo, M. and Mirza, H. (2007) 'There is nothing "honourable" about honour killings: Gender, violence and the limits of multiculturalism.' *Women's Studies International Forum 30,* 187–200.

Muslim Council of Britain (2005) *Response to the Forced Marriage Criminalisation Consultation.* London: Muslim Council of Britain.

Nielsen, F. (2005) 'Protecting youth and controlling immigration: Danish Action Plan on forced marriages and its impacts.' *Fempower.* Available at noticeboard.ucy.ac.cy/gen_announcements/Fempower11.pdf, accessed 28 April 2009.

Okin, S. (1998) 'Feminism and multiculturalism: Some tensions.' *Ethics 108,* 4, 661-84.

Parekh, B. (2000) *The Future of Multi-Ethnic Britain: Report of the Commission on Multi-Ethnic Britain.* London: Profile Books.

Phillips, A. (2007) *Multiculturalism without Culture.* Princeton, NJ: Princeton University Press.

Phillips, A. and Dustin, M. (2004) *UK Initiatives on Forced Marriage: Regulation, Dialogue and Exit.* London: LSE Research Online. Available at http://eprints.lse.ac.uk/archive/00000546, accessed on 28 April 2009.

Phillips, T. (2005) *After 7/7: Sleepwalking to Segregation.* London: Commission for Racial Equality. Available at www.cre.gov.uk/default.aspx.LocID-Ohgnew07s.reflocID-OHG00900C002.Lang-EN.htm, accessed on 28 April 2009.

Sen, P. (2008) *'Crimes of Honour': Value and Meaning.* Working Paper. London: EVAW.

Shachar, A. (2001) *Multicultural Jurisdictions: Cultural Differences and Women's Rights.* Cambridge: Cambridge University Press.

Tempest, M (2006) 'U-turn on plans to criminalise forced marriage', *Guardian,* Available at www.guardian.co.uk/politics/2006/jun/07/immigrationpolicy.gender, accessed on 28 April 2009.

Treacher, A. (2003). Reading the Other: Women, feminism, and Islam. *Studies in Gender and Sexuality 4,* 59-71.

Vertovec, S. (2006) *The Emergence of Super-Diversity in Britain.* Working Paper 25. Oxford: University of Oxford.

Walby, S. (1990) *Theorising Patriarchy.* Oxford: Blackwell

Williams, P. and Chrisman, L. (1993) *Colonial Discourse and Post-colonial Theory: A Reader.* Hemel Hempstead, UK: Harvester.

Wilson, A. (2007) 'The forced marriage debate and the British state.' *Race and Class 49,* 25-38.

Chapter 6

Continuing Control

Child Contact and Post-separation Violence

Ravi K. Thiara

Introduction

Although there have been considerable developments in responses to women and children affected by domestic violence, a focus on women's failure to protect rather than men's violence, a separation of male violence from male parenting, and a presumption of contact remain central to many professional responses (Humphreys 2006; Radford and Hester 2006; Saunders and Barron 2003). Although links between domestic violence and child abuse began to be made in the 1990s (Kelly 1994; Mullender and Morley 1994), establishing the link between domestic violence, child contact and post-separation violence has been much harder in the face of deep-rooted beliefs that contact, except in extreme circumstances, is in the best interests of the child, especially since shared or co-parenting remains the underlying presumption of family law (Humphreys and Harrison 2003).[1] Research has consistently highlighted concerns about the way abused women are denigrated in family courts, by child protection agencies and the media (Radford and Hester 2006). In particular, a lack of attention to safety after separation remains a major concern for those working to support women and children. Thus debate and concern about child contact where there is domestic violence continues to be reflected in research, which has produced an evidence base to challenge the pro-contact position and highlighted the contradictions and anomalies that exist in private and public law, and the disconnection in the approaches to domestic violence, child contact and child protection (Harrison 2006; Radford and Hester 2006; Saunders 2004). Although a study has pointed to the disproportionate number of black and minority ethnic (BME) families appearing in child contact centres in particular localities (Aris, Harrison and Humphreys 2002), and although there is currently no research on the ways in which ethnicity, domestic violence and child contact intersect, child contact and post-separation violence have increasingly been highlighted as important issues for South Asian women and children.[2]

By drawing on research conducted with twelve South Asian women, five South Asian children, and six professionals, this chapter explores the issues of domestic violence, child contact and post-separation violence. It shows that there are a group of women who continue to experience ongoing post-separation violence through a range of informal and formal child contact arrangements. It argues that child contact creates a context for continuing control of women and children by abusive partners and constitutes a powerful form of prolonged abuse in the post-separation period. The children's rights agenda, emphasising the necessity of contact with fathers, even where there is domestic violence, and a failure to consider the particular issues for South Asian women and children further serve to reinforce the victimisation of women, frustrating their attempts to move on with their lives. South Asian women often encounter complex issues and additional difficulties in relation to child contact, which are shaped by the nature of abuse experienced before separation; in order to link pre- and post-separation abuse, these are discussed in the first main section of the chapter. This provides a context for understanding the ways in which women's partners and family members use child contact to perpetrate further abuse after separation, where the continuum of abuse is maintained, discussed in the second main section of the chapter. The issues raised in this chapter have to be considered in the context of wider literature on child contact and post-separation violence. The experiences of South Asian women and children give greater nuance to existing knowledge and provide an insight into their particular issues, a necessary starting point for any effective professional responses.

Experiences of abuse

Available research reveals that South Asian women and children affected by domestic violence face similar as well as additional issues and pressures that compound their situations (Minhas *et al.* 2002; Thiara 2005). Barriers to seeking help are considered to be greater and are linked to their dis/location in wider society, their place in families and communities, and personal factors (Mullender *et al.* 2002). Although there have been some changes since the late 1990s, low levels of awareness, and a fear as well as actual experiences of insensitivity/racism from services continue to prevent women from seeking help (Izzidien 2008; Rai and Thiara 1996; Sen 1997). The regulation of behaviour in families and communities marked by collectivist values further exacerbates these barriers, leading to women staying in abusive situations or being ostracised (Gill 2004; Mullender *et al.* 2002), while patriarchal notions of *izzat* and *sharam* (honour/reputation/shame) in particular control and shape women's responses to their situations (Mullender *et al.* 2002). To prevent shame and stigma within the community, pressures to keep things within the family, and make things work by staying in abusive situations, keep women entrapped for years. Fear of being thrown out of the country and/or the threat of separation from their children, especially for women without settled immigration status, further lead to women remaining silent or being compliant.

As shown by other research, the interviewed women had experienced a range of abuse from intimate partners. In particular, with the exception of one, all women reported high levels of physical violence and for the majority, once abuse started it had been daily or almost daily. Although the physical violence resulted in serious injuries at times, women had not been able to access medical attention. Women had also been subjected to constant debilitating mental and verbal abuse, which had resulted in depression for many of them; indeed, existing studies show that between 38 and 83 per cent of abused women report depression (Cascardi, O'Leary and Schlee 1999; Humphreys 2008). Two of the women had attempted suicide as a result of the abuse, though others had had constant suicidal thoughts.[3] The effects of the mental abuse on women were especially pernicious, leading to extreme isolation, changes in their outlook as well as their sense of self:

The mental abuse was gradual, he became really controlling, I couldn't go to see my parents, I couldn't make phone calls, he was cutting me off and I became more and more isolated...All I ever got was what was bad with me...I just started to not like myself and felt...I wasn't worth anything.

Some women were forced to have children as a way of resolving the situation with their husbands, but for some, the abuse had started during pregnancy and often became worse after: 'He pushed me down the stairs when I was five months pregnant and started to argue all the time. He then made me sleep on the floor after my son was born' and 'When I was pregnant with my fourth child he was constantly hitting me and fighting and that's when I decided to call the police'.

Financial abuse or dependence – either withholding money or forcing women to go out to work – was also commonly experienced and especially exacerbated for women not allowed to go out of the house or work (see also Anitha 2008). Being in paid employment was a double-edged sword for women for while it provided an escape out of the house, they neither benefited financially nor felt less afraid. Indeed, for abusive partners, especially those who had other relationships or drug habits, employment was something to be encouraged and meant they did not have to contribute to the maintenance of homes, shopping, children or their partners. The level of economic exploitation was quite marked among the working women, whose incomes were appropriated by abusive partners and their in-laws.[4]

Sexual violence was central to the abuse experienced for over half of the women, and something they had never revealed to anyone, finding it too shameful. In cases where women had plucked up the courage to disclose to female relatives, they had been left with the feeling that *'they did not care'*. A woman spoke about being raped while she was asleep, while another said that her husband demanded sex constantly, forcing her if she did not agree. A few of the women living in refuges had spoken about it to their support workers, but others who had not accessed support talked about it for the first time in the interview.

Isolation was commonly used as a strategy for all of the women; even where women had family in the UK, they had been cut off from their support networks. Although the range and extent of abuse experienced varied among the twelve women, for eight of them, if the abuse had been assessed using current risk assessment tools, they would be considered extremely high risk. The levels of abuse and control constituted a form of 'intimate terrorism' (Johnson and Ferraro 2000), comprised of constant surveillance by men. This monitoring of women's movements had involved a man installing video cameras throughout the house, while for others not being allowed out was a common experience. Extreme sexual jealousy, common in domestic violence, and accusations of promiscuity were also levelled at women, even if they were not allowed out of the house. Women spoke about 'feeling tortured' mentally and feeling they had no options but to stay in the abusive situation. A woman subjected to severe physical, mental, sexual abuse and intimidation described her situation:

> I was not even allowed to draw curtains, he was suspicious of everything. He questioned the paternity of our son, and accused me of having sex with his father and brothers. He forced me to wear a burqa and had three cameras in the house watching me, the telephone was tapped. He used to ring me all the time and lock me inside the house.

Abuse against South Asian women is often perpetrated by multiple family members (Parmar, Sampson and Diamond 2005; Thiara 2005). In addition to partners, the involvement of parents-in-law and sisters-in-law was common for the interviewed women, resulting in abusive contexts that were totally impenetrable for many women, at least for a period of time. This is significant as the involvement of family members is a major factor in child contact contexts. Such abuse included women being constantly undermined, being treated like domestic slaves where they were forced to cook and clean for the family and denied their own rooms, not being allowed to do anything for their partners or cook without permission, being threatened with deportation or the police, and being physically abused. Such extreme abuse was especially common in contexts where the husbands were dependent on drugs and/or alcohol, had gambling habits, were verbally abusive towards their own parents, had other partners or were not in employment.

To construct women as total victims would be inaccurate as most of them had found routes out of their situations. This was, however, a difficult journey for many, especially those without family or friends in the UK, and it took these women much longer to leave than those who had been brought up in the UK. Feeling pressurised by their own families, whether in the UK or overseas, to remain with the abusive partner and his family and make things work was common to all of the women. Making things better was seen as the responsibility of women and the behaviour and actions of their husbands or wider family rarely came under scrutiny or challenge, something reinforced in the child contact arena (as discussed later in the chapter). Women also described their own need not to be stigmatised as reasons for staying, and all of the women had been scared of being separated from their children, something reinforced through constant threats from partners and family members, and something also played out in the post-separation period. Almost all of the women had wanted to make the relationship work for the sake of the children, because having two parents was seen by them to be important for their children. However, separation had occurred for the majority because they wanted to avoid psychological harm to their children caused by living with domestic violence. Despite such concerns, the abuse had continued for all of them post-separation, however, as the majority were pulled into conflictual child contact arrangements with partners and paternal grandparents, as discussed later.

Not knowing about help and support services was a common experience for the women. Some women were so isolated, they had no or little contact with the outside world, particularly those who had married British men and did not have settled immigration status. Not speaking any English, such women remained in a constant state of anxiety, believing they would be sent back and separated from their children, and believing they had no option but to stay in the situation. The following was typical of a number of the women:

> He thought nobody would help me because I don't have immigration status in this country. But I rang the police. It was hard at first but slowly I have learnt to stand on my own feet. I didn't even know how to count money.

Some of the women who were born in the UK were also unaware of domestic violence services, having dealt with their situations themselves, sometimes with some support from their own family members. A minority of the women had called the police when the physical abuse had got so severe that they feared for their own and their children's safety, something also highlighted by other research (Humphreys and Thiara, 2002). Informing teachers at children's schools, telling an employer, being thrown out, contacting the police, and telling a health visitor provided the range of routes out of the abuse for women. Seven of the twelve women had then

been supported by specialist domestic violence services while the remain-
der had tried to cope with their situations on their own.

Undermining mother's relationship with children

> He never hit my son but he didn't care about him. He hit me in front of
> him and bad mouth me in front of him... And he kept me busy all the
> time in the house and working part time so that I wouldn't spend any
> time with my son.

The issues for women in mothering through domestic violence (Hester and
Radford 2006) and in having their relationship with their children undermined as part of a strategy of abuse have been highlighted by research
(Humphreys *et al.* 2006; Thiara *et al.* 2006). In particular, the latter has
shown how the 'absent presence' of the abuser continues to impact on
women and children in the aftermath of abuse and the ways in which the
abuser is present even in his absence; it also argues that child contact
remains a key site for the abuser to maintain his damaging presence in the
lives of women and children, particularly in their relationships with each
other. However, ongoing issues experienced by women and children as a
result of this are often couched in terms of 'mother blaming' where the
abuser remains invisible (Thiara *et al.* 2006).

Although it would be wrong to stereotype all South Asian women in
this way, a key aspect of the abuse experienced by women was the systematic denial of a relationship with their children, who were seen as the
property of fathers and their families, the case for five of the interviewed
women. This is something that has also been reported by other research as
an aspect of some South Asian women's abuse experiences (Thiara *et al.*
2006). Even where abusive men were uninterested in their children, they
colluded with their parents or siblings to deny women the opportunities of
building a bond with their children. In such situations, and especially
where the children were male, though not exclusively, paternal grandparents took over the caring of the children a few weeks after birth. A woman
spoke at length about being forced to go back to work after five weeks and
having to leave her baby son:

> They only wanted me to bring in money for them... after working for 10
> hours, I had to come home and do everything, cook, clean...the only
> thing I was not allowed was spend time with my baby son, only wash his

clothes and do all the hard work. If I sat with him for even 5 minutes my mother-in-law would start saying you do this, do that.

Another young woman talked about how after returning from hospital she had been totally excluded from caring for her baby, which had been taken over by her mother-in-law:

I had been excited about having a baby but then was made to feel as if he was nothing to do with me. Those early days are so important in building a bond with your baby and I was not allowed. If I told my husband, he would just walk away and say 'What's your problem, they love him?'

A woman who was married from India had been used as a vehicle by the husband's family to have a grandchild (her husband was a drug addict) and when the child was born the family had conspired to throw her out. Another woman, who had developed a disability, was also forced to leave without her baby daughter. Both had then been engaged in protracted proceedings to secure child contact and residence of their children.

The extreme control exercised over some women also acted as a controlling mechanism over their relationship with their children:

We lived on the top floor of a tower block. I couldn't leave the house or take the kids out. He was four years old and I had never taken him out. He prevented me from taking him to play groups.

Women without settled status, and frequently threatened with deportation and separation, were grateful just to be near their children:

They threatened to send me back to India and keep my son. They would not send for my leave [to remain]...I just thanked god I could see him every day.

Undermining women's relationship with their children was common even where there was no systematic denial of a relationship. While this occurred, abusive men provided little positive input into the children's lives through their own parenting.

Fathering

Despite an increased literature on fathering, especially where fathers are absent, there has been little focus on when their presence is problematic (for a fuller discussion of the trends in the fatherhood literature, see

Mullender *et al.* 2002). Generally, most of this literature fails to consider the abuse of male power in the family, and it is only feminist studies critically engaging with notions of masculinity that have provided insights into violent men, who are rarely asked about their understanding of the impact of their violence on children. Even studies that have explored this reveal a lack of understanding of the effects of their behaviour on children (see Hearn 1998). However, despite men minimising children's responses, they are frequently present in the house when domestic violence is taking place. Based on existing studies, Mullender *et al.* (2002) suggest that:

> A picture recurs of men who regard their own needs and feelings as paramount and themselves as having a superior legitimacy; they find it difficult to see others as separate individuals with their own needs. Perhaps not surprisingly, then, they appear to reflect very little on their role as fathers. (Mullender *et al.* 2002, p.180)

The intersection of South Asian men's and their family's violence, its effects on children, and parenting in domestic violence contexts has received no attention to date. Women's narratives, and to some extent children's, reveal a picture of fathers that suggests an almost total lack of co-parenting (see also Thiara *et al.* 2006). Men disregarded the presence of children when being abusive towards their partners and appeared unconcerned about the effects of their violence on children, even though women were clear about these effects:

> The kids saw it all the time. They were small but they do remember where he hit me and where I bled. They also remember that Dad used to throw them out of the house even in the dark. He didn't like them playing around. If I said anything to him he used to hit me… he didn't care, he didn't do anything with children.

The fact that men paid little attention to children witnessing their violence suggests their parenting has to be scrutinised when making assessments about contact after separation. Clearly, such situations impacted on the children and South Asian children are often more exposed to abuse because of the greater vulnerability and isolation of their mothers. Although over half of the women said children had not seen or heard the abuse, believing they were asleep, out, or not aware, research shows that even when mothers believe they have protected children from the knowledge of abuse, children frequently know it is happening (Abrahams 1994).

Discussions with the five children revealed that all of them had been aware of what was happening at the time, as the following from a six-year-old boy reveals: 'Dad used to hit Mum. He hurt her eye and it had blood'.

In a minority of cases, the extreme abuse towards women was accompanied by direct abuse towards the children; for one child this resulted in regular beatings, the effects of which had taken over a year of counselling to start to address. Acknowledging the existence and impact of direct abuse on their children can be a painful process for many women, but for South Asian women greater support in naming and dealing with it is often needed. Children show a complex range of symptoms, including anger and violence towards their mothers, which can be difficult to fathom without support for women who believe they have protected their children. While women spoke about what are clearly the symptoms of abuse – children being hyperactive, clingy, withdrawn, not speaking, bed-wetting – few had made a connection between this and the effects of living with domestic violence. It was also evident that these conversations had rarely taken place with any support services or other professionals, and only a minority of women had been able to access some support for their children, unsurprising given the underdevelopment of services for Asian children affected by domestic violence (Imam and Akhtar 2005; Izzidien 2008; Thiara and Breslin 2007). However, this then made it harder for women to argue the link between children's behavioural problems and ongoing contact with their fathers in any convincing way to professionals during the child contact proceedings. Indeed, some women spoke about being advised not to mention domestic violence by their solicitors, as discussed later.

In addition to their violence, and sometimes also because they had drug or alcohol habits, it appears that men were both uninterested and disengaged from their role as fathers. Despite experiencing extreme abuse, women carried all responsibility for children, except where they were denied this by the wider family. The following comments in describing men were typical: 'Not interested in my daughter at all', 'He never played with my son', 'He didn't help at all with any of the children'.

While it has to be recognised that parenting practices vary greatly, based as they often are on individuals' own experiences of being parented, a lack of emotional warmth or interaction with the children on the part of the father was commonly reported by women:

> He would come in and walk straight past her. She would stand there and look at him and then at me…when he came down he would sit and watch TV with the volume turned up really high so he didn't need to speak to her.

This was reflected in what children said about their fathers – 'I never see him, he never play with me…he always fighting with Mum and making us sad'. The experiences of children in the same family varied, depending on the age of children when women left, if children were subjected to direct abuse, or if they witnessed abuse of their mothers. 'Selective mutism' was a response to their situations for some children:

> He started speaking very late, only when he was five years, he understood but didn't speak. My husband used to hit me in front of him; he used to cry and get upset.

The high levels of control over the women also extended to the children in a minority of cases, though the thread of non-caring was evident even here:

> He would beat me while I was holding the baby…he went to prison when my son was two and a half years old but he got worse in prison. He used to give my son cigarettes, lighters, and had no boundaries. He didn't send him to school but didn't allow him out to play either.

It was ironic that after she had separated and been rehoused, she was prevented from letting her son play outside because they were experiencing racism in the new area. The sense of incarceration for her son had thus continued despite leaving the abusive home.

  While some of the children were not directly abused, the denial of affection by fathers and the regulation of the mothers' time with children resulted in them having a greater bond with grandparents, which created additional issues – further abuse and conflict for women or divided loyalties for children. Other research has shown that the paternal family can be a source of support or abuse for children, depending on the responses from wider family members (Mullender *et al.* 2002). Where children were 'loved' by grandparents, though they were abusive towards the women, women felt greater guilt at leaving and pressure to enable child contact. In a number of these situations, women had attempted to make contact work through informal routes, even if it led to further abuse for them.

Child contact

It's a really risky game, children have a right to see both parents but what measures are in place to ensure abuse is not filtering down. Children are often a guinea pig.

Although women's experiences of child contact differed, they reveal ongoing difficulties, particularly for women not assisted by any support services. In all except two cases where women had been forced to leave without their children, contact had been initiated by fathers. Where women had fled to a refuge, it had taken men a number of months to make applications though, in other cases, women had received a letter from their husband's solicitor within a week of leaving. Child contact had taken between two weeks (where informal) and nine months to decide, and was ongoing for all seven women going through formal routes, and had taken between nine months and twenty months to date. These women had attended court between three and seven times, with one woman having five finding-of-fact hearings.

Five of the women had contact ordered through contact centres, three of which were supervised and two supported. For seven of the women, contact arrangements varied; where unsupervised contact was ordered or arranged by the women themselves, two women dropped off and picked up children at a police station, while five women used a range of different places including shops, eateries, library and a car park. This created a context for their abusive partners or his family members to perpetrate abuse towards women, including shouting and swearing, making threats to safety, threats that they would not see the children again, and general harassment. A number of the men with existing formal and informal child contact arrangements had drug and/or alcohol issues, with two also having past convictions for drugs.

While the pursuit of child contact was financially motivated for a minority of fathers who did not want to lose any claims over joint properties, the majority used the formal court process to slowly insinuate themselves back into women and children's lives. A number of the men applied for residence from the outset to 'up the ante' and then fought for maximum contact, which women had been advised to concede to if they wanted residence. Where women were unaware of the court process, had no support, and had solicitors advising them not to mention domestic violence, women found themselves having to leave children for up to three days with abusive partners. Only when referred by support workers were women able to get their full case heard and contact lessened.

The courts adopt an incremental approach to contact, where men 'prove' themselves to increase contact time at each court hearing. In cases where initial contact was ordered for as little as one hour per month, men had pursued the issue until they were granted more substantial contact – anything from a full day to three days per week. In a case where the man had been extremely controlling towards his partner and son, and had spent time in prison for drug offences, a woman had been to court five times and although contact was phased, he had managed to build this up gradually (domestic violence was seen not to be perpetrated towards her son, despite witnessing it repeatedly) until unsupervised contact was granted. In another case, where a child was not willing to see his father – 'He used to say that Dad hit Mum' – CAFCASS (the Children and Family Court Advisory Support Service) had convinced him to see his father. Some men used the argument of children being able to see grandparents and other family to secure unsupervised contact outside of the area. A woman who still lived in incredible fear from her partner had felt totally disempowered in the court process, when her partner had been granted unsupervised contact, despite meetings in a contact centre not having worked well. Another woman forced to leave without her child, who spoke no English, had been through the High Court to secure contact; when granted five hours a week she travelled by coach to spend time with her son, with little option but to wander around the city centre before handing him back. Not only did this create a financial strain on her but also she was subjected to ongoing abuse by her husband and his family when she collected her son. Indeed, financial hardship resulting from ensuring contact took place was experienced by a number of the women, who had to pay for travel to and from a place, sometimes outside the area they lived in.

Those women who had informal arrangements, decided through solicitors, had pursued this route to avoid their children going through the court process. Despite ongoing abuse, women stated they did 'not want things to be messy for the children' and wanted to be 'as civil as possible' though this was in the face of a great deal of harassment and abuse on the part of their partners and family members. In such cases, women had agreed to informal arrangements, in place for between two and nine months, and dealt with things 'all by myself'; not wanting to burden anyone else, they accepted the abuse and pressure that accompanied such arrangements as an inevitability.

Although none of the women was opposed to child contact, they aired concerns about its impact on children. Children viewing abuse as acceptable and being 'split in two' were common concerns for women, anxious about the long-term psychological effects on children, especially when relations between women and partners or family members remained fractious. This was especially where children were being used by partners to get back at women and where paternal grandparents wanted residence of the children:

> Court should give children to one, so children aren't split. Or he should co-parent but if he's never taken interest in children, why judges do this and why does he want contact? He doesn't even know when child was born. He never helped me to bring up children. This is only because of his parents, they never supported me, only wanted the children…He will leave them to the in-laws and not spend time with them.

While younger children were often scared of their fathers, having heard the shouting and fighting, those aged eight to twelve, especially boys, wanted contact as men frequently manipulated children with expensive presents to construct themselves as the 'good dad'. In such cases, limited contact was sufficient and children were often relieved when contact came to an end. Where contact took place in a centre, fathers were reported to 'just sit' without any form of substantial interaction but insist on children staying for the defined period of time. This was part of the process of fathers proving to professionals that they were devoted dads, what one woman termed as putting on 'a façade of a very good dad'. This was also a continuum of the fathers' approach (disengagement) to their children while still living together.

Although children responded differently, they were reported to generally become anxious before contact with fathers. A woman recounted how her very young daughter screamed and cried when handed over to her father and became extremely quiet and angry towards her after contact. In the absence of space for children to voice exactly what they felt about contact, they developed strategies to deal with it. A young boy of seven, initially very scared of his father, had been manipulated through expensive presents during weekend contact so that when the father claimed that the child did not want to return to the mother, he remained silent. Another woman, who was anxious for her son 'to be just normal', stated:

> He's restless and not settled most of the time. After contact, he seems very depressed as Dad talks to him about me. But he is also learning to manipulate the situation. If I tell him off over anything he threatens to call CAFCASS or the police.

A young teenage boy was very angry at his father for having made them live through abuse and for forcing them to have contact: 'I can't forgive him for putting my mum and us through all that and he expects me to see him and talk to him' (shaking his head). Some fathers who were especially tenacious in getting contact with their sons made it hard for children to speak up:

> They saw him every Saturday morning through the contact centre but now he has them for the day. They always get ill after and upset after seeing him. They find it hard to say no to him.

Continuum of abuse – post-separation violence

> They are trying to move on but get pulled back so the issue hangs over their heads.

Women separated after many years of abuse, with the period of abuse ranging from three to ten years. It was clear from the women's narratives that post-separation violence was a common and continuing problem, made worse when it was linked to disputes over child contact. Research has shown that child contact is often an opportunity for abusive men to reassert their control over women and children (Humphreys and Harrison 2003). It was considered by support services to be the biggest issue for which South Asian women and children needed support. Humphreys and Thiara (2003), in their work on post-separation violence, have pointed out important differences in the experiences of white and BME women, showing that though all women had difficulties in the first six months, these greatly reduced for white women while for BME women they continued to be significant after six months. Post-separation violence took varied though similar forms. Women who escaped to refuges had some reprieve before being subjected to further abuse and harassment during contact proceedings. Men often targeted women's families when unaware of their whereabouts. In the period before some form of child contact was agreed, all women except two were constantly harassed through text messages, solicitor's letters, men's presence around their homes, and harassment of their families. All of these women were clear that child contact was being used by partners to assert their control over them and their children.

Abduction and the threat of separation from their children was a fear for almost all of the women who had children living with them. This was not unfounded, based as it was on constant threats from their partners to abduct or 'take' the children. For many of the women engaged in formal proceedings, this fear had led to them insisting on supervised contact, where the actions of partners could be monitored. This is supported by research which shows that 65 per cent of resident mothers used contact centres because of actual or threatened child abduction (Aris *et al.* 2002). The fact that one woman felt totally let down by the supervised contact centre further reinforced her perceptions about the power of her partner over her. The potential of the child contact process to be used to separate them from their children by partners was a great anxiety for women.

Contact centres also created a context for abuse for some women. Even where agreements existed for men not to have any contact with women, some men ensured they were there when women arrived: 'Once he dragged my son from me to take him inside. He makes sure I see him on contact visits and CAFCASS are not paying any attention to this'. Men also used their own language to abuse women in contact centres, something not picked up by contact centre staff. Forcing women to return to an area they had fled, by snatching children during informal arrangements and filing for residence, was also a strategy used to expose them to further abuse and pressure. Where partners were professionals, this was used to persistently interfere in issues over nurseries, choice of general practitioners and potential schools for children in order to have continuing control over the women. Where men had telephone contact with children, they used this to pressurise women to return.

It was evident that the children were frequently manipulated by men and family members to perpetrate post-separation violence. Not only was this abusive towards women but also it continued to undermine the relationships between children and mothers, creating a continuum between the domestic violence and post-separation violence contexts. Some were told to hit their mothers, disobey them or call the police when they were told off – 'The children were fighting with me, their dad was telling them to treat me badly'. Giving expensive gifts was a strategy commonly used to win children over by men and their families:

> They say we'll buy you things, Play Station whatever they want. I worry they will buy the children, and make it hard for them to leave things [abuse] behind.

> My husband buys him things really not good for a child and tells him 'Why do you want to live with your mum in a small house when you can live here with me, have your own room, we can go to the park and play football'…he never did these things with him before. He's now making it hard for him to come back…He sits in the car crying and shaking his head while my husband shouts at me and tells me he doesn't want to come back.

The profound confusion for children and the resulting divided loyalties is clear to see in the case above. This was especially hard for women who had separated because of the effects they were starting to see on the children. The tension created by what they were told by their fathers or grandparents resulted in some children acting this out after contact – threatening to call the police if they did not get their own way, bribing mothers to do things they wanted, and constantly recounting the fun things they did with their fathers. The following were typical of the comments made:

> He was telling them to hit Mummy and call the police, run away from home, don't go to school. All so that my record would be bad even after the divorce.

Consequently, post-separation violence affected women and children's ability to move on from abusive men, as they found themselves caught up in child contact arrangements which not only prevented them moving from an area or country but also subjected them to close surveillance by men who used children to continue control in all aspects of women's lives. Not only did women have to endure post-separation violence from partners but also this was compounded by pressures or demands around children from paternal grandparents who believed the children belonged to them.

Use of legal process in post-separation violence

Being dragged through the court system, often a long and wearing process, was seen by support services to cause 'mental trauma' for women. It was evident that many men used the legal process itself to assert control and to perpetrate further abuse against women. Men appeared to have few concerns about the impact of this on children, though women's narratives show an overriding concern with protecting children from legal battles, even when it placed them at further risk of abuse.

Contesting women's evidence of domestic violence was common and counter-allegations of child abuse and neglect were used as a strategy by a number of the men. A key aspect of asserting the fathers' rights to contact was to undermine women's mothering and hence challenge their rights over children. If women spoke little English, this was used to challenge their ability to support children with homework. A minority of women stated that they had to answer questions in court about why they had not learnt English and 'not integrated'. Where women lived in refuges, it was asserted they could provide little or no material comforts. Additionally, emphasising the role of extended family members was central to men arguing for residence over children, especially where women had left the area and were living on their own or in crisis accommodation. As part of this undermining, women's mental capacity was also commonly used to allege their inability to care for children, and women were left to obtain reports to prove otherwise.

Allegations of child abuse were used by men to take out *ex-parte* orders for residence of the children, even though in one case the man had previous drug convictions. Another had claimed a woman was incapable of looking after the children because she kept running away (she had tried to leave because of his abuse). In a case where the grandparents were pursuing residence, there had been numerous finding of fact hearings; this for her was an attempt by them to 'steal my son through the legal system'. The family had continuously tried to 'prove' her abuse:

> They didn't used to send my son's medicine with him, they said they did but didn't to get me into trouble. My son had some bruises that have been questioned ...the dad is always making complaints.

Men seeking to secure residence often 'played games' near to court dates to provoke women to say and do things that would impact negatively on their case. Where allegations of child abuse were levelled against them, women stated that if not supported by workers they would have found what was said in court difficult to challenge.

Making women go through endless court dates, then, was a way for men to keep themselves central to women, to send them messages about the power they had over them, to carry out threats of separation from children, and to prevent them from moving on. In addition to this, the courts were considered to be unsupportive of mothers and children, as men constantly breached agreements and went unpunished whereas mothers cooperated yet were constantly dragged back to court. The use of the legal process by men coincided with the wider private law response to entrench women's disadvantage. Feeling let down by the legal and court process was a constant theme in women's accounts. The legal arena was reported to be 'a minefield' for South Asian women, who had little understanding of the legal process around child contact. The interaction of women with solicitors and CAFCASS were marked by an over-reliance on their advice, as women believed them to be working for the welfare of the children. However, responses to women were often patchy, with some solicitors advising them 'not to dig up the past' and bring domestic violence into the process, while others emphasised the rights of the father. In a case where a woman had been advised to accept unsupervised contact, a solicitor had stated: 'He's with you 24 hours a day, what will happen for a few hours?' Another had commented: 'He's his dad, you'll have to shoot him, kill him to wipe him out.'

Where engaged with CAFCASS, women's experiences ranged from very negative to positive, though even where positive, women had been surprised by the recommendations made in their reports, which appeared to be in favour of fathers. This is reinforced by recent research which shows a disconnection between the narrative and analysis in reports with the recommendations made (Prevatt Goldstein 2009). Where negative, this was because officers had little or no understanding of the complex issues for South Asian women affected by domestic violence. In a case where the father had a history of extreme control over a woman and her son, had served a prison sentence, and she had raised repeated concerns about his conduct, CAFCASS had considered the contact centre an unsuitable place to foster a good relationship between the father and son and allowed unsupervised contact (to her reminder that he smoked cannabis, she was told 'It's not a class A drug'). A few women believed CAFCASS had influenced children to have contact with fathers, with the children finding it difficult to voice their true feelings. Women also considered CAFCASS and the courts to be narrowly focused on the notion of physical harm to children. Certainly, domestic violence as a pattern of coercive control was rarely recognised by legal and court professionals.

Women also had negative experiences with judges; in particular, a woman spoke about the emphasis that had been placed on getting a routine for the child without any reference to the domestic violence and continuing post-separation violnce and control: 'It was all about me. I wasn't listened to and I couldn't say anything because I felt too intimidated'.

Playing the 'devoted dad' – 'it's about getting one up on women'

In direct contrast to their fathering while in the relationship, men constructed a very different role when dealing with professionals around child contact, portraying themselves as the 'devoted dad', so that 'he just plays games' was a typical statement made. At the same time, their conduct with women continued to be abusive, albeit verbally and mentally. It was evident that many men spent limited or no time with children during contact outside of contact centres, instead leaving grandparents to take care of them. Indeed, some men pursued contact at the insistence of their parents or to show women they had power over them:

> He took no interest in him at all so why is he interested now? His mum loves my son so he wants to get him for her, and also away from me.

Workers supporting women through the contact process also commented on the tendency of professionals to label women as obstructive or 'implacably hostile', rather than focusing on men's violence or parenting. So while women were 'expected to jump through many hoops, all men have to do is turn up for contact visits' to prove their commitment to their children. The idea of the 'invisible man' and 'responsible woman' has been shown to be powerful in the professional responses to women in situations of domestic violence (Baynes 2009). In this way, women are often endowed responsibility for controlling male violence. One study shows that when agreements were breached by men, these were seen to be breached by women (Baynes 2009). This is also an aspect of the 'absent presence' mentioned earlier. In the absence of any observation of what happened during contact, especially where informal and/or unsupervised, women's accounts were often doubted. In the words of a support worker:

> We are talking about violent and abusive men who have been given lots of chances to change by women before they leave. How can you put all that to one side and see him as a good father and then think you are looking after the welfare of the child?

Indeed, it was apparent from women's accounts that there were few connections made by professionals between male violence and male parenting, which was rarely assessed; rather, an emphasis was placed on women's 'failure to protect'. Thus, despite being violent, men's potential for being good fathers was repeatedly emphasised, and where women highlighted men's indifference and lack of interest towards children, some had been sent on parenting courses. Women's narratives provide clear evidence that an assessment of male parenting where there is domestic violence needs to be prioritised. In particular, the importance of holding men accountable for their violence and its effects on women and children before their parenting can even be considered has been emphasised by many (Eriksson and Hester 2001).

Conclusion

Research shows that despite domestic violence receiving greater emphasis in family courts, 'difficulties have remained for family courts in eliciting information about assessing the impact of domestic violence on parents and children and, consequently, in making appropriate arrangements' (Aris and Harrison 2007, p.i). Building evidence of domestic violence, and especially securing corroborative evidence, is an important aspect of the legal process around child contact, but something beset by huge problems (Humphreys and Harrison 2003). Despite experiencing quite severe abuse over long periods of time, South Asian women rarely reported this to the police or other agencies, making it hard to prove. Even where finding of fact hearings took place, unless women were supported by domestic violence services, they were often daunted by court and intimidated when giving evidence, especially through interpreters, which further served to disadvantage them. Thus, initial barriers experienced in help-seeking acted as further barriers in the court process for South Asian women.

This chapter demonstrates the ways in which state patriarchy, where an emphasis on the presumption of contact supersedes concerns for women's safety, converges with racism and patriarchal control within South Asian communities, to produce a particular experience of child contact and post-separation violence for South Asian women and children. While the importance of linking all women's experiences is recognised, this chapter has given centrality to the power and control dynamics inherent in child contact and post-separation violence processes for South Asian women and children, both in relation to their partners and family members and professionals and state agencies. In particular, the discussion has explored the links between post-separation violence and child contact and argued that child contact is a key site for the continuation of control and abuse of women and children by men and their families. Indeed, for women, threats of separation from their children formed a constant thread in both domestic violence and post-separation violence contexts. Although it has not been the intention of this chapter to essentialise Asian fathers, the complex issues around fathering before and after separation have been highlighted to show how abusive men use their role as fathers as part of the continuing abuse, especially in constructing themselves as 'devoted dads' within the legal process. Research has shown that children are often used as a weapon against mothers, with the effects of their behaviour on children being disregarded or minimised by perpetrators. The complex interplay of personal, family, community and societal dynamics which result in a par-ticular experience of abuse for South Asian women and children, some-thing inadequately understood and responded to by professionals and agencies, has also been highlighted. Moreover, the presumption of contact within family law and an emphasis on the rights of children to see both parents, bolstered by concerns about the social ills resulting from the absence of this, further serve to make the path to an abuse free life complex and difficult for many South Asian women and children.

In being able to negotiate the child contact process, being supported by specialist domestic violence services made a big difference to South Asian women and children; where this support was in place women were more informed about the process, considered they were taken more seri-ously by other professionals, had access to supportive solicitors from an earlier stage and generally felt more confident dealing with the issue, though this did not always lessen their fears about being separated from children. Women wanted more advice around child contact and the legal process as it was thought that 'our circumstances are very very different'; and that greater support was needed in such complex situations, inadequately understood by many professionals.

Finally, while women recognised the importance of children having contact with their fathers, they wanted this to happen in a way that was fair to them and their children and undertaken in supervised settings:

> They should have supervised contact in a centre and not outside. His dad does nothing constructive when he goes outside, he only does this to get back at me and show me he can still stop me from living my life.

Acknowledgements

I would like to thank Satinder Panesar for her insights and time during our numerous conversations about these issues.

Notes

1. While the development of case law, a growing research base and four Court of Appeal cases (Sturge and Glaser 2000) led to new guidelines for contact in the context of domestic violence, they have been only partly successful in challenging the disconnection between domestic violence and post-separation child contact. A pro-contact stance, still pervasive, is entrenched in the divorce literature, case law and the Children Act 1989, though the latter was amended by the Adoption and Children Act 2002, which extended the definition of significant harm and made room for an acknowledgement of domestic violence (see Humphreys and Harrison 2003). Since 2004 greater emphasis has been placed on domestic violence in family courts and a more structured referral and assessment process been recommended for contact centres; the C1A form, introduced into family court proceedings in January 2005, aims to improve safety by gathering information early in the court process related to allegation of domestic abuse, risk abduction, and other concerns about harm to children. Its completion is required for all applications under Section 8 of the Children Act 1989 relating to residence, contact, and parental responsibility where there are issues of domestic abuse, violence or harm. An evaluation of this shows that though limited, the C1A form has enabled the issue of domestic violence to be more visible in court processes and among judges, CAFCASS officers, and legal professionals (see Aris and Harrison 2007).

2. A study funded by the National Society for the Prevention of Cruelty to Children (NSPCC) is currently being undertaken on this by the editors of this book.

3. Some research has reported that many Asian women commit or attempt to commit suicide rather than seek help when experiencing domestic violence – among the reasons given by survivors for attempting suicide or self-harm were sexual and physical abuse, domestic violence, forced marriages, immigration issues and racism (Chantler *et al.* 2001, p.93). Some research in the UK shows elevated rates of

self-harm, particularly among Asian women under 30 (Merril and Owens 1986; Yazdani 1998; Soni-Raleigh 1996). A study by Bhugra *et al.*, drawn from an Accident and Emergency unit in West London, showed that young Asian women under 30 had rates of self-harm 2.5 times those of white women and 7 times those of Asian men.

4.   For a study focused on economic abuse, see N. Sharp (2008) *'What's Yours is Mine': The Different Forms of Economic Abuse and its Impact on Women and Children Experiencing Domestic Violence*. London: Refuge.

References

Abrahams, C. (1994) *The Hidden Victims: Children and Domestic Violence*. London: NCH Action for Children.

Anitha, S. (2008) *Forgotten Women: Domestic Violence, Poverty and South Asian Women with No Recourse to Public Funds*. Manchester: Oxfam Publishing.

Aris, R. and Harrison, C. (2007) *Domestic Violence and the Supplemental Information Form C1A*. December, Series 17/07, 1–68. London: Ministry of Justice.

Aris, R., Harrison, C. and Humphreys, C. (2002) *Safety and Child Contact: An Analysis of Child Contact Centres in the Context of Domestic Violence and Child Welfare Concerns*. London: Lord Chancellor's Department.

Baynes, P. (2009) 'Social Work with Violence Men: What Has Changed?' Presentation at What Do Children Need? Working with Families Involved with the Family Court, CAFCASS Research Conference, Birmingham, 27 February.

Bhugra, D., Desia, M. and Baldwin, D. (1999) 'Attempted suicide in West London, rates across ethnic communities.' *Psychological Medicine 29*, 1125–1130.

Cascardi, M., O'Leary, K.D. and Schlee, K. (1999) 'Co-occurrence and correlates of post-traumatic stress disorder and major depression in physically abused women.' *Journal of Family Violence 14*, 227–49.

Chantler, K. Burnman, E., Batsleer, J. and Bashir, C. (2001) *Attempted Suicide and Self Harm – South Asian Women*. Manchester: Women's Studies Research Centre, Manchester Metropolitan University.

Eriksson, M. and Hester, M. (2001) 'Violent men as good-enough fathers? A look at England and Sweden.' *Violence Against Women 7*, 7, 779–98.

Gill, A. (2004) 'Voicing the silent fear: South Asian women's experiences of domestic violence.' *Howard Journal of Criminal Justice 43*, 5, 465–83.

Harrison, C. (2006) 'Damned If You Do and Damned If You Don't? The Contradictions Between Private and Public Law.' In C. Humphreys and N. Stanley (eds) *Domestic Violence and Child Protection: Directions for Good Practice*. London: Jessica Kingsley Publishers.

Hearn, J. (1998) *The Violences of Men*. London: Sage.

Hester, M. and Radford, L. (1996) *Domestic Violence and Child Contact Arrangements in England and Denmark*. Bristol: Policy Press.

Humphreys, C. (2006) 'Relevant Evidence for Practice.' In C. Humphreys and N. Stanley (eds) *Domestic Violence and Child Protection. Directions for Good Practice*. London: Jessica Kingsley Publishers.

Humphreys, C. (2008) 'Responding to the individual trauma of domestic violence: challenges for mental health professionals.' *Social Work in Mental Health 7*, 1–3, 186–203.

Humphreys, C. and Harrison, C. (2003) 'Focusing on safety: domestic violence and the role of child contact centres.' *Child and Family Law Quarterly 15*, 3, 237–53.

Humphreys, C. and Thiara, R.K. (2002) *Routes to Safety: Protection Issues Facing Abused Women and Children and the Role of Outreach Services.* Bristol: Women's Aid Publications.

Humphreys, C. and Thiara, R.K. (2003) 'Neither justice nor protection: Women's experiences of post-separation violence.' *Journal of Social Welfare and Family Law 25*, 3, 195–214.

Humphreys, C., Mullender, A., Thiara, R.K., Skamballis, A. (2006) '"Talking to My Mum": Developing communication between mothers and children in the aftermath of domestic violence.' *Journal of Social Work 6*, 53–63.

Imam, U. and Akhtar, P. (2005) 'Researching Asian Children's Experiences of Domestic Violence: The Significance of Cultural Competence and Shared Ethnicities of Participants in the Research Process.' In T. Skinner, M. Hester and E. Malos (eds) *Researching Gender Violence: Feminist Methodology in Action.* Uffculme, Devon, UK: Willan.

Izzidien, S. (2008) *'I can't tell people what is happening at home': Domestic Abuse within South Asian Communities – The Specific Needs of Women, Children and Young People.* London: NSPCC.

Johnson, M. and Ferraro, K. (2000) 'Research on domestic violence in the 1990s: Making distinctions.' *Journal of Marriage and the Family 4*, 948–63.

Kelly, L. (1994) 'The Interconnectedness of Domestic Violence and Child Abuse: Identification and Prevention.' In A. Mullender and R. Morley (eds) *Children Living with Domestic Violence.* London: Whiting & Birch.

Merrill, J. and Owens, J. (1986) 'Ethnic differences in self-poisoning: A comparison of Asian and white groups.' *British Journal of Psychiatry 148*, 708–712.

Minhas, N., Hollows, A., Kerr, Y.S. and Ibbotson, R. (2002) *South Asian Women's Experiences of Domestic Violence: Pillar of Support.* Sheffield: Survey and Statistical Research Centre.

Mullender, A. and Morley, R. (eds) (1994) *Children Living with Domestic Violence.* London: Whiting & Birch.

Mullender, A., Hague, G., Imam, U., Kelly, L., Malos, E. and Regan, L. (2002) *Children's Perspectives on Domestic Violence.* London: Sage.

Parmar, A., Sampson, A., and Diamond, A. (2005) *Tackling Domestic Violence: Providing Advocacy and Support to Survivors from Black and Other Minority Ethnic Communities.* Development and Practice Report 35. London: Home Office.

Prevatt Goldstein, B. (2009) 'Why we should listen: Good practice with black minority ethnic families.' Presentation at What Do Children Need? Working with Families Involved with the Family Court. CAFCASS Research Conference, Birmingham, 27 February.

Radford, L. and Hester, M. (2006) *Mothering Through Domestic Violence.* London: Jessica Kingsley Publishers.

Rai, D. and Thiara, R.K. (1996) *Redefining Spaces: The Needs of Black Women and Children and Black Workers in Women's Aid.* Bristol: Women's Aid Federation England.

Saunders, H. (2004) *Twenty-Nine Child Homicides: Lessons Still to be Learnt on Domestic Violence and Child Protection.* Bristol: Women's Aid Federation England.

Saunders, H. and Barron, J. (2003) *Failure to Protect?* Bristol: Women's Aid Federation England.

Sen, P. (1997) *Searching for Routes to Safety.* London: London Borough of Camden Equalities Unit.

Sharp, N. (2008) *'What's yours is mine': The Different Forms of Economic Abuse and its Impact on Women and Children Experiencing Domestic Violence.* London: Refuge.

Soni-Raleigh, V. (1996) 'Suicide patterns and trends in people of Indian subcontinent and Caribbean origin in England and Wales.' *Ethnicity and Health 1*, 55–63.

Sturge, C. and Glaser, D. (2000) 'Contact and domestic violence: The experts' court report.' *Family Law 30*, September, 615–29.

Thiara, R.K. (2005) *The Need for Specialist Domestic Violence Servcies for Asian Women and Children.* London: Imkaan.

Thiara, R.K. and Breslin, R. (2006) 'Black and minority ethnic children and domestic violence.' *Community Care*, November, 32–33.

Thiara, R.K., Humphreys, C., Skamballis, A. and Mullender, A. (2006) *Talking to My Mum: Developing Communication between Mothers and their Children in the Aftermath of Domestic Violence.* Report of Key Findings. Warwick, UK: Centre for the Study of Safety and Well-being, University of Warwick.

Yazdani, A. (1998) *Young Asian women and self-harm: Mental health needs assessment of young Asian women in Newham.* London: Newham Innercity Multifund and Newham Asian Women's Project.

Chapter 7

Shariah Councils and the Resolution of Matrimonial Disputes

Gender and Justice in the 'Shadow' of the Law

Samia Bano

In 2007, a report, entitled *Living Apart Together: British Muslims and the Paradox of Multiculturalism,*[1] suggests that 37 per cent of all British Muslims are in favour of being governed by some form of shariah law. Although the methodological framework of this report has been heavily criticised, especially for the authors' presumption that the findings accurately reflect the views of all Muslims in Britain, this statistic does raise interesting questions regarding the relations between Muslims, law, religious legal practice and – perhaps most importantly – loyalty to the state. Indeed, the institution of religious, person-oriented legal systems within Western democratic societies constitutes a new and important stage in the establishment of Muslims in the West; one which not only reflects the extent of their presence and settlement in the UK, but also builds upon the multicultural policies of integration and adaptation designed to accommodate cultural and religious difference in Britain. And one of the most important issues confronting social and legal policy making in the UK today is determining the extent to which the law should accommodate cultural and religious pluralism as part of the wider multicultural project of settlement. The outcry in the media provoked by a speech by the Archbishop of Canterbury Dr

Rowan Williams on legal and cultural diversity in England in February 2008 only lends weight to the argument that, in essence, Islam cannot be reconciled with the central features of Western democracy and modernity – features such as pluralism, secularism, democracy, civil social structure, religious tolerance and gender equality.

According to this line of current social and political thinking, then, the relationship between Islam and the West has become ever-more characterised by ideological differences, practical incompatibilities and – above all – the perceived inability of Muslims to relinquish fundamentalism 'and to fully embrace the Western ideals of progress, modernity and globalization' (Sayyid 2000, p.32). Indeed, the terrorist attacks in New York on 11 September 2001, London on 7 July 2005 and Madrid in March 2005, coupled with the current conflicts in Afghanistan (2001–) and Iraq (2003–) have only further served to increase this binary opposition between Islam and the West, and to confirm, for some at least, the view that what we are witnessing nowadays is in essence a 'clash of civilizations' (Huntington 1996, p.3). And for Muslims in the West, the state-inspired 'war on terror' and the new emergence of the supposed 'home-grown Muslim terrorist' has further compounded this binary opposition, which identifies Western Muslims as 'Other': in conflict with, incompatible with and disloyal to the state.

Interestingly, the issue of gender is central to these debates, because one of the salient features that defines Islam's incompatibility with Western ideas is its supposed ill-treatment of women. From a liberal perspective, Muslim women are often presented as dominated, controlled and subordinate to archaic religious traditions and, within this discourse, it is the gendered construction of the Muslim family that is perceived to be the barrier that denies Muslim women access to the rights, equality and degree of empowerment bestowed upon other women in the West (Nussbaum 1999; Okin 1999). Conspicuously absent from these debates, however, are the voices of Muslim women themselves, and, in particular, those of Muslim women living in the West. This is surprising if we bear in mind the great diversity that exists among the generations of British Muslims, Muslims who form local, national and transnational networks and communities which in themselves generate immense differences (Werbner 2000).

It is the purpose of this chapter, then, to explore this lacuna in our understanding by focusing on the elided voices of Muslim women, and in particular to illuminate the diversity of the experiences of one specific but heterogeneous group of British Muslim women – those who choose to resolve matrimonial disputes via the community mechanisms of the Shariah Councils. Underlying this analysis is an exploration of their motivations, driven by a desire to better understand *why* these women choose to resolve matrimonial disputes within such 'privatised' forms of dispute resolution. These women present a very contrary profile to the one suggested by contemporary multicultural discourse: far from submitting passively to patriarchal systems of law, they actively draw upon it as agents, and so theirs are voices that must be heard if we are to understand the complexity of modern Muslim culture.

In trying to understand these 'new' forms of social, cultural and religious developments in resolving matrimonial disputes, I draw upon feminist critiques of community rights, multiculturalism and justice, to challenge the current representation of Muslim culture as homogenous, and also to challenge the perceived marginality of Muslim women in their interaction with these bodies. I question whether the use of Shariah Councils has indeed led to forms of (in)justice for Muslim women? If so what is the nature of this injustice? I seek to better understand the relationship between women's identity, religious law and possible conflicts with community membership and belonging. In so doing, I critique liberal feminist notions of gender equality, autonomy and choice, which constructs Muslim women's agency in rather categorical terms – seeing it as a binary opposition between 'free will' or 'force' – and which constructs the desire of Muslim women to use religious bodies to resolve matrimonial disputes as a form of 'social coercion' and 'false consciousness'. I argue that a recognition of the emergence of multiple and conflicting, socio-legal and political processes can challenge the binary opposites of state law versus religious law, integration versus separation and Muslim versus non-Muslim. It can also bring to the fore the awareness that Muslim women's identities are complex, diverse and contested. The recognition of 'multiple affiliations' of law and identity or belongings transforms the debate from one based upon conflicts between public commitments and private allegiance (the classic public/private divide) to one which illustrates how categories of law and non-law (secular and religious sources of law) and public versus private as fixed constructs that are conceptually inadequate to capture the diverse experiences of Muslim women using privatised mechanisms of dispute resolution to resolve matrimonial disputes. However, and it is important to stress that 'multiplicity' and multiple affiliations also remain conceptually inadequate in themselves when addressing questions of gender equality, agency, power and community regulation. As Shachar (2008) points out,

> these overlapping 'belongings' offer religious women a significant source of meaning and value; at the same time, they may also make them vulnerable to a double or triple disadvantage, especially in a legal and governance system that categorically denies cooperation between their overlapping sources of obligation. (Schachar 2008, p.576)

So what do Muslim women gain from using these bodies to resolve matrimonial disputes? What (if anything) do they lose and how can we move away from understanding Muslim women's agency in terms of social coercion versus false consciousness? Is this process of dispute resolution justice in the shadow of law?[2]

What is Muslim family law?

It is useful to begin with a brief overview of what we understand as *Muslim family law* and consider how it operates (as an institutionalised authority comprising of Muslim scholars) within the British Muslim diaspora. Muslim family law, like other South Asian religious and customary corpuses of law, defines the position of women in relation to marriage, divorce, child custody, dowry and inheritance (Ali 2000; Nasir 1990). In the case of Islam, Muslim family law is subject to interpretation by different religious leaders and communities. There is no single comprehensive Islamic legal system; instead, varieties exist and are demarcated according to ethnic or religious backgrounds; for example, the Islamic personal laws which exist in the Indian subcontinent vary greatly in comparison with those in Iran or Iraq. There are two main Muslim groups in Britain, Sunni and Shi'a Muslims, and the practice of Islam within these groups varies according to the different shariah schools of thought. There are also many class and sectarian divisions within these main groups, however, which operate according to different Islamic codes of laws: for example, Ismaili Muslims are part of the wider Shi'a group, but follow distinct laws applicable only to them. It is therefore difficult to speak of 'Muslim family law' in Britain when it varies so widely according to ethnic and sectarian affiliation. Nielsen (1991, p.470) for instance, notes that the discussion of Islamic family law in Britain in Muslim magazines centres on the *ethics* of the subject, rather than on the law itself. This means that it is not general principles that are under discussion: debate is focused instead on human relations. According to one interpretation, then, custom is dependent on place, time and circumstance, whereas others regard the role of religious leaders as crucial in defining current shariah practice. And Muslim feminists argue that there is a fundamental tension in Islam between its ethical or spiritual vision of sexual equality and the unequal hierarchies contained in family laws, as instituted in early Islamic society and perpetuated over time by those holding power (Ahmed 1992; Mernissi 1992).

Existing literature presents the socio-legal reality of Muslims as a complex situation, whereby official and customary laws intersect to produce a new set of hybrid laws (Bunt 1998; Carroll 1997; Pearl and Menski 1998; Poulter 1996; Shah-Kazemi 2001; Yilmaz 2002). It is through his attempts to develop a conceptual framework which embraces a 'postmodern approach' to the study of law and also recognises the pluralism and diversity in social life that Menski (1993) constructs the legal model that he terms 'Angrezi Sharia', employing the analytical framework instituted by the jurist Masaji Chiba (1986) to do so. According to Menski (1993), Asian Muslims in Britain have not simply given up Islamic law, but have combined Islamic law and English law to form 'Angrezi Sharia'. However, Menski's approach is constrained by an oversimplified and unqualified understanding of culture, religion, identity and community – one which fails to adequately engage with the multiple positions that individuals – and particularly women – occupy in relation to race, ethnicity, class, family and community (Anthias and Yuval-Davis 1992). Indeed, this approach sets Western culture against 'other cultures' (principally Islamic culture and its supposed subordination of Muslim women) and loses sight of the fact that women are social agents and so 'occupy positions in other categories of difference and location' (Anthias 2002, p.276). Furthermore, promoting a Western framework as the model of 'human rights', and the only system that can provide Muslim women with access to equality, justice and autonomy is also problematic. We should not lose sight of the fact that Muslim feminists and scholars are currently engaged in exploring the relationship between human rights, Islam and gender equality from an Islamic perspective, some of which renders such simplistic analyses virtually meaningless in relation to the complex lived realities of Muslim women's lives (see Ali 2002; An-Nai'm 2002; Mayer 1999; Mirza 2007).

Western legal scholars have long recognised the existence of different and varied social and legal orders, operating within any given 'social field'. Drawing upon social and legal theories of the nineteenth and early twentieth centuries legal pluralists challenged the centrality of state law as the single source of overarching power and authority. Moving away from viewing law as fixed, quantifiable and scientific, to a more empirical-based analysis and based upon anthropological research, these scholars highlight the social fact that state law can only be understood as one form of legal regulation which operates in any given social field and in reality there are many multiple and alternative forms of legal regulation that often the state simply has little or no knowledge of. Griffiths (2001, p.289) points out that, 'whatever the focus, legal pluralism raises important questions about power – where it is located, how it is constituted, what forms it takes – in ways that promotes a more finely tuned and sophisticated analysis of continuity, transformation and change in society'. In Britain, this critique of legal positivism also reveals a tension between the norms and values that underpin English law and the challenges it may face from the cultural and religious pluralism of multicultural Britain. Thus one theoretical challenge to the concept of law comes from 're-evaluating the concept of law in a culturally diverse, plural society' (Shah 2005, p.1). This approach draws upon a postmodern conception of the law in order to explore the relationship between cultural diversity, legal pluralism and the state response to conflicts generated by settled diasporic communities who wish to maintain their cultural and religious norms and values, a wish that can produce conflicts with official state law rules and norms. The approach summarised by Shah (2005) conceptualises contemporary legal conflict as a clash between diverse systems of law, both formal and informal, and it draws upon the origins and migration patterns of specific ethnic minority communities in Britain in order to demonstrate how conflict arises. In particular, the family and wider kin group are presented as the two key sites upon which such legal conflicts are based. As Shah (2005) argues,

> family and wider kin groups are the primary location of self-regulation, which also gives rise to conflict and negotiation in the wider British social order. Since Asian and African laws emphasise self-regulated societies rather than positivist top-down regulation, as the British state law does, there is a fundamental clash of basic values. (Shah 2005, p.19)

Shah's (2005) critical reassessment not only challenges the ontological premises on which formalist definitions of law are based, but also in so doing it reframes the discourse about the settlement patterns of dispersed communities living in the West. More recently still, discussion has centred on the relationship between law and religious identity and the move from individual notions of identity towards a communitarian notion of identity (along with its potential for undermining the legal principles of 'equality before the law' and 'common citizenship'. These issues are discussed in more depth later in this chapter, but the point here is that the shift in the terms of the debate provides us with new understandings of the relationship between pluralism, multiculturalism and legal pluralism, all of which coexist and are manifest in modern Britain.

However, this body of literature is still to some extent limiting. It pays little attention to the relationship between law and power, and in this context pluralism remains dependant upon reified definitions of cultural norms and values, as well as upon religious practice. Consequently, the problematic interaction between state law and cultural and religious customs posits that commitment and loyalty to a community are based upon immutable markers of religious and cultural difference. There is thus an underlying assumption that the spaces inhabited by diasporic communities are based upon, and can be identified by, fixed and discrete notions of culture and religious practice, which, in essence, thus define the communities as a whole. I would argue, however, that – as with the pluralism of legal diversity – cultural diversity and identity must also be understood as historically fragmented, unstable and contradictory; in Britain, this situation is well illustrated by the heterogeneity of Muslim communities and the multiplicity of meanings of Islam and Islamic jurisprudence and practice. Yet, current scholarship continues to posit Islam as being in direct, fixed opposition to Western values, especially in terms of human rights, and the scholarship pays insufficient attention to the fact that 'religious communities are internally contested, heterogeneous, and constantly evolving over time through internal debate and interaction with outsiders' (Sunder 2005, p.1403).

In Britain, Shariah Councils operate as unofficial legal bodies that specialise in providing advice and assistance to Muslim communities on Muslim family law matters. They are not unified, nor do they represent a single school of thought, but instead they are made up of various different bodies that represent the different schools of thought in Islam.[3] Many Shariah Councils are closely affiliated to mosques, and this reflects developments in Islamic religious practice in Britain. In his study of Muslims in Bradford, for instance, Lewis (1996, p.56) argues that the socio-political establishment of Muslims in Britain via mosques and community organisations such as Shariah Councils indicates a shift 'within the migrants' self-perception from being sojourners to settlers'. Indeed there has been much academic discussion taking place within minority ethnic communities, which has contributed to our understanding of citizenship, identity and national belonging.[4]

In essence, a Shariah Council has three main functions: issuing Muslim divorce certificates; reconciling and mediating between parties, and producing expert reports on matters of Muslim family law and custom for the Muslim community, solicitors and the courts. It is also significant that, in addition to providing advice and assistance on matters of Muslim family law, Shariah Councils have also been set up to promote and preserve Islam within British society (Bunt 1998), represent the socio-legal reality of Muslim communities in Britain in terms of a complex scenario of state-instituted and personal laws (and so challenge the supposed uniformity of state law, i.e. as something superior, monolithic and homogeneous), and draw upon postmodern analyses of law and legal relations that highlight 'a diversity of laws'.

Multiculturalism and community autonomy

In Britain, Muslim family law is seen as a personal law, because there have been some voices within the Muslim community in the UK demanding that a 'personal regime of law' be adopted for the Muslim community as a whole, within the area of family law. The controversy sparked by the lecture given by the Archbishop of Canterbury Dr Rowan Williams entitled 'Civil and Religious Law in England: A Religious Perspective' to the Royal Courts of Justice on 7 February 2008 reflects the viewpoint that multiculturalism promotes civic and social responsibilities from all citizens.[5] Dr Williams argued that the legal system in Britain needed to engage constructively with the religious concerns and motivations of members of the diverse communities which make up contemporary British society.

The objectification of Muslims and Islam as the 'dangerous Other' in contemporary Western democratic societies is neither new nor in the current political context particularly unsurprising.[6] Indeed the ideological underpinning of a clash of civilisations discourse now dominates a significant proportion of social and political thinking and academic analyses.[7] Perhaps nothing, however, expresses this renewed hysteria on the dangers presented by Muslims living in the West than the response to the lecture delivered by the Archbishop of Canterbury. With headlines and media commentary warning of Islam threatening the very basis upon which Western civilisation is based and shaping the perception that it is incumbent upon the enlightened modern West to see off this traditional pre-modern challenge, it is not (I would argue) an exaggeration to describe this episode as a modern day 'moral panic' directed against Islam, Muslims and in this case the archbishop himself.

In Britain there have been demands by some Muslim leaders for the establishment of religious personal law systems in Britain and to establish a single Shariah Council with state recognition to legitimise the group's autonomy in matters of family law. Undoubtedly the growth of these demands attests to increasing attempts by some individuals and groups to unify the 'Muslim community'. In this context communal autonomy takes the form of decision-making power, which maintains the group's membership boundaries vis-à-vis the larger society. This project seeks to preserve Muslim identity and it is the unique position of women within these groups as 'cultural conduits' that gives rise to the problem of gender-biased norms and practices which often subordinate women.

Such discussions primarily focus on the relationship between the family and the state and this raises questions of whether there is 'an irreducible core of family values to which everyone could subscribe' or whether English family law has the 'scope for accommodating a plurality of views about the family and family lifestyles' (Bainham 1995, p.234). More recently, the issue has moved to one of 'rights' and 'participatory democracy'. In fact the relationship between 'family' and liberal political theory has focused on the family threatening 'citizenship' and loyalty to the state. It is deemed to undermine democracy with its emphasis on loyalty to family networks, rather than the state. Kurczewski (1997) explains:

> Family, in the theory of liberal democratic politics, threatens the freedom and purity of individual judgment and decision. Under the influence of family, the citizen instead of voting according to his or her beliefs may vote for those whom he or she finds personally unworthy. Even worse,

the family presupposes a bond that rivals the bonds of interests or communality of beliefs. (Kurczewski 1997, p.24)

This raises two key questions: first, to what extent is the law committed to multiculturalism in the family context? And second, should alternative dispute resolution mechanisms such as Shariah Councils be formally recognised in English law as forums where disputing couples can resolve matrimonial disputes?

The nature and practice of multiculturalism in Britain has been extensively documented and critiqued (Anthias and Yuval-Davis 1992; Gilroy 1987; Hall 1996). These critiques have focused on the tensions between a definition of citizenship based upon liberal notions of universality and equality and one based upon the reality of a fragmentation of identities which has led to 'demands' for recognition from various groups based upon their ethnic and/or religious specificity. In particular, a critical reading of citizenship allows us to question whether a multicultural definition of citizenship undermines the liberal principles of autonomy, choice and free will for women within minority communities. This latter subject actually raises a number of important conceptual and theoretical questions about the relationship between individual and group rights, especially as to how these are to be distinguished and how clashes between them can be reconciled. At heart this raises a key question: what makes a community a community of rights? In granting individuals the right to enjoy their own culture, does the state have an obligation to foster that culture and ensure its survival? O'Donovan (1985, p.181) argues that this liberal public/private distinction is crucial to understanding the subordination of women, a subject which liberal political theory fails to investigate (cited in Phillips 2005). This distinction consigns women to the private sphere, an area of greater legal 'deregulation'; 'central to liberalism is the concept of privacy as a sphere of behaviour free from public interference, that is, unregulated by law' (O'Donovan 1985, p.181).

This also raises questions about what we mean by the term 'community'. Communities nest within one another: communities are local, national and global. They also intersect: British Muslims belong to the global Muslim *Umma*, for example. Some individuals may regard a cultural or religious practice as a 'right'; other members of the same community may see it as a means of oppression. A particular cause for concern among liberal feminist theorists has been whether the practice of recognising personal laws within the family context leads to the unequal treatment of women within these communities. Consequently, ideas about gender equality, justice and the limits of liberal multiculturalism have begun, since the 1990s, to emerge from within the disciplines of political theory, ethics and philosophy and in the context of tensions between feminism and multiculturalism. Of particular concern is the extent to which the liberal state should recognise and accommodate differences based upon cultural and religious values, or rather adhere to a single set of norms and values that apply to all citizens equally (Okin, 1999). Shachar (2001, p.6) refers to this as the 'paradox of multicultural vulnerability', 'which arises when an identity group members rights as a citizen are violated by her identity group's family law practices'. Thus, recent scholarship on the relationship between feminism and multiculturalism explores the tensions between state recognition of cultural and religious practices and the liberal pursuit of justice and equality for all female citizens. Reitman (2005) employs the term 'minority patriarchy', which she defines as

> the collective category of individual or tangible practices producing patriarchal forms of regulation which arise out of a minority's distinct set of norms or codes, submission to which is considered defining in some significant way of group membership or as a marker of identity. (Reitman 2005, p.216)

However, as Yuval-Davis (1997, p.10) points out, within these debates the notion of 'the community' is presented as having an organic wholeness and naturalness – it is something deemed to be 'out there' and to which you either belong or do not belong. This construction of 'community' has led to the designating of community leaders as representatives of the interests of 'the community' as a whole. The term 'multicultural citizenship' then becomes problematic, because it defines all cultural groups as homogeneous and operating around fixed categories, and does not take into account issues of control, power and conflict arising from conflicts of interest within those groups. Instead of this cultural homogeneity, we must view citizenship as a 'multi-tier construct' that operates in a number of different ways.

More recently, debates on the limits of the 'multicultural citizenship' have been located within the discourse of rights, and in particular on the conflict between individual and community rights. According to liberal political theory, the principles of individual choice, personal freedom and religious tolerance are grounded in the notion of individual rights. Within the liberal tradition, therefore, group rights are viewed with suspicion and seen as inherently dangerous and oppressive, particularly if they fail to acknowledge conflict and diversity within the group. More recently, however, liberals have begun to argue that group interests might in fact be accommodated within the framework of individual rights (Kymlicka 1995; Taylor 1999). The construction of a community also involves the construction of boundaries, which in turn initiates processes of exclusion as well as inclusion. The development of the individual thus becomes dependent upon the community, but this simple equation fails to recognise that individual and group rights may diverge. The issue is, therefore, how a theory of cultural minority group rights can include the recognition of difference, including gendered difference, within groups. As Van Dyke (1995, p.234) points out, the principle of recognition may open a Pandora's Box 'from which all sorts of groupings might spring, demanding rights'.

In matters of family law, the primary function of a Shariah Council is to issue Muslim women with divorce certificates in cases where their husbands fail to unilaterally divorce them.[8] Under Muslim law, and in accordance with the injunctions found in the Qur'an and in Hadith literature, a divorce can be obtained in a number of different ways: *talaq* (unilateral repudiation by the husband), *khul* (divorce instigated by the wife with her husband's agreement, and on condition that she will forgo her right to the dowry or *mehr*) and *ubara'at* (divorce by mutual consent).[9] Under any of these circumstances, a Muslim woman may contact a Shariah Council to obtain a Muslim divorce certificate. Notwithstanding the diversity of literature on Muslim divorce, however, legal scholars still point to a number of key points of conflict with English divorce law. In England, all marriages ending in divorce must be dissolved according to English divorce laws, particularly the laws contained in the provisions of the Matrimonial Causes Act 1973. Whether or not religious marriages are recognised by these laws is a complex issue, and depends upon where the marriage took place and where the parties involved are domiciled. The situation is rendered more complex by the fact that Islam permits unilateral divorce instigated by the husband, which means that even if the marriage has been registered annulled,[10] according to English law, then the female applicant remains married under Islamic law even after the divorce has gone through. Marriages affected in this way have been described by Pearl and Menski (1998, p.34) as 'limping marriages', where a civil divorce has been obtained by the woman, but her husband refuses to grant her a Muslim divorce. Yilmaz (2005, p.112) points out that if the woman is not religiously divorced from her husband, it does not matter that she is divorced under the civil law; in the eyes of the community her remarriage will be regarded as adulterous and any possible offspring will be illegitimate since it is not allowed under the religious law. So, in reality, until the religious divorce is obtained, the civil divorce remains ineffective because one party is unable to remarry.

The second function of the Shariah Councils in relation to marriage concerns the type of Muslim divorce they grant to the women, and this raises the question of fairness. For example, a *khul* can be granted only if the female applicant gives up her right to the dowry (*mehr*) in return for the divorce, and this can result in an unfair outcome for Muslim women.[11] As we can see, then, divorce *is* available to Muslim women under Shariah Council conditions, but this is neither a guaranteed nor even a straightforward matter. And interviews held with religious scholars reveal an uneasy tension between the expectations of Muslim women seeking to obtain a Muslim divorce certificate and the concerns of the religious scholars whose primary objective is usually to 'save' the marriage. Sheikh Abdullah explains:

> As Muslims, we have a duty to live according to the Qu'ran and Sunnah even though we may have chosen to live in non Muslim countries. I think it is incumbent upon us to live up to this responsibility because of the effect of Western influences upon our children and ourselves. It is easy to neglect our duties in this secular environment.

Thus the language of choice, commitment and faith, as described by the religious scholars, fits in neatly with the discourse of belonging (i.e. to a wider Muslim community or *Umma*) and demonstrates the importance attached to the development and formation of a local Muslim community identity. In this way, the community space inhabited by the Shariah Councils is deemed to be the most obvious site in which the long-established practice of Muslim dispute resolution takes place. In this respect, it seems clear that the religious scholars primarily aim to establish their authority in family law matters and require all participants to take the proceedings seriously. While the process of disputation itself reveals striking similarities to the development of family mediation in English family law, most religious scholars would also insist on its distinctiveness to state law as a unique mechanism of dispute resolution specifically directed to the needs of Muslims and providing some form of communal Muslim self-governing. In this way it is conceptualised in terms of the context of *duties* and *responsibilities* that are imbued upon all Muslims to abide by the demands of the Shariah and in turn the rulings of Shariah Councils. It seems that the mutual understanding between these two bodies stems from the belief that the secular space[12] (inhabited by the principles of English family law) cannot bring about a genuine resolution of matrimonial disputes for Muslims living in Britain. The implications of this belief are discussed in the following section, which represents findings of a study on Muslim women's interactions with Shariah Councils in resolving matrimonial disputes.

Negotiating divorce: a case study of Muslim women using Shariah Councils

I now draw upon empirical research with a group of British Pakistani Muslim women to consider whether their experience of using a Shariah Council did generate greater levels of disadvantage and inequality. The emergence of 'extra'-legal systems of law as epitomised by Shariah Councils becomes an important arena to promote civic and social integration but the Shariah Councils' existence can also be deemed a threat to this process. For women these privatised spaces of dispute resolution in matters of family law raise fundamental questions regarding agency, autonomy and whether the principles of 'common citizenship' and 'equality before the law' are undermined.[13]

In their study of Muslim legal pluralism, Pearl and Menski (1998, p.382) point to what they describe as 'the legal de-recognition of Muslim divorces…in the United Kingdom', that is the lack of provisions in English law to deal with the complexity of religious law in matters of divorce. In the current, revised form of English family law there is only one way to obtain a divorce, which is on the grounds that the marriage has irretrievably broken down, and then after a two-year separation, when the decree is made absolute. Muslim divorces granted through a 'non-judicial process' (*talaq*) are therefore generally not recognised as valid in Britain, a situation which has led to the creation of the 'limping marriages' mentioned above. This has led to situations where women divorced through civil procedures continue to be married under Muslim religious law, or where those who have been divorced abroad may not be legally recognised as divorced in the UK and thus continue to be legally married. Consequently, this has led to a conflict between legal systems, and so when husbands refuse to grant a unilateral divorce to their Muslim wives, the women contact a Shariah Council to obtain a Muslim divorce certificate.

Given that the issue of divorce is fraught with difficulties and tensions for women from South Asian Muslim communities, it is unsurprising that the women in this study adopted multiple strategies to negotiate the many obstacles they faced in order to obtain a divorce certificate. These obstacles principally involve negotiations, conflict and decision-making both within the family (immediate and extended family networks) and via the Shariah Councils. How, then, did this sample of women negotiate issues of marriage breakdown and divorce within the family, home and community?

In discussions on the reasons for the breakdown of marriage, multiple reasons included forced marriage, family interference or a 'clash of upbringing', adultery and/or domestic violence. A total of 18 women reported that they had experienced some form of emotional, sexual and/or physical abuse during their marriage, and a small percentage of women continued to face this threat. The reasons for marital breakdown were thus predicated on intra-family inequality, with discussions focusing on issues of power in the family and marriage context, lack of negotiation and continued conflict. In relation to 'family pressure', the women described relationships with their in-laws as being particularly difficult. Those who opposed or challenged their extended family's authority were ostracised, and became alienated from other members of the family. For other women, the control exercised over their physical movements meant they were given very little space to assert their own independence within the family context. In three cases, this led to increased levels of violence. The extracts below provide a brief snapshot of the effects on the women:

> My dad was never on my side; when he found out about the problems he always used to shout at me, saying that I must do everything they tell me to do. He only said that 'cause he was scared that I was going to end up divorced, and he kept saying 'Don't get divorced, don't get divorced'. (Zareena, Bradford)

Perhaps unsurprisingly, there was a close link between the decision to leave a marriage and the extent of a woman's financial independence. Those women who were financially dependent upon their husbands typically remained in the marriage for a longer period of time than those who were not. These findings confirm the work of feminist scholars, who have explored the conditions which facilitate or impede a woman's decision to leave the marriage and household. It is also useful to highlight the fact that those women who were educated to university level mentioned education as being a contributory factor in the breakdown of their marriage. Parveen described how the difficulties in the marriage were compounded by the fact that she was perceived as being too educated, and thus 'too independent':

> I did everything they wanted me to do: I cooked, I cleaned, I looked after them, as well as my husband, but still it was never enough. Just the fact that I'd been to college, that I had an education, was a problem for them. (Parveen, Birmingham)

At the same time, the interviews revealed that the women experienced specific problems relating to 'being too westernised'. Interestingly, these matters transcended class and education differences, and a number of the interviewees were keen to discuss familial expectations placed upon them.

> He started imposing things on me, like you have to wear a scarf and I'm not really comfortable with it, you know, and I told him…well, I'm not really comfortable with it and I don't believe I should do something that someone is making me do – Islam is within myself, I do it because I want to do it. I'm not saying I don't have any intention of it, I will do it, but not just yet and he was more worried about his dad than himself. The impression I got was that he wasn't really that bothered himself, he was more bothered about his family. (Nighat, London)

Prior to their decision to leave, many women embarked upon alternative strategies to save their marriages, such as reconciliation and family mediation. This fact demands that we adopt a more sophisticated approach to the analysis of matrimonial dispute resolution, and provides a clearer understanding of the conditions upon which such dispute resolution is based. As well as arranging the marriage, the family plays a vital role in organising and facilitating attempts to reconcile the parties. Of the sample, 20 women explained that they had been involved in lengthy discussions with their families, designed to reconcile them with their husbands, prior to having any contact with a Shariah Council. Shah-Kazemi (2001) points out that family mediation is of particular significance to minority ethnic communities, and this was confirmed in this study; it would seem that the importance of family intervention is closely linked to whether or not the families arranged the marriage. Arranging of marriages seemingly gives rise to a set of obligations and responsibilities for both parties. It is also clear that the women operate within a gendered environment within this relationship (cf. Griffiths 2005, p.9), and so often occupy less powerful positions in the disputation process:

> The thing with arranged marriages is that when it breaks down you're not really left alone. It's the family that arranges it, so when it breaks down they go into this motion of trying to sort things out. (Shazia, London)

> Yes, I did expect my family to help me, and yeah, I do think it was because I had an arranged marriage. I suppose the way I got married was different to how my English friends get married, and they probably don't expect the kind of help that I got. (Humeira, London)

In their management of the marital disputes, then, the interviewees were required to negotiate a complex and shifting social and legal process, continuing to fulfil the social and cultural expectations placed upon them while simultaneously negotiating the terms of their reconciliation. This demonstrates the dilemmas and conflicts that women's identities – as individuals and as members of the family group – can often generate (cf. Hellum 1999). Some interviewees discussed this:

> Well, initially I told no one, 'cause I didn't want my parents to get involved and then, you know, for things to get worse – the more people that get involved then things can get out of hand. I was a bit scared anyway, because I hadn't been married that long and if I say I've got problems, they'd be really, really worried about it...It was too difficult. I was expected to make it work, so it really had to get bad before I could tell them. (Farhana, Birmingham)

> Well, not my side of the family but his side of the family did get involved. His eldest sister-in-law did give me a lot of support. She said 'this is not right something has to be done', and then she told her husband, and they talked within the family and they told me they did speak to him, but I don't know what was said. (Shaheen, London)

Thus, the dilemma of how to preserve the 'family honour' while pursuing one's own individual choices can limit the decision-making abilities of women within the home and family. The issue of 'leaving' the marriage could never either be easily resolved or uncritically accepted, and some women grappled with the pressures of maintaining the *izzat* of the family (family honour), while others expressed the ambivalence of their feelings.

I couldn't tell my parents straight away, 'cause of the izzat thing. They were always saying that my marriage had kept the izzat of the family, so when things started to go wrong it was difficult for me to explain to them how I was feeling and what I wanted to do about the situation. (Nasima, London)

My parents aren't educated and we're not middle-class... But we're Muslims and they understand right from wrong. I wanted their help to sort things out, and in Islam they have a duty to support me in my time of need. We discussed things together, and only when they came to the conclusion that things wouldn't change did I make up my mind that it was time to go. (Zareena, Bradford)

These findings suggest that some women were able to challenge the notion of family honour, reconceptualise its meaning, reject its impact on their decision to leave and transfer this 'responsibility' to their husbands. In this way, family honour was characterised as an obligation to fulfil social and cultural expectations during the process of marriage. And, in some cases, this shift challenges the validity of the argument that women are reluctant to leave due to concerns about preserving the family honour. Nonetheless, the interview data also revealed the close connection between family intervention and the woman's decision to be reconciled with her spouse. In such cases, the failure of the family to resolve the marital difficulties was then a source of regret to those involved.

Thus, at one level, the women engaged in complex negotiations – both with their parents and with their extended family – were determined either to justify their decision to leave or to establish the grounds upon which a divorce could be sought. And it was at this point that the support provided by other female members of the family was of particular importance to the women; indeed, the extent of this support was a significant factor in their decision on whether or not to leave. The women were often able to create alliances with mothers and sisters, which highlights the importance of the solidarity between them and so challenges the dynamics of patriarchal power otherwise inherent within the family (Bhopal 1999). Notwithstanding the obvious value of these relationships, this 'collective approach' also reveals a number of ambiguities and contradictions, because this form of 'strategic essentialism' is imbued with both possibilities and limitations. It is true that the women were able to gain support and strength from these networks, but in doing so, some women reported a pressure to compromise. For example, even though some were opposed to remarrying, they agreed to accept a new marriage, arranged on their behalf by parents, in exchange for an exit from the present marriage. Thus, what at first seemed like a new space of dialogue and autonomy in the family could, in some cases, still depend upon the traditional framework of power (Anthias 2002).

For some women the impact of family mediation was a distressing experience. Nabila, for instance, complained that her parents had been unwilling to accept that her marriage was over, and her subsequent refusal to accept family mediation was met with stern opposition. This had led to a deterioration of relations with her husband and family, culminating in her parents blaming her for the breakdown of the marriage. Indeed the dynamics of 'family mediation' and the risks it may pose for vulnerable women in the family context has been extensively critiqued by feminist scholars. As Garrity (1998, p.14) questions, 'Is mediation ever appropriate to resolve any of the issues between persons where domestic violence has been perpetrated?' She also goes on to point out that 'There are many who believe that mediation is a viable and reasonable tool for resolving disputes and who include domestic violence cases as 'disputes' which can and should be addressed with mediation' (Garrity 1998, p.15). This approach is criticised by organisations such as Southall Black Sisters (SBS), who reject the idea of mediation as a tool for women's empowerment and when it was put forward as an option to combat forced marriages resigned from the Home Office Working Group on Forced Marriages. SBS argues that the best interests of vulnerable women cannot be served via a process that may include family members who may both directly and indirectly influence the behaviour of the women and possibly coerce them to reconcile with violent partners. Yet it is interesting to note that family mediation as a privatised mechanism of dispute resolution is legitimised as a forum in resolving matrimonial disputes under English law. Part II of the Family Law Act 1996 (although not enacted) seeks to clearly demarcate the public/private spheres of regulation and non-regulation in family law matters and legal practioners may seek to encourage couples to resolve disputes outside the traditional adversarial system of law. Eekelaar (1997) describes this development of social and legal norms as one which exists within society a network of social norms which is formally independent of the legal system, but which is in constant interaction with it. Formal law sometimes seeks to strengthen the social norms. Sometimes it allows them to serve its purposes without the necessity of direct intervention; sometimes it tries to weaken or destroy them and sometimes it withdraws from enforcement, not in an attempt to subvert them, but because countervailing values make conflicts better resolved outside the legal arena. (Eekelaar 1997, p.25)

Feminists have extensively critiqued this tenuous relationship between family and state intervention across a wide spectrum of disciplines. For example, Thornton (1991) points out that unofficial family mediation ensures that the state absolves itself of responsibility to adequately protect vulnerable women. She explains: 'In mediating interests which appear to be irreconcilable, the task of the liberal state is made easier if there are some areas conceptualized as "private" with which it does not have to grapple'. (Thornton 1991, p.167). In other words privatised family mediation allows the state to avoid intervention on the grounds of respecting cultural and religious difference. For SBS the multiculturalists treat racial minority women in a way that they would not treat white women, that is, 'ignoring the violence directed against them in the interest of respecting culture' (Razack 2007, p.142).

Yet it is precisely the fact that women have such divergent experiences of family mediation that renders problematic any proposals to develop family mediation as a more formalised process to suit the specific needs of minority ethnic communities (cf. Shah-Kazemi 2001). There seems to be an inherent conflict between recognising identities as multiple and fluid and formulating social policy initiatives that are based upon specific cultural practices, precisely because cultural and religious practices are open to change, contestation and interpretation. At the very least, we must ensure that mechanisms are in place so that those who choose not to partake in such processes are not compelled to do so. It is in this context that concerns have been raised about how such proposals will lead to delegating rights to communities to regulate matters of family law, which is effectively a move towards some form of cultural autonomy. Maclean (2001, p.137) rightly asks: 'What are the implications for family justice of this move towards private ordering? Is this form of "privatization" safe?' Undoubtedly, in this context formal law provides protection against abuse in the 'private' sphere – the sphere in which this legal ordering operates. Maclean (2001) goes on to ask:

> is it dangerous to remove disputes from the legal system with the advantage of due process, plus protection of those at the wrong end of the far from level playing field, and visible negotiation and settlement which takes place of not in court than in the shadow of the law? (Maclean 2001, p.136)

Contact with the Shariah Councils

With the exception of one interviewee, all the women had contacted a Shariah Council voluntarily, notwithstanding any guidance they may have received from family, friends and/or the local Imam. In most cases, initial contact had been made via the telephone, and this was followed up with an application form citing the reasons for seeking a religious dissolution of marriage. The most obvious question for us concerns the autonomy and independence of the women during this process. In particular, we are interested in assessing the effectiveness of the mediation and evaluating the response of the women towards reconciliation practices. Existing literature does not present consistent evidence to support the view that women are marginalised and denied equal bargaining power during official mediation processes (Davis and Roberts 1988). On the other hand, there is evidence to suggest that there is deep anxiety among all women at the prospect of initiating both official and unofficial mediation, an anxiety that persists throughout the process (Bottomley 1984; Roberts 1997).

This ambivalence is reflected in the data: some women described the initial advice they received as helpful and sympathetic, enabling them to pursue the divorce, whereas others were critical of the initial impression given by the scholars at these bodies. Sameena explained:

> I rang the number of this Shariah Council that our Maulvi [religious scholar] had given to us. I told them what had happened to me and that I wanted to divorce my husband, but that he wasn't happy with it and wouldn't agree to it. They were very helpful; they explained that divorce was wrong, but that in Islam, in some circumstances, it was allowed…they took my address and contact details and told me they would send me some forms to fill in and then decide whether it would be possible.(Sameena, London)

In cases where documents such as proof of marriage (i.e. a copy of the *nikah* certificate or certificate of civil marriage) were unavailable, the women were required to provide an affidavit to confirm that the marriage had taken place. Notably, most women did not have a copy of their *nikah* certificate, and in these cases they provided an affidavit instead. Unsurprisingly, perhaps, what we ascertain quickly from the interview data is the desire of all the women to complete the process with minimal disruption and conflict. Despite this, a total of 23 women complained about the process as being incoherent, time-consuming and at odds with the Shariah Council's own claims that it is sympathetic to the needs of women.

> I got a letter back from them saying they were looking into the case, and in the meantime I think they had met with my husband and heard his side of the story. But I'm not sure – every time I asked what was going on I never got an answer. (Rabia, Birmingham)

Mediating at Shariah Councils

For all the Shariah Councils, the process of reconciliation and/or mediation is principally an investigation into the possibility of reconciling the parties. It is by no means an uncomplicated process, and it actually gives rise to an interesting set of cultural and religious practices which are overlapping and, at times, in conflict. What becomes clear, when the process is examined closely, is the centrality of gender relations, which frame the terms of the discussion upon which the basis for reconciliation is sought. These 'common understandings' regarding the position and representation of Muslim women are in fact crucial to the outcome of the dispute.

Interviews with religious scholars reveal the importance attached to reconciling the parties. In this context, reconciliation is understood both as a moral duty (to preserve the sanctity of the Muslim family) and a religious obligation (a divorce cannot be pronounced without reconciliation). Mohammed Raza explains:

> We do not just distribute divorces on a footpath…we are not encouraging divorce – that's not our role. When a woman rings here to find out about divorce or to request an application form, we are initially reluctant to issue a divorce application. We ask her that you should try to rethink your position, because divorce is something that is considered a stigma in society and divorce is nothing good for you, and if they have children that will be another problem after divorce so we discourage it.

With the exception of one Shariah Council, all female applicants are expected to participate in the reconciliation and/or mediation process. One important question is whether or not the characteristics and parameters of this alternative dispute resolution process can determine specific outcomes for Muslim women. Although religious scholars are associated with sources that claim divine authority, interview research also revealed that religious scholars were keen to promote the idea of the Shariah Council ADR framework as a system whose authority, legitimacy and validity can mirror that of state law. To this end, each religious scholar was keen to avoid persuading female applicants to reconcile with estranged husbands:

> They wanted me to meet with my husband. In fact they said that I couldn't have a divorce unless we both met with the Imam. But it wasn't as bad as I thought. My husband took it very seriously…what the Imam was saying. I think he needed a religious person to explain to him where he was going wrong and why I was leaving him. (Sabia, London)

> I needed to explore the possibility of us getting back together from an Islamic perspective. I'm a Muslim, so it helps if you can get advice and assistance from another Muslim. I think a Muslim woman would have been able to understand where I was coming from. (Humeira, London)

Feminist scholars have warned of the dangers of trying to resolve marital disputes outside the protection of formal law. This may include situations where 'cultural norms deny women decision-making authority' (Roberts 1997, p.129) or where the mediator is not neutral and yet still provides the 'normative framework for discussion' (Roberts 1983, p.549), a situation which can transform the nature of the discussion and curtail the autonomy of the disputant. Brunch (1988, p.120) raises concerns that negotiations might well occur in private, 'without the presence of partisan lawyers and without access to appeal'. Numerous studies point to the fact that official mediation places women in a weak bargaining position, and encourages them to accept a settlement considerably inferior to one that they might have obtained had they gone through the adversarial process. In their study of mediation and divorce, Greatbach and Dingwall (1993, p.208) found that mediators do not act in a neutral way, and they enter the mediation process and guide the participants towards particular outcomes, with the consequence that there is a strong imbalance of power – the parties are not equal and cannot respond in an equal way. Furthermore, Bottomley (1984, p.45) reminds us that conciliation 'has not arisen in a vacuum and is not practised in one', and that we need to explore the dynamics of power which underpin this process. Thus, we can say that mediation promotes a particular familial ideology that is based upon social control and patriarchal norms and values, and operates through subliminal, covert forms of power and coercion. In contrast, formal law provides protection against abuse in the private sphere, and so in response to the move towards private legal ordering, critics argue that mediation fails to deliver on the key issue of 'justice'.

Conclusion

At a time where the relationship between Muslims and the British state is predicated on notions of loyalty, belonging and 'Britishness', a culturally relativist notion of multiculturalism fails to acknowledge heterogeneity within communities. Muslim identities are complex, negotiated, contested and historically unstable: Purdam (1996, p.130) points out that 'Muslims themselves are debating and contesting exactly what it means to be a Muslim, what Islam means and how it should be constructed and reproduced both in the West and in the rest of the world'. Western laws are perceived as mutable, evolving and contested, whereas cultural and religious practices are presented as fixed and immutable. Sunder (2003) states:

> Exposing this actual diversity reveals religion and religious law as a choice; they are not natural and unchanging as fundamentalists (and cultural relativists) would have us believe. In short, cross-cultural dialogue opens up space in a community for reasoned deliberation and dissent, and makes internal opposition of oppressive norms harder to justify. (Sunder 2003, p.903)

In an apparent attempt to unify women's experiences, it would seem that relativist approaches fall into the trap of 'identity politics' – the construction that liberal feminists demarcate as the space that symbolises and brings to the fore tensions between multiculturalism and feminism, and is defined by the moral frameworks of universal rights and the politics of cultural relativism. This research demonstrates the ways in which identities are fluid, multiple and changing. The women in this study identify themselves variously as Muslim, British and as Pakistani according to context. Cultural, religious and legal diversity must, if it is to respond to this individual complexity, also be in flux, contested and open to change. As Hall (2000) points out:

The temptation to essentialize community has to be resisted – it is fantasy of plentitude in circumstances of imagined loss. Migrant communities bear the imprint of diaspora, 'hybridization' and difference in their very constitution. Their vertical integration into their traditions of origin exist side by side with their lateral linkages to other 'communities' of interest, practice and aspiration, real and symbolic. (Hall 2000, p.209)

The real conflicts are not so much down to the theoretical debates about multiculturalism and feminism or state law versus unofficial law, but about power, and how the voices competing voices for power and representation ignore the internal voices of dissent and change, most often the voices of women. And we should not forget that complexity, difference and ambiguity open up the conceptual spaces to allow us to explore the interrelationships between law, gender, community, diaspora and identity, and the contests over cultural and religious meanings. As Bauman (1999, p.13) points out: 'From whatever side you look at it, difference is today an asset rather than a liability and those different from the dominant majority may reasonably expect to gain rather than lose.'

Notes

1. The report was produced by the Conservation think tank Policy Exchange, and was published in May 2007. For a copy of the report, go to www.policyexchange.org.uk/Publications.

2. This term was first developed by Mnookin, R. and Kornhauser, L. (1979) 'Bargaining in the shadow of the law.' *Yale Law Journal 88*, 950–97.

3. The four ancient Islamic schools of Sunni thought can be broadly categorised as *Hanafi, Maliki, Shafi'i* and *Hanabali*. For an in-depth analysis of the historical development of these schools, see Coulson (1969) and Schacht (1964).

4. On the demands made by the 'new generation' of South Asians in Britain, the debates on social cohesion, poverty and deprivation and how the concept of citizenship is articulated within South Asian communities see Bagguley and Hussain (2003).

5. A copy of this lecture can be found at *Archbishop – UK law needs to find accommodation with religious law codes* www.archbishopofcanterbury.org/1580 posted on Thursday 7 February 2008.

6. The Runnymede Commission Report, *Islamophobia: A Challenge For Us All* (1997) is generally considered to be the first detailed report on Islamophobia. Islamophobia was defined as 'an unfounded hostility towards Islam, and therefore fear or dislike of all or most Muslims' (p4).

7. The phrase was first coined by Samuel Huntington in his book, *The Clash of Civilizations and the Remaking of World Order*. New York: Simon and Schuster (1996).

8. There is extensive literature on the extra-judicial nature of the *talaq*. See the Women Living Under Muslim Laws Dossier, 'Knowing Our Rights: Women, Family, Laws and Custom in the Muslim World' (2006).

9. There is, of course, great diversity within these approaches and huge variations in relation to the timing of divorce, whether it can be issued verbally or only in writing, and the minimum number of witnesses present. See Hamilton, C. (1995) *Family Law and Religion*. London: Sweet and Maxwell.

10. I.e. according to the Marriage Act (1949).

11. Menski describes this process thus: 'Usually the wife will offer to pay a certain sum, normally the amount of the dower either given to her or promised to her, in return for the agreement of the husband to release her from the marriage tie' (1993, p.284). Again, this is a complex area of Muslim law and one that contains a degree of confusion as to the precise size of the dowry that the husband should receive for the *khul* (1993, p.234).

12. This perception of English law as secular is patently erroneous: a recent White Paper on constitutional reform reiterated the centrality of the Church of England in state-law relations. It stated that 'the Church of England is by law established as the Church of England and the Monarch is its supreme governor. The government remains committed to this position'. See *The Governance of Britain* (2007), a report presented to Parliament by the Secretary of State for Justice and Lord Chancellor, Jack Straw, MP, July 2007, Para.25.

13. Part of a doctoral thesis entitled 'Muslim Women, dispute resolution and Shariah Councils in the UK' shortly to be published as a book monograph entitled *Islamic Dispute Resolution and Family Law in the UK* (Palgrave Macmillan, Spring 2010). This study was completed at the University of Warwick, School of Law in 2005.

References

Ahmed, L. (1992) *Women and Gender in Islam*. New Haven, CT: Yale University Press.

Ali, S. (2000) *Gender and Human Rights in Islam and International law: Equal Before Allah? Equal Before Man?* The Hague: Kluwer Law International.

An-Na'im, A.A. (2002) *Islamic Family Law in a Changing World: A Global Resource Book*. London and New York: Zed Books.

Anthias, F. (2002) 'Beyond feminism and multiculturalism: Locating difference and the politics of location.' *Women's Studies International Forum 25*, 3, 275–86.

Anthias, F. and Yuval-Davis, N. (1989) 'Introduction.' In F. Anthias and N. Yuval-Davis (ed.) *Woman-Nation-State*. London: Macmillan.

Anthias, F. and Yuval-Davis, N. (1992) *Racialized Boundaries: Race, Nation, Gender, Colour and Class and the Anti-Racist Struggle*. London: Routledge.

Bainham, A. (1995), 'Family law in a pluralistic society.' *Journal of Law and Society 22*, 234–47.

Bauman, Z. (1999) 'On Universal Morality and the Morality of Universalism.' In C. Lund (ed.) *Development and Rights: Negotiating Justice in Changing Societies*. London: Routledge.

Bhopal, K. (1999) 'South Asian Women and Arranged Marriages in East London.' In R. Barot, H. Bradley and S. Fenton (eds) *Ethnicity, Gender and Social Change*. London: Macmillan.

Brunch, C.S (1988) 'And how are the children? The effects of ideology and mediation on child custody law and children's well-being in the United States.' *International Journal of Law and Family 2*, 1, 106–126.

Bunt, G. (1998) 'Decision-making concerns in British Islamic environments.' *Islam and Christian-Muslim Relations 19*, 1, 103–13.

Bottomley, A. (1984), 'Resolving Family Disputes: A Critical View.' In M.D.A. Freeman (ed.) *State, Law and the Family: Critical Perspective*. London: Sweet and Maxwell.

Carroll, L. (1997) 'Muslim Women and "Islamic Divorce" in England.' *Journal of Muslim Minority Affairs 17*, 1, 97–115.

Chiba, M. (ed.) (1986) Asian Indigenous Law in Interaction with Received Law. London and New York: KPI.

Davis, G. and Roberts M. (1989) 'Mediation and the battle of the sexes.' *Family Law 305*, August.

Eekelaar, J. (2000) 'Uncovering Social Obligations: Family Law and the Responsible Citizen.' In M. Maclean (ed.) *Making Law for Families*. Oxford: Hart Publishing.

Garrity, R. (1998) *Mediation and Domestic Violence: What Domestic Violence Looks Like*. Available at www.biscmi.org/documents/Mediation_and_Domestic_Violence, accessed 3 August 2009.

Gilroy, P. (1987) *There Ain't No Black in the Union Jack: The Cultural Politics of Race and Nation*. London: Verso.

Greatbatch, D. and Dingwall, R. (1993) 'Who is in charge? Rhetoric and evidence in the study of mediation.' *Journal of Social Welfare and Family Law 17*, 199–206.

Griffiths, A. (2001) 'Gendering culture: Towards a plural perspective on Kwena women's rights.' In J. Cowan, M-B. Dembour and R .Wilson (eds) *Culture and Rights: Anthropological Perspectives*. Cambridge: Cambridge University Press.

Griffiths, A. (2005) 'Using ethnography as a tool in legal research: An anthropological perspective.' In R. Banakar and M. Travers (eds) *Theory and Method in Socio-Legal Research*. Oxford: Hart Publishing.

Hall, S. (1996) 'When was the "Post-colonial"?: Thinking at the Limit.' In I. Chambers and L. Curti (eds) *The Post-Colonial Question*. London: Routledge.

Hall, S. (2000) 'Conclusion to the Multi-cultural Question.' In B. Hesse (ed.) *Unsettled Multiculturalisms: Diasporas, Entanglements, Transruptions*. London: Zed Books.

Hellum, A. (1999) 'Women's Human Rights and African Customary Laws: Between Universalism and Realitivism – Individualism and Communitarianism.' In C. Lund (ed.) *Development and Human Rights: Negotiating Justice in Changing Societies*. London: Frank Cass Publishers.

Huntington, S. (1996) *The Clash of Civilizations and the Remaking of World Order*. New York: Simon & Schuster.

Kurczewski, J. (1997) '"Family" in Politics and Law: In Search of Theory.' In J. Kurczewski and M. Maclean (eds) *Family Law and Family Policy in New Europe. Onati International Institute for the Sociology of Law*. Aldershot: Dartmouth.

Kymlicka, W. (1995) *The Rights of Minority Cultures*. Oxford: Oxford University Press.

Lewis, P. (1994) 'Being Muslim and Being British: The Dynamics of Islamic Reconstruction in Bradford.' In R. Ballard (ed.) *Desh Pardesh: The South Asian Presence in Britain*. London: C. Hurst and Co.

Maclean, M. (2000) (ed.) *Making Law for Families. Onati International Series in Law and Society*. Oxford: Portland.

Mayer, E. (1999) *Islam and Human Rights*. Boulder, CO: Westview Press.

Menski, W. (1993) 'Asians in Britain and the question of adaptation to a new legal order: Asian laws in Britain?' In M. Israel and N.K. Wagle (eds) *Ethnicity, Identity, Migration: The South Asian Context*. Toronto: University of Toronto Press.

Mernissi, F. (1992) *Women and Islam: An Historical and Theological Enquiry*. Oxford: Blackwell.

Mirza, Q. (2007) (ed.) *Islamic Feminism and the Law*. London: Routledge-Cavendish.

Nasir, J. (1990) *The Islamic Law of Personal Status*, 2nd edn. London: Graham and Trotman.

Nielsen, J.S. (1991) 'A Muslim Agenda for Britain: Some Reflections.' *New Community* 17, 3, 467–75.

Nielsen, J.S. (1997) 'Muslims in Europe: History revisited or a way forward?' *Islam and Christian-Muslim Relations 8*, 2, 135–43.

Nussbaum, M.C. (1999) *Sex and Social Justice*. Oxford: Oxford University Press.

O'Donovan, K. (1985) *Sexual Divisions in Law*. London: Weidenfield and Nicholson.

Okin, S.M. (1999) *Is Multiculturalism Bad For Women?* Princeton, NJ: Princeton University Press.

Pearl, D. and Menski, W. (1998) *Muslim Family Law*, 3rd edn. London: Sweet and Maxwell.

Phillips, A. (2005) 'Between norms and practicalities: A response to Sawitri Saharso.' *Ethnicities 5*, 2, 271–273.

Poulter, S.M. (1986) *English Law and Ethnic Minority Customs*. London: Butterworth and Co.

Purdam, K. (1996) 'Settler Political Participation: Muslim Local Councillors.' In W. Shadid and V.S. Koningsveld (eds) *Political Participation and Identities of Muslims in Non-Muslim States*. Netherlands: Kok Pharos.

Razack, S.H. (2008) *Casting Out: The Eviction of Muslims from Western Law and Politics*. Toronto: University of Toronto Press.

Reitman, O. (2005) 'Multiculturalism and feminism: Incompatability, compatability or synonymity?' *Ethnicities 5*, 2, 216–47.

Roberts, M. (1983) 'Mediation in family disputes.' *Modern Law Review 46*, 5, 337–57.

Roberts, M. (1997) *Mediation in Family Disputes: Principles of Practice*. London: Arena.

Sayyid, S. (2000) 'Beyond Westphalia: Nations and Diasporas – the Case of the Muslim Umma.' In B. Hesse (ed.) *Unsettled Multiculturalisms: Diasporas, Entanglements, Transruptions*. London: Zed Books.

Shachar, A. (2001) *Multicultural Jurisdictions: Cultural Differences and Women's Rights*. Cambridge: Cambridge University Press.

Shah, P. (2005) *Legal Pluralism in Conflict*. London: Glass House Press.

Shah-Kazemi, N.S. (2001) *Untying the Knot: Muslim Women, Divorce and the Shariah*. London: The Nuffield Foundation.

Sunder, M. (2003) 'Piercing the Veil.' *Yale Law Journal 112*, 1399.

Sunder, M. (2005) 'Enlightened constitutionalism.' *Connecticut Law Review 37*, 891, 165–198.

Taylor, C. (1999) 'Democratic exclusion (and its remedies?)' In R. Bhargava, A. Bagchi and R. Sudarshan (eds) *Multiculturalism, Liberalism and Democracy.* New Dehli: Oxford University Press.

Thornton, M. (1991) 'The Public/Private Dichotomy: Gendered and Discriminatory.' *Journal of Law and Society 18*, 4.

Van Dyke, V. (1995) 'The Individual, the State, and Ethnic Communities in Political Theory.' In W.W. Kymlicka (ed.) *The Rights of Minority Cultures.* Oxford: Oxford University Press.

Werbner, P. (2000) 'Divided Loyalties, Empowered Citizenship? Muslims in Britain.' *Citizenship Studies 4*, 3, 307–324.

Yilmaz, I. (2002) 'Challenge of post-modern legality and Muslim legal pluralism in England.' *Journal of Ethnic and Migration Studies 28*, 2, 343–54.

Yuval-Davis, N. (1997) *Gender and Nation.* London: Sage.

Chapter 8

Protection for All?

The Failures of the Domestic Violence Rule for (Im)migrant Women

Kaveri Sharma and Aisha K. Gill

The position of women of uncertain immigration status 'without recourse to public funds' who are suffering domestic violence remains desperate. The government appears to be in breach of Article 2 of the Human Rights Convention in providing these women with no access to funding should they need to leave a violent relationship. (Womankind 2008, p.11)

Introduction

In this chapter, we examine the discriminatory nature of present UK immigration laws against immigration women facing domestic violence. Specifically, current immigration policy, practice and legislations offer few options for these women to escape abuse. We first review the racialisation of the immigration laws historically. We next explore the negative impact of this official discourse on (im)migrant women suffering from domestic violence.[1] We will conclude with a discussion of the recent changes implemented by the government in this area since 1999. The new policies do little to address the human rights violation of these female victims, a situation exacerbated by poorly conceived laws and policy excluding (im)migrant women from most official aid sources limiting their ability to escape domestic violence and avoid destitution upon leaving such circumstances.

Case studies of recent women seeking help from Newham Asian Women's Project (NAWP) will be used to support this argument.[2] Finally we will offer policy recommendations stressing the responsibility of the UK toward female (im)migrant victims of domestic violence and their children. We contend that upholding the human rights of all people within its border, such as ensuring aid to abused (im)migrant women, should be prioritised over desires to minimise unwanted and illegal immigration.

Background

The Immigration Rules, governing the administration of the Immigration Acts, demand that immigration and entry-clearance officers carry out their duties without regard to the race, colour or religion of individuals. Section 19B(1) of the Race Relations (Amendment) Act 2000 legally prohibits a public authority from being discriminatory. However, section 19C states that section 19B of the Act does not apply to 'immigration and nationality functions'. This exception indicates that in matters of immigration, unlawful discrimination based on race may be legitimately allowed, demonstrated in section 19D of the Act permitting officials in some cases to discriminate on the basis of ethnicity or nationality.

This omission regarding immigration opens the space for the racialisation of the British immigration control, reflected in legal and administrative measures, introduced by successive British governments, to reduce Black immigration. Tellingly all post-war British governments have encouraged immigration from the Old Commonwealth (i.e. Canada, Australia and New Zealand) while discouraging it from the New Commonwealth (i.e. India, Pakistan and the Caribbean) resulting in a reduced number of visas, passports and work permits issued to (im)migrants from these countries. Furthermore, the government's increasing linking of immigration restrictions to ancestry, evidenced in both the Immigration Act 1971 and the British Nationality Act 1981, which granted the right to freedom from immigration control only to British nationals with at least one parent or grandparent born, adopted or granted citizenship in the UK disproportionately benefited individuals from the Old Commonwealth while disadvantaging those from the New Commonwealth (Geddes 2003; Pearson 2002).

The racialisation of British immigration control is linked historically to rising popular concerns over immigration within the UK, specifically targeted at individuals arriving from the New Commonwealth. These widespread objections were fuelled by fears that such (im)migration would lead to increased crime and unemployment, putting further stress on the NHS and official housing resources (Miles 1990). Immigration restrictions were consequently connected to a racist rhetoric concerning the need to preserve Britain's ethnic make-up from those (im)migrants perceived to be culturally incompatible with British norms and values. Specifically, official policies, evidenced in the 1971 and 1981 Acts, based freedom from immigration control on ancestry thus indirectly equating concerns over excessive immigration to skin colour, reinforcing the notion that the archetypal unwanted (im)migrant is either Black or Asian.

UK immigration control also unfairly bases their decision on gendered stereotypes concerning the likely behaviour of both male and female (im)migrants, especially those from the New Commonwealth (Gilroy 2002). Historically, the government and media have portrayed immigration as a predominantly male phenomenon with women playing a secondary role. Yet despite the fact that following the Immigration Act of 1971 exclusively male immigration into the UK all but ceased, it is still understood as a male phenomenon. The portrayal of female (im)migrants as merely an accessory to their husbands has negatively affected their status within UK immigration controls (Gilroy 2002). The Immigration Act 1971 for instance assumes that wives and children would accompany male deportees while allowing husbands to remain in the UK if their wife was deported. Moreover, it wasn't until the British Nationality Act 1981 that women could automatically pass on their British citizenship to their children. This discriminatory legacy has continued to presently undermine the position of women within the immigration and asylum sphere. The close relationship between race and gender makes it impossible to examine these forms of discrimination separately in terms of the British immigration system. Black feminist theory and activism began the process of systematically documenting Black women's individual and collective histories, creating what Segal (2001) described as a powerful new feminist voice. We contend that mono-causal explanations of gender and racial oppression are overly simplistic, overlooking the fact that people are often simultaneously gendered and 'raced'. Central to Black feminism is the belief that 'ethnicity is gendered and gender relations are ethnically distinct' (Barot, Bradley and Fenton 1999, p.4). Hence, ethnicity intersects with gender to create experiential diversity. The realisation of this diversity has directed UK immigration away from discussions of a typical female (im)migrant experience and toward an acknowledgement that it is more accurate to speak of a range of women (im)migrant experience, distinguished by ethnicity. For example, often women's gender-specific roles within their ethnic groups (e.g. their roles as wives) are utilised, in immigration regulations, to effectively exclude the wider group from entering or remaining in Britain, creating a situation 'where racism meets sexism, where patriotism meets patriarchy' (Cohen 2001, p.145).

Public versus private acts of persecution

The concept of gender-specific persecution is vital in understanding how women are treated as a social group.[3] Feminist legal studies have made important critiques concerning the role of gender-specific persecution in UK asylum and immigration law. Two themes are central: the distinction between the public and the private domain, and the tendency to conceptualise women as a homogenous social group. The first theme relates to the way in which asylum privileges 'public' acts of persecution and subordinates 'private' acts of persecution. Pateman (1992) argues that liberalism promotes a public/private dichotomy that is gendered where women's activities are relegated to the private realm of domesticity while men's are promoted to the public world of power and politics. In her essay on UK asylum, Crawley (1999) draws on Pateman's (1992) work to show that human rights policies and laws rest 'on the reproduction of various dichotomies between the public and private spheres' (Crawley 1999, p.310). She goes on to argue that because 'traditional rights law has so sharply distinguished the public sphere from the private sphere of the home, courts are likely to characterise familial violence as a personal dispute' (p.319).

The implication for women applying for asylum is that their experiences of domestic violence 'are conceptualised as "private" – private to personal relationships, private to cultures and private to states – and therefore beyond the scope of international protection efforts' (Crawley 1999, p.329). Gender persecutions, such as domestic violence, forced marriage and female genital mutilation, are considered to take place in private institutions, such as the family, making legal redress via international instruments impossible within a discourse of rights that only considers public acts of harm worthy of enforcement. If women's persecution is private, and men's public, it follows that international law will discriminate against female rights violations.

Women as a social group

The second theme emerging from feminist legal studies emphasising gender-specific persecution in UK asylum and immigration law relates to the fact that persecution becomes a legitimate basis for asylum claims *only* if women are understood as a distinct social group. International agreements, such as the 1951 Refugee Convention and its 1967 Protocol, currently do not recognise gender-specific persecution as a criterion for granting asylum status. Instead, gender-specific persecution has overwhelmingly fallen under the rubric of 'membership in a social group'.

Under asylum law, being part of a social group is taken to mean membership of 'a group of persons, all of whom share a common, immutable characteristic' that 'members of the group cannot change, or...should not be required to change because it is so fundamental to the members' individual identity or conscience' (Kelly 1993, pp.648–9). However, there is some dispute as to how useful this concept is for adjudicating gender-based asylum claims. Some legal scholars, such as Neal (1988), argue that the legal framework for adjudicating gender-based claims is already in place, provided that women are conceptualised as a social group. By contrast, others, like Kelly (1993), claim that seeing women as a social group is androcentric and that adjudicating gender-based claims under this rubric is thus problematic. Although both Neal (1988) and Kelly (1993) assume that it is possible (even if undesirable) to treat all women as a homogenous social group, neither despite their differences discusses the practical implications of such a homogenous understanding of women.

Critical scholars have theoretically investigated the adverse effects of viewing women as a homogenous as opposed to heterogeneous group. Transnational feminists pay particular attention to how gender is central to understanding the asymmetries and inequalities of power in global processes such as race (William-Crenshaw 1992), citizenship, culture (Narayan 2000), human rights, migration (Walsum and Spijkerboer 2006) and knowledge production (Mohanty 1991). A significant body of feminist scholarship critiques Western feminists for speaking on behalf of im(migrant) women in the name of feminist solidarity (Mohanty 1991). Postcolonial feminist scholars critique Western feminists for using their own culture as the yardstick for measuring (im)migrant women's experiences and status. Transnational feminist scholars challenge Euro- and US-centric feminist scholarship uncritical of dualities such as West and non-West, modernity and tradition, and global and local (Grewal and Kaplan 1994), arguing that these binaries are problematic for feminist scholarship as they allow gender to operate explicitly within a specific framework that 'dangerously corresponds to the colonial-nationalism model that leaves out certain subaltern groups' (Grewal and Kaplan 1994, p.11). These writers emphasise how the public/private dichotomy and the notion of women as a homogenous social group subordinates differences based on race, class and nation to differences based on sex. Postcolonial theorists are particularly sensitive to these issues, evidenced in their discussions of cultural essentialising of (im)migrant women's experiences and how othering is used to frame specific forms of gender-based harms. Regarding essentialism, scholars like Anthias and Yuval-Davis (1993) warn against homogenising the category of 'woman.' This deconstruction of the category 'woman' has long been a staple of feminist theorising (Collins 2002; Mohanty 1991). Mohanty (1991) states that 'treating "woman" as a category of analysis assumes that all of us of the same gender, across classes, cultures, are somehow socially constructed as a homogenous group' thus perpetuating a unified notion of 'woman' (Mohanty 1991, p.56). Admittedly the term 'woman' as an analytical category does not necessarily imply that all women are identical nor that they have no other significant attributes. Yet Mohanty (1991) remains critical of how some Western feminists use of 'woman' ignores diversity, specifically national and racial differences within the category. These critical interventions can be employed to construct a more diverse and sensitive conception of 'women' when used analytically. British immigration policy reflects these problematic gender assumptions, reflected in the inadequate implementation of the guidelines provided by the (im)migrant Appellate Authority and the Border and Immigration Authority (BIA, the institution that determines who gains entry to the UK). The guidelines state that although gender does not constitute proper grounds for determining an individual's refugee status under the 1951 Geneva Convention, it may nevertheless inform official judgements as to whether any one of the five criteria given by the Convention (i.e. race, religion, nationality, political opinion or membership of a social group) are applicable. Some of these guidelines reflect the House of Lords decision in the landmark case of Shah and Islam in 1999, which ruled that women subject to domestic violence in their countries of origin may qualify for refugee status as members of a social group[4] provided that their own state has failed to protect them.

The BIA also recognises that anyone not entitled to international protection under the 1951 Convention could still qualify for an asylum claim under a human rights application on the basis of the same set of facts, i.e. abuse faced and subsequent persecution. However, despite these changes, women subject to gender-related persecution continue to be refused full refugee status. Although some have successfully appealed these rulings, many do not want to undergo the trauma of a formal hearing, particularly if they are granted leave on other grounds, like humanitarian protection, which may restrict or limit their rights and entitlements.

Immigration and marital status: policy and procedure

Since the 1960s, successive UK governments have imposed restrictions on immigration (Miles 1990). In the early 1980s, the government introduced rules to prevent foreigners from entering the UK based on marriage to a UK resident. These restrictions were predominantly intended to contain immigration from Commonwealth countries. These policies must be understood within the context of the British government's official encouragement to Commonwealth citizens to immigrate to Britain after the end of the Second World War in order to replace the lost workforce. The most significant of these rules restricting marriage-related immigration were, first, the primary purpose rule, second, the one-year immigration rule, and third, the no recourse to public funds (NRPF) rule.

The primary purpose rule

The primary purpose rule required applicants to prove that the primary reason for their marriage was not settlement in the UK. All marriages between UK and non-UK citizens were seen as potentially suspect (Joshi 2003).

One- and two-year immigration rule

The one-year rule mandated that anyone joining their spouse in the UK must be married for a minimum of a year before being able to apply for permanent residence in Britain. It also required that a married (im)migrant's application for indefinite leave to remain in the UK had to be supported by the resident spouse. Consequently (im)migrant spouses who did not apply for indefinite leave *before* the expiry of the one-year spousal visa automatically became an overstayer hence committing a criminal offence making them liable to deportation; (im)migrants whose marriages break down during the one-year period may also be liable to deportation; (Southall Black Sisters 2007).

Consistent pressure by women's groups led to the abolition of the primary purpose rule in 1997. Following the successful campaigning of black women, a concession was made in 1999 allowing (im)migrant spouses to live in the UK permanently if their marriage breaks down as a result of domestic violence within the one-year probationary period. The problem with this concession was that the evidentiary level required to prove domestic violence was very high, having to take the form of a criminal caution or injunction, prohibiting many women from making use of it as most felt uncomfortable approaching the police or the courts due to fears of further violence, destitution or deportation. The concession also did not help women who had become overstayers.

The probationary period for the primary purpose rule was extended in April 2003, to two years, causing it to be renamed 'the two-year rule'. The domestic violence rule (which replaced the concession) also applies to same-sex and co-habiting couples. However, victims still must obtain a civil court injunction, a caution or a conviction against their spouse, or other family member(s) perpetrating this violence, in order to prove abuse has occurred. In the absence of such evidence, victims are required to provide either a medical report or letter from a hospital, a general practitioner, the police, social services, a woman's refuge, or a civil court undertaking (Gill and Sharma 2006). Reporting domestic violence can be very difficult for (im)migrant women, who may not know the language and may be unaware of their rights. Some women are kept in isolation, making it even more difficult to report abuse. This stringent evidentiary requirement thus makes it difficult for women to make successful applications under this rule.

This application process is further complicated by the fact that many applicants are also dealing with both an unfamiliar system and an unfamiliar language, a problem particularly affecting female (im)migrants. Lawyers representing these victims note how they frequently encounter problems accessing authorities such as doctors and police in order to obtain formal corroboration of the violence they have suffered. The new two-year rule moreover protects only women who enter the UK as spouses or partners as well as those who apply for indefinite leave to remain in the UK within the accepted probationary period. Women who are 'overstayers' are not entitled to indefinite leave and are subject to immigration control despite having possibly suffered domestic violence.

No recourse to public funds rule (NRPF)

(Im)migrants coming to the UK on spousal visas are subject to the NRPF rule.[5] The rule, defined under Section 115(9) of the Immigration and Asylum Act 1999, requires that an (im)migrant spouse must be either financially supported by their sponsoring spouse or self-supporting. An (im)migrant spouse is not entitled to any welfare benefits, council housing, or access to public funded services or facilities. The NRPF rule adversely affects several categories of women facing domestic violence, including those on spousal visa, overstayers, visitors, students, individuals on work permit and their dependants.

Joint impact of 'two-year rule' and NRPF rule on women facing domestic violence

Although the two-year rule has allayed women's fears of deportation if their marriage or relationship breaks down, it has not decreased these female (im)migrant concerns of destitution or of being trapped in a violent home. The continuing restriction on public funds preserves the economic dependency of abused women on violent spouses (or partners, or relatives) and prevents a significant number of women from escaping spousal abuse. In the 2003 consultation paper *Safety and Justice* the government acknowledged that welfare benefits and access to housing are essential prerequisites for all victims of violence, as they provide a safety net for victims of domestic abuse. Yet the NRPF rule denies this provision to women who have an insecure immigration status, leaving them unprotected by existing

UK domestic violence legislation and policy. These female victims are also excluded from access to refuge spaces by the NRPF rule thus defeating the very purpose of adding a domestic violence rule to existing immigration laws.

NRPF has had a devastating impact on women and their safety. Many female abuse victims, fearing destitution caused by not having access to public funds, feel they have no choice but to stay in an abusive relationship. Moreover, some women return to their abusive partner due to lack of available resources, leaving them even more vulnerable to escalated abuse and control by their violent spouse. In other cases, women who have successfully escaped from their situation are forced to rely, because of a lack of public support, on personal social networks (composed primarily of family and friends) opening them to pressure from these individuals to return to their partner. This may also result in these women being made a servant to their supportive friend or relative, or suffering further abuse at these individuals' hands. For instance, a client at NAWP was forced to live with an aunt as she was denied a refuge space and was ineligible to work after her abusive husband sent her away from the marital home. For almost a year she was subjected to physical abuse, financial control and domestic servitude from her aunt and her family before finally escaping to a police station after a particularly severe incident. She later reported that she felt it was 'safer' to return to her aunt's home instead of reconciling with her husband due to fears of sexual abuse by her former spouse. This example shows the limitations that this rule places on women making a choice about their safety.

Legal developments on proof required

Under the new domestic violence rule, a considerable amount of evidence is required to prove a relationship has broken down due to domestic violence. While the evidential standard is ambiguous within Immigration Rules themselves, they are listed clearly in the Immigration Directorate's Instructions, serving as guidelines for government caseworkers about how to apply these rules when making decisions on individual cases. These guidelines have occasionally come under scrutiny, as in the case of Ishtiaq ([2007] EWCA Civ 386) heard by the English Court of Appeal in 2007. Ishtiaq, a citizen of Pakistan, was granted leave to remain in the UK as the wife of a British resident. She applied for indefinite leave to remain in the

UK on the grounds that her marriage had permanently broken down due to domestic violence. Although she was able to prove that her marriage had broken down within two years, she was unable to produce the documents specified by the secretary of state in section 4 of chapter 8 of the Immigration Directorate Instructions ('IDIs') for proving the occurrence of domestic violence. The principal issue in the appeal was whether the inability to produce such evidence should automatically bar an individual's application to remain in the UK indefinitely under the domestic violence rule. This led to a reconsideration of the evidentiary standard mandated by the IDIs. The Home Office argued that the list of evidence in the IDIs constitutes an inflexible prescription without which false allegations of domestic violence could otherwise be made in order to obtain leave to remain in the UK. The Court of Appeal, however, was unconvinced by these arguments, noting that Home Office caseworkers, like judges, are often charged with a difficult fact-finding task, and are therefore legally required to use their own judgement to determine the veracity of a case. The Court of Appeal concluded that while the IDIs provide a strong guideline as to the proper evidence standard for proving domestic violence, they are not exhaustive for such decisions.

The Court of Appeal further held that it was not the purpose of the rules to deny leave to victims of domestic violence who despite being able to prove their case could not do so in the ways prescribed by the secretary of state within the official instructions. Preventing an applicant from proving her case using different evidence than that mandated by the guidelines would defeat the purpose of the rules, created to ensure that victims should not feel forced to remain in an abusive relationship simply to qualify for leave to remain.

This judgment has significant bearing on the Instructions given by the Border and Immigration Authority (BIA) on how to deal with immigration applications. Dyson LJ presented the court's judgment:

> It is obviously highly desirable that BIA caseworkers should be given clear guidance as to how they should perform the difficult tasks that they have to perform. But for the reasons I have given, I do not consider that they can be given inflexible instructions which have the effect of depriving them of the right to consider what evidence they should require when they consider the question of domestic violence in an individual case. ([2007] EWCA Civ 386 Paragraph 41)

This decision is to be applauded as a common-sense decision which acknowledges the difficulties that (im)migrants face when making a formal application. Despite this decision, the Home Office regularly rejects applications where the proof of domestic violence is not in the prescribed format. The application of a client at NAWP was rejected by the Home Office based on lack of proof. The client faced severe domestic violence, including sexual abuse which she could not report as she was kept isolated in her house. Upon leaving this abusive marriage, she reported the abuse to police but the charges were dropped by the Crown Prosecution Service (CPS) due to insufficient evidence. Her application for leave to remain in the UK was subsequently rejected on the grounds that there was no proof of domestic violence. In the appeal, it was argued that for a woman in her circumstances, it was impossible to report abuse as she was imprisoned in her home and further did not know how to call the police and could not even speak to her own family in privacy. NAWP provided statements of support from her counsellors and therapists while the refuge worker provided evidence stating that the client's testimony was consistent with that of a domestic violence survivor. NAWP also offered expert evidence on the specific nature of domestic violence within South Asian communities and the impact that has had on women being able to seek assistance. On the basis of this evidence, the client's appeal was accepted.

Prohibitive fees

Despite the positive judicial decision in the case of Ishtiaq, the ability of (im)migrant victims of domestic violence to seek protection is currently threatened in two important ways. In the same month as the Ishtiaq decision, the government introduced a £750 application fee, restricting many women entitled to such protection by the 'domestic violence rule' from even applying for such benefits. An individual is exempted from this fee only if he or she is proved destitute by a letter from an official source, usually from social services. However, obtaining such a letter can be difficult because social services will issue one only if it is directly involved in the case. For many female (im)migrants surviving on minimum and low wages, this fee is prohibitive, forcing many vulnerable women to choose between remaining in an abusive relationship, 'disappearing' underground, or becoming unwillingly destitute solely to qualify for this fee exemption. A client at NAWP told us how after borrowing £750 from a relative to pay the Home Office fees, she had to work for them for almost a year, doing domestic work and taking on the family's childcare responsibilities.

One-size-fits-all approach

The second threat to the protection of immigration is the BIA's 2007 proposal to 'minimise the need for [Home Office] caseworkers to exercise discretion', set out by the recent consultation document for the purpose of 'simplifying' immigration law (BIA 2007, para 3.1). The Court of Appeal in the Ishtiaq case (in 2007) affirmed the role of discretion in Home Office decision-making. For immigration practitioners, the leeway granted to caseworkers for exercising discretion promises that the individual facts of a client's case will be considered, allowing for an appeal if such discretion is not exercised properly. Yet the Home Office proposes to reduce the use of discretion across the board in immigration cases. If legislation is to be 'simplified' in the manner proposed by the government, then the most obvious alternative might be a 'one-size-fits-all' approach eliminating the discretion given to case workers for deciding applications. This approach would be highly inappropriate as the complexities of an individual (im)migrant's particular circumstances requires careful individual scrutiny and should not be subject to a box-ticking exercise. The Immigration Law Practitioners' Association (2007), representing the UK's leading immigration practitioners, has rightly criticised the short-sighted tactic of reducing discretion:

> Whether viewed from the perspective of European Union law, human rights law or UK administrative law, both proportionality and regard to all the relevant circumstances of the individual case are fundamental requirements of a lawful decision. Reducing discretion for decision makers to be able to meet these requirements will cause their decisions to fail to command public confidence and lead to litigation; this in turn may add complication and further undermine public confidence. (Immigration Law Practitioners' Association 2007, p.6)

The methods for assessing these cases must reflect the diversity of women's experiences and the fact that each claimant's experience is unique. For this reason case workers should be given discretionary powers to ensure that they are able to take into account the specific circumstances of each application in their decision-making.

The scale of the problem

Home Office (2003) figures show that, while on average 44,000 spouses were granted settlement each year between 2000 and 2002, only 119 women applied for indefinite leave to remain under the domestic violence concession, of which only 60 per cent were granted. The NRPF rule is likely to be a major factor in preventing women from making use of the domestic violence rule. Presently there has been no comprehensive UK-wide research on the effect of the NRPF rule on the number of women fleeing gender-based abuse. National research, carried out by Southall Black Sisters (2007), indicates a consistent level of about 800–900 domestic violence cases a year, though it is believed to be closer to 1000 cases a year as many go unreported due to the difficulties women face in seeking help. Some do not (or are unable to) make an application under the domestic violence rule while others are unwilling or unable to leave their abusive relationship.

According to Roy (2008), only 9 per cent of women subject to NRPF who seek support from refuges, domestic violence organisations, social services or housing departments are housed; leaving 91 per cent without any public aid. Similar findings were also reported by other research, such as Anitha et al. (2008), who found the following:

> Preliminary information from refuges catering to South Asian women indicate that they are only able to offer a space to under 10 per cent of the women with NRPF who have been referred to them. (Anitha et al. 2008, p.30)

Research from the Women's Resource Centre (2007) shows that during the period 2006–07, 238 women with NRPF were supported by fifteen providers. Seven of these providers were women's organisations, four were BME women's organisations, three were BME housing associations, and one was a general housing association. Less than 20 per cent of the 238 women were given accommodation. These studies show the urgent need for more resources and services, particularly in terms of housing, to be provided to women subject to the NRPF rule.

Ray of hope?

Section 21 of the National Assistance Act (NAA) 1948 grants discretionary power to local authorities for providing assistance to destitute individuals, irrespective of their immigration status. Under this provision, women subject to the NRPF rule fleeing domestic violence can apply for support, both in terms of accommodation and sustenance, from a local authority for the period during which the Border and Immigration Authority is adjudicating their application for indefinite leave to remain. However, in 2000, an amendment was introduced to make the requirements for qualifying as destitute stricter. Those subject to immigration control were no longer eligible for assistance if their need stemmed either from 'destitution alone' or from the consequences of destitution. The key criterion became whether or not there was an imminent risk that the individual would be exposed to significant harm *not* arising from financial or accommodation reasons, if support were not provided. This 'harm' had to be a consequence of additional, extraneous circumstances, such as ill health, disability, or other vulnerability, making it even more difficult for (im)migrant women to successfully apply for assistance under section 21 of NAA. For a woman to be eligible for support under this provision she has to prove that she continued to suffer mental and/or physical abuse after escaping domestic violence. This can be difficult to prove, as demonstrated in the case of Khan vs. Oxfordshire (2004) where the applicant suffered repeated violence and was abducted twice after fleeing violence. The court rejected her argument that she needed support to protect against further abuse, ruling that she could achieve this goal through applying for injunctions and pursuing a criminal prosecution.

In 2006, the Home Office wrote a letter to local authorities highlighting the need for them

> to be mindful that some victims of domestic violence could have specific needs for care and attention and/or have dependent children, which may make them eligible for assistance under section 47 of the NHS & Community Care Act, the Local Government Act s.2, Children Act 1989 or other relevant legislation.[6]

The letter also reminded local authorities to consider the case of Khan vs. Oxfordshire (2004) when making individual assessments. As described above, although this was a disappointing decision on the facts of the case the court nevertheless upheld the principle that a woman's need for care arose as a result of suffering the domestic violence, over and above her destitution caused by her lack of accommodation. The court, therefore, acknowledged her right to funding under section 21 and accordingly the need for each case to be judged on its merits as opposed to a 'one-size-fits all' approach.

Unfortunately, the Home Office guidelines are interpreted and applied very differently from one local authority to another. Due to this inconsistency, women remain uncertain regarding the level of support they can expect and consequently whether or not they should challenge such provisions if their application under Section 21 is successful. This problem is compounded by the fact that Section 21 is not directly linked to the need for accommodation funding. For a single woman with NRPF, Section 21 is often her only path for accessing any kind of financial support. However, this avenue is severely limited by the stringent eligibility requirements and the failure to include domestic violence within such criteria.

Furthermore, women supported by local authorities under this provision often do not receive enough financial assistance to support themselves or their children. Anitha *et al.* (2008) examined the economic situation of 11 single women who were being supported by social services or refuges. The research found that:

> the women were living on between £25 and £35 a week; the poverty threshold for adults is £101 per week. Four women with one child each were living on an average of less than £60 a week; others with one or two children were living on between £80 and £100. One family, comprising of a woman and four children, were struggling to survive on £55 per week; their poverty threshold was £266. Five women, who were not in receipt of any support, were living on nothing and relying on the charity of others for food and shelter (often in return for labouring in their homes). Two women, who were employed, were living on between £40 and £70 a week. (Anitha *et al.* 2008, p.67)

The inconsistent and less than adequate support given to women by local authorities under current legislation demonstrates that, at present, there is no comprehensive, effective policy for successfully escaping domestic violence.

Undermining gender justice

The statutory framework on violence against women has made advances in addressing domestic violence and closing some of the existing provision gaps. For some (im)migrant women fleeing domestic violence, the legislation now provides sufficient support to allow them to leave abusive relationships. While many ambiguities remain, this framework is a significant improvement the situation in the late 1990s. However, it needs to be extended to comprehensively assist all women in these situations. Specifically, effective protection offers an avenue for (im)migrant women to remain in the UK on the grounds of domestic violence.

Yet conflicts between the principles behind female immigration policies continue to prevent women from achieving financial independence and freedom from their abusive spouse. The legal system must recognise the economic realities (im)migrant women face when leaving abusive marriages and introduce practical measures to tackle these problems. An effective response to these issues always requires the government to recognise and properly address the individual circumstances and backgrounds of these women, especially in relation to race, culture, socio-economic status and language. Acknowledging the effect of these factors on an abused (im)migrant woman's assessment of her options must be a key part of any effective solution.

In 2004 the Home Office incorporated gender guidance into its asylum policy instructions for caseworkers. The policy instruction provided a framework for caseworkers to interpret the Refugee Convention properly, particularly in relation to gender-related violence. It states that asylum seekers at risk of these forms of violence may qualify for asylum if they can show that the mistreatment is likely to occur for one of the reasons set out in the 1951 Refugee Convention. The purpose of these guidelines is to ensure that the UK asylum process is sensitive to the needs of women. Particularly, it recognises that women who have suffered trauma may have difficulty in processing their experiences. It therefore advises that the interview be conducted by a same-sex interviewer and instructs caseworkers to try to avoid interviewing women in front of children or male relatives, who may not be aware of all the reasons why the woman is claiming asylum.

Many of the practitioners advocating for vulnerable women working in the field of immigration and asylum law understandably view the passing of gender-based asylum laws and policies as a feminist victory. Gender-based persecution laws and policies now allow (im)migrant women to claim asylum based on forms of harm that, historically, were not considered private matters and therefore not as persecution. The BIA presently recognises sex equality as central to its mission, a move welcomed by all those concerned for the rights of women. Yet these gains are bittersweet.

The implementation of these policies and laws exhibits a limited under-standing of gender. While these guidelines and the acknowledgement of gender bias in asylum decision-making is commendable, nevertheless there is still much to be done in order to adequately protect all women from domestic abuse. A study published in 2006 by the Refugee Women's Resource Project on the implementation of the Home Office's Gender Guidance concluded that the guidance is 'far from being systematically implemented when processing and assessing women's asylum claims in the UK or dealing with women asylum seekers', suggesting that the Home Office is paying mere 'lip service' to gender issues. The report details specific incidents of neglect regarding the measures proposed in the Gender Guidance, including a lack of provision of female interviewers and interpreters and an overall absence of awareness of gender issues by decision makers within the asylum process. These measures are necessary to ensure that the particular needs of women asylum seekers are fully understood and appropriately considered in the assessment of their claims.

When immigration officers assume that women are persecuted solely on the basis of their gender, and then go on to engage in an ethnocentric understanding of harm in their decisions, this 'feminist victory' starts to look more like a gendered defeat. The above analysis on asylum policy for (im)migrant women fleeing domestic abuse reveals the situation to be worsening. Especially troubling is that access to public resources and support has been denied to activists as a result of the state ignoring the way in which immigration, asylum and domestic violence policies combine to affect vulnerable women.

Domestic violence legislation and the failure to protect (im)migrant women

The following case studies demonstrate the impact of immigration laws on the lives of two women currently (i.e. in 2008) being assisted by Newham Asian Women's Project. The women's names have been changed to protect their safety and privacy.

'Puja' first travelled from her native country of Kenya to the UK in 2002. Her family comes from an Indian background as does her British ex-husband. Puja was forced into her marriage, believing that she had no choice but to agree to her family's wishes. She came to the UK on a spousal visa where soon afterward she began being sexually, physically, emotionally and verbally abused by her husband. Within the first year of the marriage, her husband had abandoned her, leaving her with a distant relative. Puja made a police complaint about the abuse she had suffered from her husband. Although the CPS brought charges of marital rape, after two years of waiting and a long-drawn-out trial, the case fell through and her husband was found not guilty due to insufficient evidence.

Meanwhile, her family in Kenya started threatening her, claiming that if she came back to Kenya, they would force her into another marriage. At this time Puja also started being abused by her aunt. With no money, family or friends, and no means of support, Puja approached a refuge (with the assistance of the police) and found a place to stay despite not having recourse to public funds. An application for indefinite leave to remain was made on her behalf in 2004 for which she is still waiting for the BIA's decision on. Puja has gained several qualifications, including NVQ level 3 in childcare, but is not allowed to work in the UK because of immigration restrictions. She is now facing eviction from the refuge, because she has reached the end of her maximum period of stay.

'Firoza' travelled from Pakistan to the UK in 2004, under almost identical circumstances to Puja. She faced abuse from her husband, who kept her in isolation so that she could not complain to authorities. Eventually, her husband sent her back to her family in Pakistan; the journey to and from Heathrow was the only time she had been allowed out of the house in the fourteen months that she lived in the marital home. She was delighted to be going to Pakistan as she believed that she would be safe there. However, her family also began abusing her extensively. Firoza finally arranged for a ticket to London. When she reached the UK, at the end of 2005, she sought support from Newham Asian Women's Project and made an application for indefinite leave to remain under the domestic violence rule. Like many women in her situation, Firoza had not reported the abuse perpetrated on her to anyone. So, when she made the application under the domestic violence rule, she did not have any evidence to prove the abuse. Consequently, both her initial application and subsequent appeals have been rejected.

> Firoza has the right to work in the UK, so she is supporting herself. However, she is now on the verge of being deported to Pakistan, where she will be unable to obtain refuge from her abusive family. She fears she may have to accept a second forced marriage. It is clear from this case study that there needs to be a separate measure for women in Firoza's situation who have not been able to report abuse while being in situations of abuse.

These examples show that although several measures have been taken to address violence against women, the challenges facing one of the most vulnerable groups of women – (im)migrants – remain large. The barriers in accessing sources of help for these women are substantial, and the support and resources available to them, severely limited. The consequences of this insufficient support and resources mean that many of these women face a continuing violation of their human rights, that is, their right to protection and safety from violence. Since in these cases, the abuse takes place in the UK, the responsibility of upholding the rights of abused women lies with the host country rather than the country of immigration.

A violation of human rights

The failure of the UK government to extend the domestic violence rule, and the very existence of the NRPF rule, violates the fundamental human rights of women with insecure immigration status. This is in direct breach of a number of the international treaties that the UK is a signatory to, including the Convention on the Elimination of All Forms of Discrimination Against Women, and the European Convention of Human Rights (incorporated into the Human Rights Act 1998). In particular, they infringe on a women's right to life, to freedom from inhuman and degrading treatment, and to family life (for example, the right to be accommodated with their children when leaving violent situations). Moreover, to ignore the plight of (im)migrant women subject to violence makes the law discriminatory in its outcomes, since the effect is to render some women worthy of protection, but not others.

Gender Equality Duty

Gender Equality Duty (GED) is a legal obligation which came into force in April 2007. It was introduced by the Equality Act 2006, which amended the Sex Discrimination Act 1975. The GED requires public authorities to promote gender equality and eliminate sex discrimination. The NRPF rule has a greater negative impact on women than men, as women are more likely to face domestic violence than men. Furthermore, since it impacts on women facing domestic violence, it violates the GED. A challenge under the Equality Act 2006, combined with the Human Rights Act 1998, could be advanced in order to create an exception within the NRPF rule for women attempting to escape domestic violence. The new Equality and Human Rights Commission, responsible for the implementation of the Equality Act 2006, must guarantee its support for activists, women's groups and affected (im)migrant women. This would ensure that the NRPF rule does not negatively impact on women escaping domestic violence, especially those most vulnerable among them such as asylum seekers.

New initiatives on domestic violence for (im)migrants

The Home Office report *Tackling Domestic Violence: Providing Advocacy and Support to Survivors from Black and Other Minority Ethnic Communities* (Parmar, Sampson and Diamond 2005) was until recently the official report addressing domestic violence as experienced by members of Black and minority ethnic communities. Although the report recognised that immigration functions as an aggravating factor in preventing abused women from accessing help, it did not mention the impact that the NRPF rule has on these women. On 10 March 2008, while answering a question in the House of Commons, Vernon Coaker, a Member of Parliament and under-secretary of state in the Home Office, provided an overdue announcement to address the issue of NRPF. He said:

> We have also commissioned the development of a step-by-step guide for women in black and minority ethnic communities who are victims of domestic violence. It will provide practical advice on how victims, and agencies supporting victims, can protect themselves and their children. Soon we will be announcing a new scheme where victims of domestic violence who have no recourse to public funds may be able to have their

housing and living costs met linked to indefinite leave to remain (ILR) criteria. The proposals under the new scheme will strengthen the way in which domestic violence cases are considered enabling those victims who are vulnerable to access further support. (Coaker 2008)

This marks an unprecedented shift in government policy on the issue of NRPF. The new guidelines and scheme will need to be scrutinised to assess their effectiveness. However, presently it seems that retrospectively linking housing and living costs to ILR criteria may provide little additional support to vulnerable women with little to no resources. The potential awarding of the costs after their ILR application is accepted defeats the very purpose of these guidelines since women will not be able to make an application without first getting the requisite support.

Implications

For the Domestic Violence, Crime and Victims Act (2004) to have a positive impact on (im)migrant women, it must be extended to all victims subjected to both domestic violence and immigration control. The domestic violence immigration rules will not be fully effective until the restriction on recourse to public funds for female asylum seekers is abolished or radically reformed. While any proposal that suggests providing financial support for women with NRPF is welcome, the most successful way of providing this support is to ensure that these women can claim essential welfare and housing benefits. Such proposals need not result in a huge injection of extra funds as the number of claimants would be very small (approximately 800–900 per year).

In addition to financial and housing-related assistance, there should be a stipulated period of two weeks within which decisions on applications under the domestic violence rule should be made. This would minimise the cost of maintaining and accommodating applicants during the pendency of their applications. However, public funds should be made available for unsuccessful applications undergoing an appeal or judicial review proceedings. Notably such a reform, while costing little, would have enormous social benefits for reducing the human and economic costs of domestic violence for this particularly vulnerable group. Furthermore, these reforms would demonstrate the government's commitment to upholding the human rights of all domestic violence victims.

Conclusion

The UK government has gone to great effort to provide assistance to (im)migrant women experiencing domestic violence. The most progressive changes have been prompted by women's groups campaigning for greater legal protection and economic assistance, a notable case being the June 1999 abolition of the primary purpose rule. We recognise that changes in legislation have all been well meaning (Gill and Sharma 2006). However, despite such good intentions, these measures have been limited in their effectiveness due to continuing implementation problems, as well as a number of unintended consequences. The most important fault lies in the conflict between the humanitarian aim of the government to protect those suffering from domestic violence and the political need to be publicly seen as tough on illegal immigration. The present system largely prohibits rather than assists an abused (im)migrant woman's struggle for independence and security. As Lewis (2004) argues: 'The Government appears to be trying to tackle the issue of domestic violence but the legislation is discriminatory when considered holistically' (Lewis 2004, p.14). The government's sharp conservative shift towards more conservative immigration and asylum laws has put vulnerable (im)migrant women at an extreme disadvantage compared to female victims of abuse who are British citizens, particularly in regards to social support and the response of the criminal justice system.

The campaign to change laws and policies that provide access to justice for these women is long overdue. The application of these laws shows that there is also a limited understanding of the role of gender in this process for those who implement immigration laws and policies. When immigration tribunals take for granted that women are persecuted solely on the basis of their gender and engage in ethnocentric understandings of violence against (im)migrant women in their decisions, the cases that become 'case precedents' seem less of a feminist victory and look more like a defeat.

The need to protect (im)migrant women experiencing domestic violence is a prime social duty of the legal system and should therefore take priority for the government over the need to prevent potential illegal immigration (Joshi 2003). While the central government claims to be committed to maintaining fair and just immigration policies it is clear that fairness and justice do not extend to guaranteeing that the needs of some of the most vulnerable people within its border are addressed or even recognised.

We end with a quotation, taken from our earlier article on this issue from one of the women who was assisted by Newham Asian Women's Project, which amply expresses the frustration experienced by abused (im)migrant women with no recourse to public funds:

> What is my fault in all this? I left my home, country, family and everything that I had ever known and came to the UK to live with my husband. In the last seven years that I have been here, not only have I been abused by my husband but by the State as well. I have been discriminated against only because I belong to a culture where women as upholders of family honour are expected not to complain against their husband and so I did not leave him even though my visa had expired. Now that I have left him, I have no support from the State because I did not leave him soon enough. (Gill and Sharma 2006, p.200)

Notes

1. We have used the term '(im)migrant' as opposed to 'immigrant' to distinguish between the intention of migration between cases where the person seeks asylum, thus it is not by choice from cases where a person intends to migrate, for example owing to marriage.

2. Newham Asian Women's Project is a charity based in the London Borough of Newham and provides advice, information, support, training, counselling and safe accommodation to women and children fleeing all forms of gender-based violence including domestic violence.

3. Gender-specific claims may be brought by either women or men, although due to particular types of persecution, they are more commonly brought by women. In some cases, the claimant's sex may bear on the claim in significant ways. In other cases, however, the refugee claim of a female asylum seeker will have nothing to do with her sex. Gender-specific claims typically encompass (although are by no means limited to) acts of sexual violence, domestic violence, coerced family planning, female genital mutilation, punishment for transgression of social mores, and discrimination against gays and lesbians.

4. The 1951 Geneva Convention defines an asylum seeker as follows:

   > A person having a well-founded fear of being persecuted for reasons of religion, nationality, membership of a particular social group or political opinion, is outside the country of his nationality and is unable, or owing to such fear, is unwilling to avail himself of the protection of that country.

   A person is a refugee only when the Home Office has accepted his or her asylum claim. While a person is waiting for a decision on his or her claim, he or she is called an asylum seeker.

5. This also includes several other types of visas, including student, student dependant, migrant worker, holders of work permit or Highly Skilled Migrant Programme (HSMP) visa holders or their dependants, and so on.

6.   No Recourse To Public Funds Network Briefing on Domestic Violence July 2007, written by Islington Council in consultation with Southall Black Sisters.

References

Anitha, S., Chopra, P., Farouk, W., Haq, Q. and Khan, S. (2008) *Forgotten Women: Domestic Violence, Poverty and South Asian Women with No Recourse to Public Funds.* Manchester: Saheli.

Anthias, F. and Yuval-Davis, N. (1993) 'Connecting Race and Gender.' In F. Anthias and N. Yuval-Davis, *Racialized Boundaries: Race, Nation, Gender, Colour and Class and the Anti-Racist Struggle.* London: Routledge.

Barot, R., Bradley, H. and Fenton, S. (eds) (1999) *Ethnicity, Gender and Social Change.* London: Macmillan.

Border and Immigration Agency (BIA) (2007) *Simplifying Immigration Law: An Initial Consultation.* London: Home Office.

Coaker, V. (2008) *Written answer in the House of Commons.* Available at www.publications.parliament.uk/pa/cm200708/cmhansrd/cm080310/text/803 10w0016.htm#08031033000793, accessed on 28 April 2009.

Cohen, S. (2001) *Immigration Controls, the Family and the Welfare State.* London: Jessica Kingsley Publishers.

Collins, P. (2002) 'Defining Black Feminist Thought.' In P. Essed and D.T. Goldberg (eds) *Race Critical Theories.* London: Blackwell.

Crawley, H. (1999) 'Women and Refugee Status: Beyond the Public/Private Dichotomy in UK Asylum Policy.' In D. Indra (eds.) *Engendering Forced Migration: Theory and Practice.* New York: Berghan Books.

Geddes, A. (2003) *The Politics of Migration and Immigration in Europe.* London: Sage.

Gill, A. and Sharma, K. (2006) 'Marriage Migration in the UK: Response and Responsibility.' In S. Walsum and T. Spijkerboer (eds) *Women and Immigration Law: New Variations on Classical Feminist Themes.* London: Glass House Press.

Gilroy, P. (2002) *There Ain't No Black in the Union Jack: The Cultural Politics of Race and Nation.* London: Routledge.

Grewal, I. and Kaplan, C. (eds) (1994) *Scattered Hegemonies: Postmodernity and Transnational Feminist Practices.* Minneapolis, MN: University of Minnesota.

Home Office (2003) *Safety and Justice: The Government's Proposals on Domestic Violence.* London: Home Office.

Ishtiaq v Secretary of State for the Home Department [2007] EWCA Civ 386.

Immigration Law Practitioners' Association (ILPA) (2007) *Response to Consultation on Simplifying Immigration Law.* London: ILPA.

Islam (A.P.) vs. Secretary of State for the Home Department Regina vs. Immigration Appeal Tribunal and Another Ex Parte Shah (A.P.) (Conjoined Appeals) [1999] 2 WLR 1015.

Joshi, P. (2003) 'Jumping Through Hoops: Immigration and Domestic Violence.' In R. Gupta (ed.) *Homebreakers to Jailbreakers: Southall Black Sisters.* London: Zed Press.

Kelly, N. (1993) 'Gender-related persecution: Assessing the asylum claims of women.' *Cornell International Law Journal 26,* 625–74.

Khan vs. Oxfordshire (2004) CC [2004] HLR. 41.

Lewis, K. (2004) *Victims of Domestic Violence: Disparities Accessing Legal and Social Welfare Assistance under EU and Domestic Legislation.* London: Joint Council for the Welfare of Immigrants.

Miles, R. (1990) 'Whatever happened to the sociology of migration?' *Work, Employment & Society 2,* 2, 281–98.

Mohanty, C. (1991) 'Under Western Eyes: Feminist Scholarship and Colonial Discourses.' In C.T. Mohanty, A. Russo and L. Toures (eds) *Third World Women and the Politics of Feminism.* Bloomington, IN: Indiana University Press.

Narayan, U. (2000) *Dislocating Cultures: Identities, Traditions, and Third-World Feminism.* London: Routledge.

Neal, D. (1988) 'Women as a social group: Recognizing sex-based persecution as grounds for asylum.' *Columbia Human Rights Law Review 20,* 203, 218.

Newham Asian Women's Project (NAWP) (2003) *Response to Safety and Justice: The Government's Proposals on Domestic Violence.* London: NAWP.

Parmar, A., Sampson, A. and Diamond, A. (2005) *Tackling Domestic Violence: Providing Advocacy and Support to Survivors from Black and other Minority Ethnic Communities.* Development and Practice Report 35. London: Home Office.

Pateman, C. (1992) 'Equality, Difference, Subordination: The Politics of Motherhood and Women's Citizenship.' In G. Bock and S. James (eds) *Beyond Equality and Difference: Citizenship, Feminist Politics, and Female Subjectivity.* London: Routledge.

Pearson, D. (2002) 'Theorizing citizenship in British settler societies.' *Ethnic and Racial Studies 25,* 6, 989–1012.

Refugee Women's Resource Project (2006) *'Lip Service' or Implementation? The Home Office Gender Guidance and Women's Asylum Claims in the UK.* London: Home Office.

Roy, S. (2008) *No Recourse – No Duty to Care? Experiences of BAMER Women and Children affected by Domestic Violence and Insecure Immigration Status in the UK.* London: Imkaan.

Segal, L. (2001) 'Only contradictions on offer: Anglophone feminism at the millennium.' In M. Dekoven (ed.) *Feminist Locations: Global/Local/Theory/Practice in the Twenty-First Century.* New York, NY: Rutgers University Press.

Southall Black Sisters (SBS) (2007) *How Can I Support Her? Domestic Violence, Immigration and Women with No Recourse to Public Funds.* Resource Pack. London: SBS.

Walsum, S. and Spijkerboer, T. (eds) (2006) *Women and Immigration Law: New Variations on Classical Feminist Themes.* London: Glass House Press.

William-Crenshaw, K. (1992) 'Mapping the margins: Intersectionality, identity politics, and violence against women of color. *Stanford Law Review 43,* 1241–2.

Womankind (2008) *Shadow Report to CEDAW.* London: Womankind.

Women's Resource Centre (WRC) (2007) *Funding to London Women's Refuges: Report to London Councils.* London: WRC.

Conclusion

Looking to the Future

Aisha K. Gill and Ravi K. Thiara

This collection reveals the ongoing failure of mainstream policy and support systems, as well as violence against women (VAW) and domestic violence (DV) agencies to address the comprehensive and contextually specific needs of South Asian women. It draws on an intersectional approach to highlight the complex realities of South Asian women's experiences of gender-based violence. As Crenshaw (1992) suggests, the intersecting and mutually reinforcing systems of race and gendered subordination work together to alter BME women's interactions with a wide range of public support systems. Structural intersectionality, defined here as the unique location of South Asian women at the intersection of 'race'/ethnicity, gender, class, religion and nationality, distinguishes their experiences of gender-based violence from those of white women. The concept of intersectionality remains paramount in understanding the experiences of South Asian women, and offers a useful analytical framework for tracing how various axes of oppression intersect.

The failure of society to properly address the needs of some of its most vulnerable members is underlined by a more general tendency to overlook the specific socio-economic and socio-cultural factors affecting marginalised South Asian (and other BME) women who are victims of VAW. In particular, too often such abuse is separated from the wider political and socio-economic environment in which it emerges. Popular movements in support of women's rights, empowerment and equality have identified multiculturalism, community cohesion and 'culture' as sites of contestation and political struggle as well as domination, something often ignored within the broader public discourse. The notion of culture, whether in its orientalist or occidentalist guise, as argued by Ertürk (2007), has become a tool of new forms of oppression, (Ertürk 2007). By legitimising cultural practices which subordinate women, recent and proposed legislation serves to reinforce the construction of women as victim-subjects (Kapur 2005). This, in turn, has invited protectionist responses from the state; for instance, immigration law in the UK has recently increased the minimum age at which a person may marry to 21, when one partner is from overseas. The inability of the law to recognise the multiple ways in which women exercise agency within (and despite) constraints, and its preoccupation with the victim-subject, have led feminists to argue that it offers an insufficient route to gender justice (Baxi, Rai and Ali 2008; Coy, Kelly and Foord 2009; Kapur 2005). This is complicated by protectionist policies, which are aimed at stricter immigration controls (as argued by Gill, Mitra-Kahn and Sharma (Chapters 5 and 8) in this volume); however, these policies have significant implications for state or institutional responses to gender-based violence in South Asian communities and also the application of human rights conventions to these issues.

A more victim-centred, intersectional approach to South Asian women affected by VAW has to facilitate women's agency through a recognition of their needs and experiences. Such an approach must include provisions to do the following:

- Establish victim safety, including safe child contact (Thiara and Roy 2009; Thiara (Chapter 6) in this volume).

- Offer women and their children the opportunity to access specialist support, including therapeutic assistance, which recognises the importance of allowing women to express the impact of their experiences in their own words, without fear of implicit or explicit censure.

- Create structures and responses that recognise women's agency and their desire to have choices.

- Give women from BME communities the right to citizenship in cases of gender-based violence.

- Provide outreach services to implement preventative measures.

Public support providers working in the field of VAW often fail to address the reasons why they are ineffective in responding to the experiences of South Asian women (Gill 2008). Since providers are working in a sensitive area, it is important for them to willingly explore their own beliefs, values and influences in relation to the problem of VAW in South Asian (and BME) communities if they are to ensure that their personal biases do not negatively influence their responses to their clients (Coy *et al.* 2009). This is a critical aspect of the wider intersectional, victim-centred approach that is advocated in this volume. A further aspect of this approach is the need to be more sensitive to women's perspectives in understanding how intersectionality influences victims and survivors in their response to VAW. For example, we must address why violence and abuse in South Asian communities is under-reported, and why women often flee marital homes without seeking support from relevant authorities.

Taking action to end VAW in South Asian communities is not easy, because the phenomenon of VAW cannot be extricated from the many socio-cultural forces that sustain it. The chapters in this volume offer a range of promising ways forward by exploring the theoretical background of gender-based violence in South Asian communities *alongside* the work of activists and the development of human rights and legal responses. Given the fact that this grave problem stands at the intersection of multiple social forces, it is important to remember that these potential solutions must be viewed as only *part* of a mosaic of necessary responses to VAW.

What ways does this volume offer for moving forward? Perhaps the most important implication of the research gathered in this volume is that the criminal justice system must change in order to recognise the ways in which differing forms of VAW intersect. The employment of such a framework would do much to ensure a coordinated, joined-up, interdisciplinary response, which would also prevent South Asian (and other BME) women from 'falling through the cracks' in the matter of legal redress. All recent legislative initiatives related to VAW need to be reviewed, in order to determine their effectiveness, as part of a wider process of examining whether the criminal justice system exists as a 'resource not a solution' in women's struggles to end violence in their lives (Menon 2004; Robinson 2007;

Stanko 1992). Seeking help is a complex, ongoing process for South Asian women facing gender-based violence. It is the quality, consistency and reliability of the responses that abused women receive which has the greatest influence on whether or not they achieve effective outcomes for themselves and their families (Kelly 2006).

In exploring the promise and limitations of both criminalisation and civil remedial responses to VAW, the critical issue remains the challenge of integrating diverse types of legal responses in order to better flag, detect and punish these crimes. This requires going beyond criminal justice solutions in order to more fully engage with social justice approaches to gender-based violence, given the evidence that these offer the most promising avenues for effectively combating and preventing such forms of violence in the long term (Gill and Anitha 2009; Coy *et al.* 2009; Gangoli 2007; Robinson 2007). However, implementing such changes would require all those working in public support systems to understand the larger picture, with regard to the complexity of the VAW issue, in order to adopt a more holistic viewpoint. Although different agencies and services work within distinct parts of the criminal justice, health, educational and social care systems, these parts should operate as part of larger whole.

Moreover, every agency and local authority must acknowledge the complexity of South Asian (and other BME) women's experiences of, and responses to, gendered forms of violence and abuse. Poverty, health status (both mental health and physical well-being), 'race'/racism, class, language ability, sexual orientation, religious beliefs, disability and place of residence (whether urban or rural), all have a profound effect on South Asian women's ability to access the services and resources they need (Anthias 2009; Crenshaw 1992). Victims of VAW may have a disability or may be poor, trafficked, asylum seekers or refugees fleeing war and conflict with their children. All of these circumstances contribute to an individual's unique, gender-based 'herstory,' and such complicating factors need to be taken into account when designing preventative, protective and interventionist responses to VAW and especially to individual victims. The need to respect human rights and encourage the meaningful participation of all citizens is central to addressing violence against South Asian women.

In order to effect changes, more resources need to be directed towards adopting preventative measures and providing financial security for specialist support services, many of which are currently under threat from a lack of funding. Criminal justice institutions, health care providers, educationalists, teachers and policy makers are facing ever more stringent restrictions on spending related to violence against women. At the same time, community resources, such as specialist BME refuges and outreach services, are facing imminent cutbacks, and, in some cases, closure, at a time when their clients' situations are becoming more acute and complex (Imkaan 2008; Newham Asian Women's Project 2008). Funding allocation has to take into account the diverse requirements and claims of different individuals and groups on the understanding that, for example, safety planning for women and children has to include work with violent men. Insufficient funding leads to allocation becoming a competitive process, which marginalises some groups (often the most vulnerable) in favour of others (Imkaan 2008; Thiara and Hussain 2005). This raises an important question: to what extent are individuals empowered to make choices, and to what extent are their actions mediated by their socio-economic, structural location (i.e. by the range of choices available to them)? How do local authorities encourage criminal justice agencies, the health services and specialist service providers to work together in order to provide a comprehensive, multilayered strategy to tackle all forms of violence against women, especially when resources are scarce? A situation characterised by scarcity of funds is the context in which policy decisions, actions and services are implemented; even if these policies and services are developed and improved, these require funds in order to execute their duties effectively.

This argument is borne out by considering the ways in which asylum-seeking and refugee women with no recourse to public funds have been treated in the UK (see Chapter 8). At a time when the government has embarked on a nationwide consultation exercise to develop a national strategy for tackling VAW, the specialist BME sector is very concerned at the government's continuing failure to help women trapped in abusive relationships simply because their insecure immigration status does not allow them access to support. This issue has been identified by a host of service providers as one of the most pressing issues and yet no effective measures have been adopted to ensure that all women can access help to escape violence. Specialist BME organisations (refuges in particular) are facing increasing funding pressures due to the rise in referrals of women with no recourse to public funds (Women's Resource Centre 2009).

In order to build a system which consistently and effectively addresses the needs of South Asian (and other BME) women, it will be necessary for social and legal approaches to stop viewing the issue through a 'culturalist' lens and, instead, address the fact that many so-called 'cultural' practices – such as so-called 'honour' crimes and forced marriage – constitute specific types of violence against women. The fact that agencies and state departments often disregard the perils facing abused women is a reflection of the way in which they are 'racialised'; in other words, their experiences are dismissed as manifestations of cultural difference rather than expressions of VAW. South Asian women's suffering is thus treated as a cultural problem that cannot be addressed by agencies outside their given community. Multiculturalism, for all its good intentions, has become a force of repression for the very women it aims to help as it fails to recognise that VAW is a pan-cultural, human rights problem that can and should be dealt with on a universal level. Intersectionality – especially in our awareness of how socio-cultural inequalities construct victims – is vital if we are to transcend the narrow vision provided by multiculturalism.

While the state continues to treat VAW in South Asian communities as a cultural issue, there has recently been an alarming escalation in policy that emphasises the importance of seeking the views and consent of community 'gatekeepers'. Usually, the men consulted are religious leaders, who are also involved in debates on security and terrorism, and who view these additional requests for dialogue as an opportunity to advance an agenda which undermines the rights of women. As recently as September 2008, the state has empowered these 'gatekeepers' to further the 'community cohesion' agenda by facilitating 'their' communities' rights to use shariah law in civil arbitrations if both parties consent (see Chapter 7). The use of Muslim Arbitration Tribunals is currently being monitored by leading women's groups in the UK, and it is hoped that campaigning initiatives will be launched during 2009 to block legislation hindering women's access to the law in matters related to marriage, divorce and child contact.

We do not suggest that cultural contexts should be ignored, especially when dealing with VAW in South Asian (BME) communities; however, when the cultures of these communities are invoked in essentialist ways, and seen as something static, remaining unchallenged and isolated from the politics and history which shape it, then women from these communities are constructed as perpetual victim-subjects, completely defined by their cultures. The need for a human rights approach to be universal intersects with the need for approaches (both to combat and prevent VAW) to be sensitive to different socio-cultural contexts in a particularly powerful way with regard to VAW in South Asian communities.

Three key themes resonate throughout the book. The first is the issue of intersectionality – the understanding that VAW in BME communities is multifaceted and complex, involving the intersection of 'race', class, religion, ethnicity, citizenship, and sexuality which entrench historical disadvantage. As Crenshaw (1992) argues, the unique location of minority women at the intersection of race and gender, distinguishes their experience of rape, sexual violence and domestic violence from that of Caucasian women. The South Asian VAW movement in the UK suggests mainstream support services systematically fail to address the specific needs of South Asian victims of VAW; this failure results from a lack of understanding about the particularly complex political, socio-cultural and socio-economic intersections that characterise South Asian women's experiences. The second key theme focuses on the need to recognise the importance of gender for understanding VAW. A number of chapters in this volume focus on the implications of a gendered power imbalance, particularly in terms of the location of power and responsibility, and gendered rights concerning what may be voiced, and what may be silenced, and by whom. Finally, the third key theme revolves around the implications for public support systems in terms of the most promising avenues for developing a responsible, responsive, rights-based response to violence against women in South Asian communities.

Change is possible, to adopt President Barack Obama's phrase. VAW in South Asian communities is not inevitable; it is a social problem that can be remedied. For VAW to be permanently eradicated, there has to be both political will and socio-cultural motivation, coupled with investment in effective interventions. Specifically, there must be renewed efforts to ensure that the government provides intervention and tertiary prevention, recourse to the law, and specialised resources for South Asian and other BME communities. Given the extent of gender-based violence, commitment to prevention and early intervention can no longer be postponed. Each of the chapters in this book has highlighted a number of different areas that must be addressed in order to effectively combat VAW in South Asian communities, especially through policy-related interventions. Such responses are dependent upon the ways in which violence, abuse and oppression are commonly viewed, and how underlying assumptions about rights and responsibilities are treated. The needs and rights of all people not to be subject to violence is the foundation of all the strategies discussed in this volume. Approaches for tackling VAW must be founded on inclusive policies and practices, in conjunction with socially just laws implemented through welfare, social, health and legal services, and encompassing community education, professional education, community development, early intervention and prevention programmes, crisis intervention, statutory activity, legal action and recovery programmes. Ultimately, what is required is a comprehensive response to VAW in which the voices of those experiencing violence are central to the action taken. In this way, professionals can be alerted to their needs, and can also gain knowledge about the possible unintended consequences of particular interventions.

One of the major stumbling blocks to responding to violence in South Asian communities is the insufficient coordination of legal, health and social service responses to VAW; focusing on one aspect of VAW (usually the legal response to such crimes) often results in further suffering for victims, since it tends to come at the expense of offering general advocacy and more holistic support. Safety planning has to be prioritised; however, as Patel and Siddiqui argue in Chapter 4, the intentional or unintentional association of 'safety' with external control can create further difficulties, serving to reconfigure and compound abusive situations. Even more critical is the lack of adequate funding for VAW specialist support services. There exist countless documents and evidence, from academics, activists and human rights lawyers, that demonstrate that specialist provision is a 'postcode lottery' (Coy *et al.* 2009). This research further shows that the significant gaps in service provision relate to misconceived legislation and social policy. Significant resources have been invested in the 'community cohesion agenda'. The unintended consequence of this initiative is that South Asian (and other BME) women have been excluded from the support services set up to help them to escape family and community violence (Gill 2008; see also Patel and Siddiqui (Chapter 4); Wilson (Chapter 2) in this volume). The UK government's failure to provide sustainable funding for specialist BME VAW support services has reinforced fears that this represents a move towards mainstreaming VAW services: a development that would threaten rights-based political endeavours in the quest for justice and gender equality. In this way, it would appear that the UK government is undermining the gains that groups like the Asha Project, Ashiana, Imkaan, Newham Asian Women's Project, the Nia Project, Roshni, Saheli, Southall Black Sisters and others have fought for since the 1970s.

We would like to conclude with a dedication to all the victims and survivors of VAW and all the activists, past and present, who have inspired our feminist activism and academic pursuits. These activists have sought to foster a politics of 'struggle not submission', pursuing a goal of 'working for women and children; working against all forms of gendered violence' – a passion that satisfies the thirst for justice and humanity without sacrificing critical reason and responsibility. They have created the foundation on which present-day activism continues to challenge the state and its constituent parts, demanding safety, justice, and citizenship rights for all women affected by gender-based violence. In exploring VAW in the context of South Asian communities, we have demonstrated the importance of viewing gender-based violence, not as a specific socio-cultural issue, but as a widespread problem that involves a complex interweaving of many different socio-economic and socio-cultural forces. Only an approach that embraces the intersectionality of violence against women can offer hope for the future.

References

Anitha, S. and Gill, A. (2009) 'Coercion, consent and the forced marriage debate in the UK.' *Feminist Legal Studies 17*, 2, June.

Anthias, F. (2009) 'Hierarchies, Belongings, Intersectionality: Problems in Theorising Diversity.' Professorial Lecture, Roehampton University, January.

Baxi, P., Rai., S. and Ali. S. (2008) 'Legacies of Common Law: "Crimes of Honour".' In A. Cornwall and M. Molyneux (eds) *The Politics of Rights: Dilemmas for Feminist Praxis*. London: Routledge.

Coy, M., Kelly, L. and Foord, J. (2009) *Map of Gaps: The Postcode Lottery of Violence Against Women Services in Britain*. London: End Violence Against Women.

Crenshaw, K. (1992) 'Mapping the margins: Intersectionality, identity politics, and violence against women of color.' *Stanford Law Review 43*, 1241–2.

Ertürk, Y. (2007) *Elimination of All Forms of Violence Against Women: Follow-up to the Secretary-general's in-depth Study at National and International Levels, 1 March 2007.* Available at www.un.org/womenwatch/daw/csw/csw51/panelvaw/YE_CSW_Statement_07.pdf, accessed 28 April 2009.

Gangoli, G. (2007) *Indian Feminisms: Campaigns Against Violence and Multiple Patriarchies.* Aldershot, UK: Ashgate.

Gill, A. (2008) '"Crimes of honour" and violence against Women in the UK.' *International Journal of Comparative and Applied Criminal Justice 32*, 2, 243–63.

Gill, A. and Anitha, S. (2009) 'The Illusion of Protection? An Analysis of Forced Marriage Legislation and Policy in the UK.' *Journal of Social Welfare and Family Law 31*, 3.

Imkaan (2008) *Celebrating 'Herstory'*. London: Imkaan.

Kapur, R. (2005) *Erotic Justice: Law and the New Politics of Postcolonialism*. New Delhi: Permanent Black.

Kelly, L. (2006) 'Why Violence Against Women is an Equalities Issue.' Keynote speech: Association of London Government, London, December.

Menon, N. (2004) *Recovering Subversion: Feminist Politics Beyond the Law.* Champaign, IL: University of Illinois Press.

Newham Asian Women's Project (NAWP) (2008) *Annual Report: Transforming Young Lives, Creating Futures without Violence.* London: NAWP.

Robinson, A. (2007) 'Improving the civil-criminal interface for victims of domestic violence.' *Howard Journal of Criminal Justice 46*, 4, 356–71.

Stanko, E. (1992) 'Domestic Violence.' In G. Cordner and D. Hale (eds) *What Works in Policing? Operations and Administration Examined.* Cincinnati, OH: Anderson Publishing.

Thiara, R.K. and Hussain, S. (2005) *Supporting Some People: Supporting People and Services for Asian Women and Children affected by Domestic Violence.* London: Imkaan.

Thiara, R.K. and Roy, S. (2009) *BAMER Women and Children and Domestic Violence: Recent Findings.* London: Imkaan.

Women's Resource Centre (WRC) (2009) *Campaign to Abolish No Recourse to Public Funds.* London: WRC.

List of Contributors

Marzia Balzani is a reader in social anthropology at Roehampton University, the Chief Examiner for Social and Cultural Anthropology with the International Baccalaureate and an associate lecturer with the Open University. She also prepares expert reports for asylum seekers from South Asia with a focus on religious persecution and gendered violence. Her monograph *Modern Indian Kingship* (2003) is an examination of tradition and politics within a high caste Hindu community in Rajasthan, India. She is currently researching a book on the Ahmadi Muslims in London, a diasporic South Asian community.

Samia Bano is a lecturer in family law in the School of Law, University of Reading. She obtained her PhD in 2005 at the University of Warwick, where her doctoral thesis explored the practice of Muslim Family Law in the UK and the experiences of Muslim women. Her research interests include Islamic family law in the UK and Europe, Islamic jurisprudence and human rights and issues concerning the rights of Muslim women. Her current work explores the relationship between informal systems of dispute resolution within Muslim communities, state law and gender relations in the UK and is due to be published in 2009 (Palgrave Macmillan).

Aisha K. Gill is a senior lecturer in criminology at Roehampton University. Her main areas of interest and research are health and criminal justice responses to violence against Black, Minority Ethnic and Refugee (BMER) women in the United Kingdom. Since 1998 she has been involved in addressing the problem of violence against women (VAW) at the grassroots and activist level. She is Chair of Newham Asian Women's Project, management committee member of Imkaan (a second-tier national VAW charity) and a member of Liberty's Project Advisory Group and End Violence Against Women (EVAW) campaign. Aisha has extensive experience of providing expert advice to government and the voluntary sector on legal policy issues related to so-called 'honour' killings and forced marriage, and has challenged politicians to be more inclusive of BMER women's voices in policy-making on issues of gender-based violence and human rights. Her current research interests focus on rights, law and forced marriage, crimes related to patriarchy, 'honour'-based violence and femicide in Iraqi Kurdistan and the Kurdish/South Asian Diaspora, post-separation violence and child contact, trafficking, missing women and sexual violence. She has also published widely in refereed journals and is currently co-editing a book on *Forced Marriage: Introducing a Social Justice and Human Rights Perspective.*

Trishima Mitra-Kahn is currently a doctoral student in social anthropology at Roehampton University with a particular interest in the feminist politics of the Indian women's movement in India.

Pragna Patel is a founding member of Southall Black Sisters (SBS) and Women Against Fundamentalism (WAF). She worked as a co-ordinator and senior caseworker for SBS from 1982 to 1993, when she left to train as a solicitor. She has remained active in the group in respect of its policy, training and campaigning work and has, over the years, been centrally involved in SBS and WAF's most high profile campaigns around gender-based violence, racism, the criminal justice system, immigration law and religious fundamentalism. She has also written extensively on race, gender and religion and is currently chair of SBS.

Kaveri Sharma is a lawyer trained in India and has represented women fleeing violent situations in India. She is currently doing a PhD at London Metropolitan University and is researching the interaction of Asian women escaping domestic violence with the legal system in the UK. She also works at Newham Asian Women's Project as manager of the Legal Advice Service.

Hannana Siddiqui has been involved in working on race and gender issues since the early 1980s. She has worked at Southall Black Sisters since 1987 and is currently a joint coordinator. Her work has ranged from undertaking casework, policy and campaigning on violence against black and minority women, and has included domestic violence; battered women who kill, in particular the famous case of Kiranjit Ahuwalia; immigration, asylum and no recourse issues, which included helping to reform the law on domestic violence and immigration in 1999 and in creating the pressure leading to the recent government proposals on reforming no recourse; forced marriage, including helping to introduce the forced marriage guidelines and the Forced Marriage (Civil Protection) Act 2007, and was an original member of the Home Office Working Group on Forced Marriage in 1999; suicide and self-harm; and so-called 'honour killings' or honour-based violence. Hannana has also undertaken some international work, such as lobbying on the Convention of All Forms of Discrimination Against Women. She was a founding member of Women Against Fundamentalism and is currently involved in fighting the use of religious courts or tribunals on women's issues.

Ravi K. Thiara is currently a senior research fellow at the Centre for the Study of Safety and Well-being at University of Warwick, UK. She has been working in the violence against women field since the late 1980s, holding numerous positions on committees and advisory groups. Since 1996 she has worked as a researcher and specialist adviser to services in this area. Having undertaken extensive research in this field, Ravi has a particular expertise in gendered violence, children, and black and minority ethnic communities. She has published widely on these issues. In addition, she has written and conducted research on the Indian diaspora in South Africa, bride price and marriage rights in Uganda, and black and minority ethnic youth in the UK.

Amrit Wilson is a writer and activist on issues of gender and race in Britain and South Asian politics. Her books include *Finding a Voice: Asian Women in Britain* (Virago 1978) and *Dreams, Questions, Struggles: South Asian Women in Britain* (Pluto 2006). She is currently a visiting research fellow at the University of Huddersfield and honorary research fellow at Royal Holloway College. She is also chair of Imkaan, a national second-tier organisation working with Black, Asian, minority ethnic and refugee women's refuges and domestic violence projects.

Subject Index

Author Index